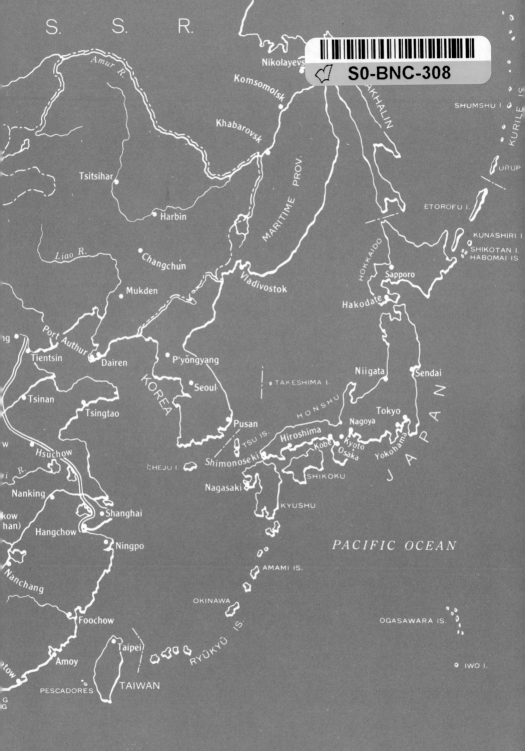

S.S.R.

Amur R.

Nikolayevs

Komsomolsk

SAKHALIN

SHUMSHU I.

Khabarovsk

URUP

Tsitsihar

ETOROFU I.

KURILE IS.

Harbin

KUNASHIRI I.

Liao R.

Changchun

MARITIME PROV.

SHIKOTAN I.
HABOMAI IS.

Vladivostok

HOKKAIDO

Sapporo

Mukden

Hakodate

Port Authur

Tientsin

Dairen

P'yongyang

Niigata

Sendai

Tsinan

KOREA

Seoul

TAKESHIMA I.

HONSHU

Tokyo

Nagoya

Tsingtao

Hsuchow

Pusan

Kyoto

Kobe

Osaka

Yokohama

JAPAN

R.

Shimonoseki

TSU IS.

Hiroshima

Nanking

CHEJU I.

Nagasaki

SHIKOKU

kow
han)

Hangchow

Shanghai

KYUSHU

Ningpo

PACIFIC OCEAN

Nanchang

AMAMI IS.

Foochow

OKINAWA

OGASAWARA IS.

Taipei

Amoy

RYUKYU IS.

IWO I.

PESCADORES

TAIWAN

G

EAST ASIA

S0-BNC-308

The Emergence of Japan
as a World Power
1895-1925

THE EMERGENCE
OF JAPAN
AS A WORLD POWER
1895-1925

by Morinosuke Kajima

CHARLES E. TUTTLE COMPANY
Rutland, Vermont & Tokyo, Japan

Representatives

Continental Europe: BOXERBOOKS, INC., *Zurich*
British Isles: PRENTICE-HALL INTERNATIONAL, INC., *London*
Australasia: PAUL FLESCH & CO., PTY. LTD., *Melbourne*
Canada: M. G. HURTIG LTD., *Edmonton*

Published by the Charles E. Tuttle Company, Inc.
of Rutland, Vermont and Tokyo, Japan
with editorial offices at
Suido 1-chome, 2–6
Bunkyo-ku, Tokyo, Japan

© *1968 by Charles E. Tuttle Co., Inc.*

Library of Congress Catalog Card No. 68-11079
International Standard Book No. 0-8048-0166-5

First printing, 1968
Third printing, 1971

Book design by Keiko Chiba
PRINTED IN JAPAN

Table of Contents

5

Preface

THIS BOOK, originally published in Japanese under the title
of *Nippon Gaiko Seisaku no Shiteki Kosatsu*, is based on ex-
haustive research into the fundamental features of Japan's
foreign policy during the crucial years from 1895 to 1925,
beginning with the Triple Intervention and ending with the
restoration of diplomatic relations between Japan and Soviet
Russia.

This period may aptly be described as the golden age of
Japanese diplomacy, a period which saw Japan, a tiny isolated nation lying off the Asiatic mainland, attain parity
with other powers and after overcoming countless difficulties
advance resolutely along a path which eventually won her a
place among the most powerful nations of the world.

In the ensuing years, however, with the ascendancy of the
militarists in Japan, the country became embroiled in the
Manchurian Incident, followed by the North China Incident
that quickly led to the capture of both Shanghai and Nanking, the occupation of French Indo-China, and finally the
surprise attack on Pearl Harbor, plunging the entire nation
into World War II.

Although the nation as a whole and the Ministry of Foreign
Affairs as well as the National Diet were clearly opposed to
these military actions, the militarists acted arbitrarily, almost
as if they were completely under the hypnotic charm of

Hitler's spectacular military successes in Europe. The apparently irresistible train of events marked one of the most nightmarish chapters of modern Japanese history.

It is inconceivable that these developments reflected the normal course of Japan's foreign policy, but rather the dictatorial policy of the militarist elements. From this point of view, I believe that this diplomatic survey covering the critical period of three decades will reveal the truth about the principles which normally guided Japan's foreign policy.

The author, while serving in the Ministry of Foreign Affairs, was assigned with the task of arranging the secret diplomatic documents and compiling Japan's diplomatic history. The compilation was made in order to provide information and facilitate the performance of official duties by the Japanese diplomats.

After completing the compilation of the documents relating to Anglo-Japanese Relations and Japanese-American Relations, I was transferred to the Japanese Embassy in Rome. Since I had made a comprehensive study of Japan's diplomatic history from the early years of the Meiji Era up to World War II, I published *A Diplomatic History of Japan and Great Britain* in 1957, and *A Diplomatic History of Japan and the United States* in 1958. ·

The materials for this book entitled *Nippon Gaiko Seisaku no Shiteki Kosatsu* have come not only from Japanese diplomatic documents which came to my attention, but also from existing documents relating to the Far Eastern policy of the Western powers as well as autobiographies, memoirs, and biographical works of many outstanding statesmen, diplomats, and soldiers of both Japan and the West who were closely associated with the events in question.

After carefully comparing the respective documents of Japan and the other countries concerned, I have tried to ascertain the hitherto conflicting claims, and to deal with the motives, course, and outcome of the fundamental policy of Japan's diplomacy.

Originally published as *Teikoku Gaiko no Kihon Seisaku (Fundamental Policy of Imperial Japan's Foreign Policy)* in 1938, this book was printed in three editions and became a best-seller, being recommended by the Ministry of Education. When the fourth edition was printed in 1951, shortly after the end of the war, the title of the book was changed to *Nippon Gaiko Seisaku no Shiteki Kosatsu*. It is now in its fifth edition.

As a modest scholar and a historian, I have tried in this book to be objectively accurate, fair and reasonable in my judgment, upholding a historical value that would not be swayed by political considerations of the time.

It was, therefore, extremely gratifying to me that this book, together with *A Diplomatic History of Japan and Great Britain*, was awarded the Japan Academy Award in 1959, the highest honor in this country for books belonging to the field of academic research.

Although the world of today continues to suffer from the cold war waged between the free and communist blocs, Japan, as a member of the free and democratic community of nations, is striving to win peace and prosperity for herself and the world.

The author earlier published in English *A Brief Diplomatic History of Modern Japan*, but decided to publish an English version of this book not only because of its academic value but also to advise intelligent readers in other countries that Japan, looking back contemplatively on her brilliant diplomatic successes in the past, is making earnest efforts—for her own sake as well as for the welfare of mankind—not to lose her footing again along the path of righteousness.

In conclusion, I should like to express my sincere gratitude to Mr. Yuichiro Isobe, to whom I entrusted the laborious task of translating the *Nippon Gaiko Seisaku no Shiteki Kosatsu*, and to Mr. Seiichiro Katsurayama for his invaluable assistance. To Mr. Charles E. Tuttle, who undertook to publish this book, I owe my heartfelt appreciation.

Tokyo, 1967 MORINOSUKE KAJIMA

PART   I
Analysis

CHAPTER **1**

The Triple Intervention
1895

~~~~~~

1

AT the height of the boundless jubilation over the conclusion
of the Treaty of Shimonoseki, which formally terminated the
Sino-Japanese War, a sudden and cruel turn of events—in
the form of the so-called "Triple Intervention"—threatened
to deprive Japan of the fruits of her hard-won victory. The
unexpected intervention and the events that followed proved
to be one of the most agonizing chapters in Japan's diplomatic history.

On April 23, 1895, the ministers of Russia, Germany, and
France, carrying out instructions from their respective Governments, visited the Japanese Vice-Minister for Foreign Affairs, Tadasu Hayashi, at Kasumigaseki, Tokyo, presenting
in turn a memorandum advising Japan to restore to China
the Liaotung Peninsula that the latter had ceded to Japan
under the terms of the Sino-Japanese Peace Treaty. Maintaining that Japanese possession of the territory in question
would menace Peking, render illusory Korean independence,
and adversely affect the permanent peace of the Far East, the
Russian and French memoranda advised Japan "as an expression of sincere friendship" to give up Liaotung.

Count Hayashi's memoirs reveal that, while the gist of the
Russian and French memoranda was to advise Japan in a

15

spirit of good neighborliness to return the ceded territory, the German Minister's memorandum called on Japan to accept the advice of the *Dreibund* as she could hardly hope for victory in a war against the three powers. This surprisingly threatening attitude of Germany as reflected in the German Minister's memorandum prompted Count Hayashi to remark to the German Minister as follows: "Although both the Russian and French Ministers have advised Japan in a friendly manner, contending that the advice was given in the interest of peace in the Far East, and urging mature deliberation on the part of Japan, your memorandum could be construed as a warning to Japan to obey the overture or risk a clash of arms. If that is the case, Japan's national honor and the feelings of the people must be taken fully into account. As the German memorandum is written in Japanese, Japan desires to be informed whether or not there has been a mistranslation."

According to Count Hayashi's memoirs, the perplexed German Minister attempted to disguise his embarrassment by replying that "the memorandum of the German Government had no intention of implying the application of any pressure against Japan. Should there be any words that give such an impression, that is due to faulty diction. I wish to state that the purport of the German memorandum is no different from those of the Russian and French Ministers."

The facts concerning this attitude of the German Minister are also roughly borne out by official German records. Whereas the German Minister had adopted a stringent attitude in his memorandum, the other two Ministers had made a preliminary dressing of their instructions. They favored conveying the advice to Japan with courtesy and decorum, but the German Minister insisted that they should perform their duties strictly in compliance with official instructions.

2

TELEGRAPHING the nature of the diplomatic representations of the three foreign envoys to Premier Ito in Hiroshima and Foreign Minister Mutsu, then recuperating from an illness at Maiko, Vice Foreign Minister Hayashi requested instructions.

To Mutsu, the urgent communication came as no surprise. He had earlier been informed of possible intervention against the Treaty of Shimonoseki by certain leading European powers through Minister Nishi in Russia and Minister Aoki in Germany. He consequently sent the following message to the Premier: "Since Japan gave no prior notification to the leading powers in Europe of the demands she would make of China, they had to await publication of the treaty before being able to raise their objections to its terms. In the present situation, Japan has no alternative but to show a firm determination not to yield a step even at the risk of creating a new crisis."

Meanwhile, Russia was concentrating a greater number of naval vessels in the Far East, a move which had become apparent a year previously, especially in the coastal waters of Japan and China. There were reports that the Russian Government had also instructed units of her fleet to be ready to go into action on twenty-four-hour notice. In these circumstances, the Japanese Government's attitude was a matter of vital importance to the nation's welfare and integrity. The Government could hardly be in a worse quandary. Unable to countenance the loss of the prizes of war, won after bloody military sacrifices and the untold sufferings of the people on the home front, the Government was unable to decide on a direct course of action. Conscious of the uncontrollable wrath of the armed forces and the people if the Government were to adopt a weak-kneed policy, Foreign Minister Mutsu con-

cluded that the most pressing need was, first of all, to reject
the advice of the three powers, thoroughly sound out their
innermost thoughts, and correctly gauge the feelings and
emotions of the Japanese nation.

A series of crucial conferences was immediately summoned, the first of which was the conference held before the
Throne at the Hiroshima Imperial Headquarters on April
24, 1895. The conference was attended by Prime Minister
Ito, War Minister Yamagata, Navy Minister Saigo, and
several senior staff officers of the army and navy, upon whom
devolved the important task of overcoming the national
crisis.

At the conference Prime Minister Ito outlined the three
possible courses open to Japan: (1) to reject the demands at
the risk of creating new enemies; (2) to refer the question to
an international conference; or (3) to accept the tripartite
advice and return the Liaotung Peninsula to China as a
favor.

Concerning the first proposal, the conference believed that
recourse to arms was out of the question as the flower of
Japanese soldiery was already stationed in Liaotung Peninsula, and all of Japan's naval vessels were in the Pescadores.
Moreover, the protracted war had exhausted both the nation's
manpower and her war supplies, and there appeared only a
very slender chance of victory over the Russian fleet, not to
speak of the combined naval forces of the Three Powers. The
first course of having new enemies was, therefore, considered
inadvisable.

As for the third proposal, that of unconditional submission, this was considered to be so humiliating that it would
lead to dangerous internal dissensions.

It was finally decided that the only course open would be
to submit the entire question to a congress of major powers.

Hurrying from Hiroshima to Maiko, where Foreign Minister Count Mutsu was recuperating, Ito was joined by
Finance Minister Matsukata and Home Minister Nomura

from Kyoto. At the Maiko Conference, held on the following day, Mutsu, opposing the decision of the Hiroshima Conference, reiterated his stand that Japan must initially reject the advice of the three powers, sound out their innermost thoughts, and then completely revamp her diplomatic policy.

Refuting Mutsu's ideas, Premier Ito argued that "it was hardly necessary to inquire further into the motives of the Three Powers, not to mention those of Russia which have already been clearly manifested since the previous year. It would be very dangerous to offer any excuses for hostilities by rejecting their representation without reflecting on the circumstances. The situation is very delicate and highly explosive. This being the case, there could be no room for adopting a complete change in our foreign policy." Seeing both Matsukata and Nomura inclined to support Ito's view, Foreign Minister Mutsu assumed a more conciliatory tone, but vehemently continued to oppose the idea of submitting the question to an international conference. The Maiko Conference, after repeated discussions, adopted the policy of granting "concessions to some extent to the three powers, but nonconcession to China." Home Minister Nomura hurried from Maiko to Hiroshima on the night of April 25 and obtained the Imperial sanction to this course of action.

At the Maiko talks, the conferees agreed that before making any final decision Japan should resort to every conceivable measure to save the situation, such as attempting to induce the three powers either to withdraw or to moderate their representation by May 8, the date for the exchange of ratifications of the Sino-Japanese Peace Treaty, failing which to enlist the support of certain other powers to restrain the interventionists. They recognized, too, the necessity for Japan to take all steps that would contribute towards improving Japan's position vis-à-vis the tripartite powers.

3

IN line with the newly adopted policy, Foreign Minister Mutsu instructed the Japanese Ministers stationed in the leading capitals of the world to feel out the attitude of the powers on the question of intervention. Realizing the paramount need to ascertain the attitude of Russia, the key figure in the *Dreibund,* Mutsu instructed Minister Nishi in St. Petersburg to inform the Russian leaders that, since the Sino-Japanese Peace Treaty had been ratified, it would be exceedingly difficult to abandon the Liaotung Peninsula. Japan, therefore, desired that Russia reconsider her representation. The Japanese Government would even, in case of permanent occupation of Liaotung Peninsula, guarantee the safety of Russian interests as well as Korean independence.

Foreign Minister Mutsu's instructions to Minister Nishi had a twofold purpose. Firstly, by her proposal Japan could test the genuine intention of the Russian Government on which to establish her own future policy. Secondly, Japan would be afforded the opportunity to hear the views of other powers, including Great Britain, and might receive unexpected support from certain quarters.

Mutsu then instructed Minister Kato in London to confidentially ascertain to what extent Japan could rely on British support in meeting the grave situation posed by Russian designs on northeastern Manchuria and northern Korea and so blatantly demonstrated by her intervention. Japan considered that Britain's interests were far more involved than those of other Western powers.

Minister Kurino in Washington was ordered by Mutsu to urge the United States, which had hitherto endeavored to restore peace, to go a step further and prevail on Russia to reconsider her intervention and to induce China to ratify the Shimonoseki Treaty.

On April 27, Minister Nishi, who was the first to report back to his Government, revealed the unshakeable determination of Russia, and the stand taken by the Russian Tsar that he was unable to accept Japan's overture because he found no compelling reason for Russia to act otherwise. On the same day, Minister Kato cabled Britain's reaction as follows: "While the British Minister for Foreign Affairs, Lord Kimberley, expressed very friendly sentiments towards Japan, he felt that the act of interceding in behalf of Japan could also be interpreted as intervention."

Furthermore, on April 29, Lord Kimberley drew Kato's attention to the fact that the British Government considered it proper to adhere to a policy of neutrality. In the present circumstances, despite Great Britain's feelings of friendship, she was unable to lend any support to Japan as her own interests must take precedence. The Japanese Government, however, should be aware of the fact that Russia was truly determined to persist in her stand. Thus, the British Government politely but unmistakably declined to accept Japan's request for assistance.

As for the United States, she took a similar attitude to that of Great Britain. Minister Kurino informed his Government that the United States would, within the limits of neutrality, cooperate with Japan and instructed the United States Minister in Peking to urge China to immediately ratify the Treaty.

On the other hand, the Italian attitude came as quite a surprise to Japan. The Italian Government, which had always entertained goodwill towards Japan, became the first power to express a desire to join Great Britain and the United States in opposing the *Dreibund*. Yet, this possibility was doomed to failure as a result of the passiveness of the Anglo-American attitude.

4

WHEN the Japanese Government realized that it could expect neither leniency from the *Dreibund* nor any sympathetic intercession by the other powers, it presented the following proposal to Russia, Germany, and France on April 30, 1895, through Nishi, Aoki, and Sone, the respective Ministers to the three powers: "The Japanese Government, after duly considering the friendly advice of the Russian Imperial Government (German or French Government) and in order to confirm the importance it attaches to the friendly relations between Japan and Russia (Germany or France), agrees, after safeguarding the national honor and dignity of Japan by exchanging the ratifications of the Shimonoseki Treaty, to the following amendment in an additional convention: The renunciation of the Liaotung Peninsula, in return for an additional indemnity from China, as well as the occupation of the said territory as a security for the faithful fulfilment of the terms of the Shimonoseki Treaty."

Russia, of course, rejected the Japanese proposal. In his cable, Minister Nishi revealed that the Russian Cabinet had passed a resolution, sanctioned by the Tsar, to the effect that Russia would not withdraw her original advice to Japan as she deemed that Japan's occupation of Port Arthur would constitute an obstacle.

Minister Nishi's reply was not unexpected, for Mutsu had earlier been informed by his Minister on April 29 as follows: "Russia seems to be in constant fear that her territories would be threatened by land and sea if Japan possessed a powerful, strategic harbor in the Liaotung Peninsula. Japan, using the said harbor as a base of operations, could wield her power not only over the Peninsula, but also over the whole of Korea as well as the fertile lands of northern Manchuria." Negotiations with Germany and France also met with a similar disappointing response.

Meanwhile, elated over Japan's failure to win effective support in countering the Triple Intervention, or more probably instigated by Russia, China proposed on May 2 the postponement of the exchange of ratifications. Consequently, Mutsu came to the conclusion that the time was now ripe for Japan to make a final decision without delay to pursue a policy of "concession to the three powers, but nonconcession to China," a policy which Premier Ito, Finance Minister Matsukata, Navy Minister Saigo, Home Minister Nomura, and the Chief of the Naval Staff Kabayama had agreed to during their discussions.

The conference summoned for the purpose spent nearly an entire day to work out the details for the return of Liaotung Peninsula. Foreign Minister Mutsu advocated that Japan's reply to the three powers should be confined to an expression of willingness to accept their advice, leaving the details to future discussion without referring to the precise terms of the retrocession of the Peninsula.

Premier Ito immediately approved the Foreign Minister's view, and other members of the Cabinet also expressed their agreement. It was against this background that Japan's reply, drawn up by Foreign Minister Mutsu and immediately sanctioned by the Emperor, was adopted. The three powers were notified by the respective Japanese envoys that "the Japanese Government agrees to renounce the permanent possession of Liaotung Peninsula in response to the friendly advice offered by the Governments of Russia, Germany, and France."

On May 9, the Ministers of the *Dreibund* visited in turn the Foreign Office in Tokyo and presented their memoranda, declaring that "the Government of Russia (Germany or France), upon being informed of the renunciation of the right of permanent occupation of Liaotung Peninsula, notes with satisfaction the views of the Imperial Japanese Government, and wishes to express its felicitations in the interest of world peace." In this manner, the acute crisis over the Triple Intervention was eventually surmounted, but related problems still remained.

An outstanding problem was the Chinese postponement of the exchange of treaty ratifications under the pretext of the Triple Intervention. Japan had once allowed a deferment of five days, but through the good offices of Great Britain, the United States, and Germany, and Li Hung-chang's retraction of the postponement, the ratified copies of the Treaty of Shimonoseki were finally exchanged at Chefoo between Miyoji Ito, the Japanese plenipotentiary, and Wu Ting-fang, the Chinese plenipotentiary.

5

THE maintenance of the status quo in the Far East was one of the pivots of Russian policy until she had completed the Siberian Railway, acquired a satisfactory ice-free port in the Pacific, and established a commanding position in Manchuria and Korea. This Russian desire to preserve the status quo was plainly indicated before the Sino-Japanese War when the Russian Minister in Tokyo was instructed to advise Japan to withdraw Japanese and Chinese troops from Korea. At the height of the Sino-Japanese controversy, Russia, like other Western countries, did not believe that the situation would become extremely grave and, in the event of hostilities, expected Chinese victory over Japan.

Even after the two antagonists came to grips, Russia was still convinced that the conflict between Japan and China could easily be settled through ordinary diplomatic measures. However, as the tide of war began to turn in Japan's favor with her unexpected victories in the battles of Pyongyang and the Yellow Sea, the Russian Government and people realized the danger of relying on ordinary diplomacy. Thereupon,

Russia began steadily reinforcing her fleet in the Orient and, at the same time, transporting additional troops to Vladivostok. It was clearly evident that Russia had become fully aware of the necessity to be adequately prepared to back diplomacy with strength in case of an emergency.

It appears that Russia did not originally have any clear-cut Far Eastern policy, a fact that was known to Premier Ito and Foreign Minister Mutsu. According to Witte's memoirs, the ringleader of the Triple Intervention was none other than Witte himself. Writing in his memoirs, he said: "We cannot allow Japan to sink her roots deep into the Chinese continent and to possess an area like the Liaotung Peninsula which could seal the fate of Peking in certain circumstances. Based on this conclusion, I have proposed the necessity of preventing the effectuation of the new Treaty concluded between Japan and China."

Regardless of Russian ambitions, the intervention could hardly have had the desired results without German participation. It might also be said that Russia surely would have hesitated to institute the intervention had she not been assured of the positive cooperation of Germany and France, especially the former.

In the final analysis, could Russia have stood by when the Liaotung Peninsula was about to pass from the hands of China to Japan? Obviously, there were cogent reasons for Russia to intervene. In order to defend her Siberian Railway interests, Russia felt that it was imperative for her to acquire an advantageous terminus on the Pacific coast. Japanese occupation of South Manchuria would reduce the importance of the Russian outpost and seriously obstruct the shortest Russian sea route.

At the time Japan was already in occupation of Korea. It was, therefore, Russia's view that Japan's acquisition of a strategic stronghold, such as the Liaotung Peninsula, would give her a key to determine the destiny of Peking, Manchuria, and Korea, and by seizing supreme power over the Far East make Korean independence little more than a mere name. Adopting this stand, Russia regarded Japan's advance in the Far East as a great menace to her entire Far Eastern policy, a menace that might eventually spell the forfeiture of Russia's substantial interests in the Far East, not to speak of her prestige as a great power. Russia felt, however, that it would be essential to enlist the cooperation of at least two or three nations before taking this momentous step of evicting Japan from the Asian continent.

6

IN becoming a party to the *Dreibund,* France took into consideration not only the European situation resulting from the Franco-Russian Alliance (1891–1893), but also her colonial interests in the Far East.

After the Franco-German War (1870–1871), France diverted her attention to her overseas colonies in an attempt to compensate for her lost territories in Europe and to restore her national prestige. Thus, her participation in the Triple Intervention may be viewed as a continuation of her policy of colonial expansionism. The intervention afforded France the opportunity to gain limited advantages. There was also the need to consider the interests of her ally, Russia.

Despite the relative unimportance and indefiniteness of the interests involved, France took the attitude that she could not be indifferent to the balance of power in the Far East. Hence, France felt that it was necessary to act in order to restore parity in the Far Eastern power balance, which had become disadvantageous to Russia.

In summarizing, it would appear that French participation in the Triple Intervention was based on preserving her colonial interests, and that, far from wishing to join in any common action with Germany, France reluctantly joined the tripartite demands out of loyalty to her Russian ally.

7

COMPLICATED factors also attended Germany's position. If Germany, like Great Britain, had not participated in the *Dreibund,* there was scant likelihood that Russia would have intervened with only French acquiescence. Political interests did not figure in German policy on Far Eastern questions, though admittedly she did have a certain amount of economic interests.

Consequently, in the early stages of the Sino-Japanese War, the German attitude was marked by moderation. When the British Government approached the German Government in an attempt to have Germany associate herself with Great Britain for the peaceful settlement of the Sino-Japanese conflict, the German Government declared that Germany was not obliged to intervene; but in order to avoid an Anglo-Russian clash, Germany would, in light of her commercial interests in the Far East, welcome any undertaking by the Western powers for peaceful mediation.

Recognizing the difficulty of achieving a satisfactory solution, Germany stood aloof from allied maneuvers at the beginning, avoiding any intrigues by Britain or Russia to utilize her as a tool. Moreover, she had no desire to make sacrifices without commensurate compensation.

Germany also realized that she could hope for no success against a victorious Japan without overwhelming strength to back up the delivery of any challenge.

The German Government's attitude, however, began to undergo a profound change from around November, 1894, due mainly to German recognition that the time was opportune to seize a base of operations in the Orient. In February of the following year, the German Government began seriously examining the question of acquiring an anchorage in the direction of the Far East, either at Kiaochow Bay, the Pescadores, or the Chu Shan Islands.

The German Foreign Minister felt that, while the Chu Shan Islands were the most ideal, Germany should not press for the acquisition of this berth if Great Britain had already acquired a treaty right to its possession. Should this not be the case, Germany should immediately institute secret negotiations with the Chinese Government for the purchase of the said islands before the validation of the Sino-Japanese Peace Treaty.

On March 1, 1895, Count Hatzfeldt, the German Ambassador at London, filed a representation with the British Government on the question of the Far East. This German overture vaguely hinted at a joint intervention against Japan. Count Hatzfeldt suggested that, although the real "break-up" of the Chinese Empire still seemed to be a remote possibility of the future, Germany would not hesitate to demand indemnification to offset any disadvantages or loss of interests that might result from any significant changes in the present situation or from the actions of third powers who might exploit the situation to their own advantage. Should such a contingency arise, Germany desired to take common action with Great Britain. She would not, therefore, at the outset oppose any design for joint intervention. Germany, moreover, declared that she was prepared to negotiate whenever Britain desired to open such talks. Taking a very negative attitude, the British Foreign Minister Lord Kimberley, in reference to the German proposals, stated that any nation dealing with important questions would hardly exclude Germany from the discussions.

In this complicated situation, Germany continued to maintain a neutral stand until the middle of March, 1895. The German Foreign Office, on the other hand, was gradually contemplating Germany's involvement in allied actions in the Far East. Although Germany claimed her action was based on Japan's rejection of German advice and against the former's territorial ambitions on the Chinese continent, the simple truth was that Germany was afraid that Japan's action might unloose a scramble for concessions in China among the Western powers.

Before making any positive move, the German Government instructed Count Hatzfeldt to ascertain British intentions. Having concluded that Britain was solely interested in maintaining the status quo, Germany resolved to act in unison with Russia. On March 23, Germany approached Russia with the proposal for a joint action, an approach which inspired the Triple Intervention.

Extremely delighted at the German proposition, the Russian Tsar and Foreign Minister Prince Lobanoff began to incline heavily towards intervention against Japan on the basis of Witte's advice.

The German Government did not know the entire contents of the Shimonoseki Peace Treaty until it received a telegram from the German Minister in China on April 4, 1895. Immediately communicating the contents of the Treaty to the German Ambassadors in Russia and Great Britain, the German Foreign Minister instructed them to inquire privately whether there were any indications that Russia, Great Britain, and France had come to an agreement on the partitioning of China.

Ambassador Hatzfeldt's cable from London indicated that there appeared to be no agreement among the three powers on either the partitioning of Chinese territory or on a common action, but it remained a constant source of anxiety to the German Government that, while Germany acquired nothing, Russia, Great Britain, and France might secretly attempt to secure rights and interests in China. These were the circumstances under which Russia delivered to Germany her intervention proposal.

On April 8, 1895, Russian Foreign Minister Lobanoff suggested an intervention formula to the various powers, requesting common action with the Russian Minister in Tokyo. Russia intended that this representation would be couched in friendly terms, advising Japan that "the annexation of Port

Arthur by Japan would be a lasting hindrance to the re-establishment of good relations between China and Japan, and a perpetual menace to the peace of Eastern Asia." At the time this proposition was made, Russia doubted the possibility of achieving complete success.

At the same time, Great Britain, anticipating an approach by Russia, decided at a Cabinet meeting on April 8 against intervention, declaring that Japan's peace terms did not damage British interests in the Far East sufficiently to warrant intervention, and that in any event such intervention must probably be based on strength.

But German action was far from negative. In a master stroke, even before ascertaining the British response, the Kaiser had already pledged German support to Russia's proposal. On learning about Japan's peace terms in early April, however, the Kaiser had remarked "they are not excessive demands," but shortly thereafter he completely reversed his stand because of his obsession over the bogey of Yellow Peril. The Far Eastern dispute became a convenient example of what was described then as a great clash between the white and yellow races, between Christianity and Buddhism.

We should allude here to the influence which the former German Minister to China, Max von Brandt, who was then living in retirement in Wiesbaden, exerted on the Kaiser and the German Government leaders. His statement of April 8, 1895, is said to have given a new direction to German Far Eastern policy. His analysis of the situation in China may be summarized as follows:

"The primary reasons for the Russian Government to maintain interests on the Chinese continent are political and military. Any radical change in the economic situation there caused by China's subordination to Japan is bound to seriously affect all nations with commercial relations with China. This reason alone should be sufficient for Germany to unconditionally accept the Russian proposition."

This view of Brandt's is said to have completely convinced the Kaiser.

Since the German Government had originally hoped to win British support, the latter's refusal came as a disappointment. The British stand was a matter of sincere regret to France who, through her Ambassador in London, had made a strong appeal to Great Britain to reverse her attitude, but had been firmly refused by Lord Kimberley.

As a result of Britain's refusal to intervene, France, after showing some hesitation, finally accepted the Russian invitation. On April 20, Russian Foreign Minister Lobanoff was formally notified of France's decision to become a party to the *Dreibund* by her Ambassador in St. Petersburg.

Aware that Russia had vital interests in the Far East, Japan had grave forebodings that Russia would oppose her occupation of Liaotung Peninsula. It was also no surprise to Japan that France would honor her alliance obligation and join forces with Russia. The actions of the German Government, on the other hand, were somewhat mystifying to Japan in view of the friendly relations which had so far existed between the two nations. It was even more bewildering to know that Germany was one of the chief proponents of the Triple Intervention.

Germany alleged that she participated in the intervention partly because of her resentment over Japan's indifference to Germany's unselfish advice, and partly in order to prevent Japan's continental advance, fearing that this development would hamper the future expansion of German commerce and industry. However, German complaint that the Sino-Japanese Peace Treaty would obstruct her commercial activities can only be described as childish in view of the actual magnitude of German industrial interests compared to those of Japan.

The assertion that Japanese indifference to German display of goodwill had compelled Germany to participate in the intervention can hardly be substantiated by facts. Whatever the ostensible reasons, it is obvious that German policy was dictated by the situation in Europe and the desire to acquire territorial interests, or at least a coaling station in China. It is hard to pinpoint which of the two factors played the most decisive role in Germany's policy; but without any ulterior motive, such as a desire for territory or a coal depot in China, Germany would hardly have even considered being a party to the Triple Intervention. Consideration of a general political nature most certainly must have weighed heavily in Germany's decision to act jointly with Russia regardless of Britain's attitude on the question of intervention. Subsequent events clearly corroborate the fact that Germany's aim was to kill two birds with one stone by participating in the *Dreibund*.

8

COUNT Mutsu, in his memoirs, alludes to his personal forebodings about the possibility of an intervention. If this were actually so, were there any preventive measures taken to forestall this eventuality? So far as the views of Premier Ito and Foreign Minister Mutsu were concerned, they appear to have held the opinion that, even if intervention were unavoidable, they would adopt a wait-and-see policy, sound out the views of the Governments concerned, when such an action did take place, and act according to the circumstances.

By taking no adequate countermeasures and adopting a laissez-faire attitude, the statesmen responsible for directing the ship of state can hardly escape the charge of gross diplomatic negligence. In sharp contrast to this nonchalant policy were the diplomatic maneuvers which the Iron Chancellor, Bismarck, skillfully and methodically executed at the time of the Austro-German War (1866) and the Franco-German War (1870–1871) in order to nip in the bud any attempts at intervention by neighboring powers.

Although Foreign Minister Mutsu did negotiate with Russia in the hope of arriving at some understanding, it is easy to imagine the almost insurmountable difficulties he must have faced, since the Russian Foreign Minister Lobanoff was only poorly informed about Far Eastern affairs. At the same time, it may be said that Russia's lack of a definite Far Eastern policy could, if properly utilized, have been turned to Japan's advantage in obstructing the intervention.

The Japanese Government, however, made no concrete proposal to Russia. Neither did it attempt to take advantage of its diplomatic relations with Britain, which was definitely hostile to Russia, in an effort to manipulate Russia. But there appears to have been very little protracted negotiation in this field until the Triple Intervention had actually materialized.

Six months before the Triple Intervention, the London *Times* published a significant editorial on September 24, 1894, declaring that a report was circulating that, whatever the outcome of the Sino-Japanese War, a diplomatic intervention was being planned. If, in the face of such an intervention, the representatives of the two countries did not support one another at least on important issues, said the *Times,* it would be strange indeed.

If Foreign Minister Mutsu, anticipating an intervention, was determined to forestall it, this editorial would have afforded a splendid chance for Japan and Great Britain to exchange views on the question. A number of courses could easily have been taken, such as requesting the British Ambassador in Tokyo to call at the Foreign Ministry, or instructing Japanese Ambassador Kato in London to feel out the views of the British Government regarding the certain "important issues" referred to by the *Times.*

There also appears to have been every reason for the Japanese Government to seek Britain's advice on how to prevent the rumored intervention. Should such conversations have been held on the extent of British support, it was within the limits of possibility to have reached some sort of an agreement between Japan and Great Britain before the intervention occurred.

After the Triple Intervention became a reality, both Premier Ito and Foreign Minister Mutsu took a number of generally convincing countermeasures. It is understandable that, having confirmed that both Great Britain and the United States had no intention of opposing the intervention by force of arms, Japan had no recourse but to make concessions to the tripartite powers.

In restoring Liaotung Peninsula to China, it should have been possible for Japan to receive Chinese assurance not to transfer or lease the said peninsula in whatever form to any third power. In fact, this step should have been regarded by Japan as a prerequisite. If Japan had put forward such a proposition to Britain and the United States, she might have received their strong diplomatic support on an issue which the Three Powers would have found little or no reason to oppose.

Lastly, there remains a hypothetical question. What would have been the consequence if Japan had rejected the *Dreibund?* Admittedly, Japan's chances of victory over the Three Powers were almost negligible. Count Mutsu gave a depressive assessment of Japan's position in his memoirs. "Under existing circumstances," he wrote, "Japan had only a very faint hope of successfully coping with the Russian fleet, not to speak of the combined naval strength of the Three Powers."

Thus, the Japanese Government concluded that it would not be in her best interests to break off relations of friendship with the Three Powers, and gain new enemies for Japan.

This Japanese decision reached at the Hiroshima Imperial Conference may be considered as sound and beyond reproach. Great Britain, for her part, in view of the conflicting interests of the Three Powers, expected a split to occur—a split which she hoped to seize as an opportunity to cooperate with one or two nations of the coalition.

Germany, on one hand, was interested in wooing Russia away from France through her role in the *Dreibund,* but France, on the other, was maneuvering to avoid the formation of a united front with Germany. If Japan had rejected the tripartite representation, what concrete assurances are there that the Three Powers would have been able to effectively enforce their demands?

The Sino-Japanese War was an important question of world politics. Keenly aware of the heavy interests involved, the Western powers kept a vigilant eye on the course of the conflict. Foreign Minister Mutsu, however, consistently held the view that it was a regional affair of the Far East and attempted to solve the issue within its confines.

I am not necessarily opposed to Mutsu's thought of confinement. Moreover, I believe that he was justified in rejecting the idea of referring the question to an international conference as a remedial measure.

However, subsequent events clearly demonstrated that Japan could not possibly have confined the issue to the Far East. Having anticipated Russian intervention and, at the same time, realizing that regional compromise would be difficult to attain, should not Japan have concentrated her efforts on Great Britain, the traditional enemy of Russia, in a bid to enlist her support against Russia? It was also a matter of great importance to have considered fully in advance how Japan could have won German support of her policy.

It is ironic that Premier Ito and Foreign Minister Mutsu, who were both deeply humiliated by Russia, later became opponents of the Anglo-Japanese Alliance. This fact might be attributable to their lack of understanding of the shifts in Britain's Far Eastern policy, or to their overrating of Russian strength or underestimation of British power. The truth is that probably they were guilty on both counts.

Indications of this unsound assessment were seen in the Sino-Japanese War and Japan's diplomatic policy in dealing with the Triple Intervention. No doubt miscalculation, misjudgment, and the absense of sound understanding, as well as the flagrant negative diplomacy pursued in the Sino-Japanese War, all contributed to having brought the Triple Intervention into existence.

CHAPTER 2

Origins of Japanese Treaty Negotiations 1891-1898

∿∿∿∿∿∿∿∿∿∿∿∿∿∿∿∿∿∿∿∿∿∿∿∿∿∿∿∿∿∿∿∿∿∿∿

Russia and France vs. Great Britain in the Far East —The Revision of Japanese Treaties—

THE YEAR of 1891 was marked by the conclusion of the diplomatic agreement between Russia and France as well as Russia's decision to construct the Trans-Siberian Railway. The fact that Russia proclaimed this ambitious project throughout the realm could not but have far reaching effects on the Far Eastern policies of the big powers. A perceptible change soon became apparent in the foreign policy of Great Britain, who had hitherto consistently led the opposition to Japan's legitimate demands for treaty revisions. Now on her own initiative Britain began ameliorating the oppressive policy that she had followed in the past towards Japan.

Both Shuzo Aoki, Japanese Minister to Germany, and Munemitsu Mutsu, Japanese Minister of Foreign Affairs, seized the opportunity to begin bargaining with Britain for the revision of treaties, with a view to extending at a later date the treaty revision talks to other powers. During the later stages of the negotiations, the British Minister in Japan, on the one hand, repeatedly charged the Japanese Government with a lack of "earnestness" in the treaty revision negotiations. On the other hand, the British Foreign Minister in his negotiations with Minister Aoki in the spring (March–

April) of 1893 on many occasions used the word "concession." In order to discover the reasons for this mystifying
attitude on Britain's part, confidential inquiries were instituted by Japan. The findings revealed that the British Government's attitude was based on the fear and suspicion that
both the Russian and French ministers in Japan were scheming to win over Japan in a plot to undermine Britain's position in the Far East by isolating her.

Furthermore, it is reported that a certain official of the
British Foreign Office voiced similar suspicions to Baron
Siebold, who had been requested by Minister Aoki to accom-
pany him from Berlin to London, while making inquiries into
the possibility of Japan transferring one island to England.
Great Britain's suspicions about Japan were again revealed
when Minister Aoki in London on May 2, 1893 sounded
Assistant Secretary of Foreign Affairs Bertie about the British
Government's sentiments towards China. Bertie questioned
Aoki about the latter's knowledge of the ambitions of the
Russian and French ministers in Japan. When the Japanese
Minister gave a negative reply, Bertie posed two questions:

1. Should a treaty between Japan and Britain be concluded, was it likely that Russia and France would be prepared to conclude identical treaties without demanding concessions?

2. What would be Japan's reaction if Russia and France
were to demand a coaling station in Japan?

These moves amply illustrate the apprehensions felt by
Britain regarding a Russo-French alliance and its collusion
with the Empire of Japan. Then on May 25, 1893, during the
treaty revision negotiations, Bertie requested the inclusion of
Hakodate as an interport trade harbor. To this proposal,
Japan objected on grounds solely of economy, explaining that
since only one or two British ships—according to statistics
available—entered the said port annually, it would be highly
uneconomical to set up a customhouse and other facilities
necessary to operate such a port. Despite the unaccommodat-

ing Japanese stand, not only did the British Government persist in this demand but even proposed the inclusion of Nemuro, thereby revealing that her policy was motivated by special political considerations. There is no room to doubt that, anticipating the completion of the Trans-Siberian Railway, the British Government was adopting countermeasures.

In transmitting his views to the Japanese Foreign Office, Minister Aoki expressed his belief that the success of the treaty revision depended on the extent to which Japan was prepared to go in conceding to British views. Should the British proposals be accepted, according to the words of Bertie, Great Britain would not only entirely renounce her consular jurisdiction in Japan but would, in addition, approve the restoration of the Japanese right of taxation.

Consequently, on the basis of Minister Aoki's report, Foreign Minister Mutsu, in consultation with Prime Minister Hirobumi Ito, decided to adopt a positive policy, aimed at the early conclusion of the treaty. Full advantage, however, would be taken of Britain's restlessness and uneasiness in order to assert Japan's rights, but on matters where persistence would be of no avail concessions would be made affirmatively.

Thus, the greatest difficulties obstructing the revision of the treaty with Britain were removed and the treaty finally realized. It was the success achieved by the Japanese Government in signing the treaty that led the way to the successive revisions of similar treaties with the United States, Germany, France, and Russia. The gigantic task of revising the unequal treaties which had heretofore plagued Japanese foreign policy since the early years of Meiji was now accomplished.

This British change in policy towards Japan may be attributed to the growing realization that it was vitally important for her to court Japan's goodwill and friendship, to hurriedly win Japan over to her side as a means of counteracting the steady inroads of Russia and France in the Far East following their alliance.

Britain, motivated also by the fear that the completion of

the Trans-Siberian Railway would pose a serious challenge to her Far Eastern trade, hoped for economic and political reasons to gain a foothold on the Sea of Japan area to meet the grave situation. Determined not only to defend her paramount interests but to maintain the balance of power in the Far East, Britain took the initiative in currying Japan's favor. But the conclusion of an alliance with Japan was not the immediate objective, for it was rather with China that Great Britain cherished a desire to enter into an alliance. If the idea of an alliance with Japan began to steadily gain ground, it was for the purpose of reinforcing the Anglo-Chinese alliance.

This thinking was evidenced by the fact that in 1885, when a clash between Great Britain and Russia appeared imminent over the Afghanistan affair, the London *Times* special correspondent, Archibald R. Colquhoun, advocated an Anglo-Chinese alliance, to be augmented by an Anglo-Japanese alliance.

In his report, Colquhoun described Russia as a nightmare for all politicians—one that would linger on. Its agonizing omnipresence in Manchuria could not be swept aside, and China, he felt, would earnestly welcome an alliance with Great Britain to deal with the Russian menace. In addition, such an alliance would give Britain substantial control over the Chinese military and naval forces, and contribute towards the maintenance of British status in the Far East at comparatively low cost and decreased responsibility. It went without saying that British trade prospects in China would also vastly improve. Japan, the writer asserted, strongly supported the conclusion of such an alliance. Should war be proclaimed between Great Britain and Russia, there were possibilities that the following alliances would shape up:

a. An Anglo-Chinese alliance related to Afghanistan, Kashgar-Kuldia, and Korea.

b. A tripartite Anglo-Chinese-Japanese alliance for the sole protection of Korea.

It is clear even from the foregoing report of A. R. Colquhoun that Great Britain's primary objective was to form an alliance, not with Japan, but with China, and that the Anglo-Japanese Alliance concluded in 1902 cannot correctly be regarded as the first treaty of alliance which Britain had with another power. During the Napoleonic and Crimean wars, Britain had an alliance with Turkey. For more than a century, with the firm intention of ensuring the security and pre-eminence of the British Empire as well as to protect her expansion in India, Great Britain spared no efforts in allying herself with various nations of the East. This British policy, following the same pattern in limited areas of Persia and Central Asia, was the fundamental basis for the English rule in India.

Projected Anglo-Chinese Alliance Against Russia

In order to understand the origin of the Anglo-Japanese alliance, it is essential to take a glance at Anglo-Chinese relations. Although prior to the Sino-Japanese War there were many intellectuals who rated China as a militarily weak nation and had practically no faith in her dependableness, the more astute of the British newspapers entertained the idea that, by applying strong pressure, China could be molded into a formidable fighting force.

British public opinion, on the other hand, not only placed confidence in China's capabilities, but recognized that the two nations had interests which they shared mutually. It felt that since Russia's advance was made at the sacrifice of Chinese territories, China regarded Russia as her real enemy. Neither did the Chinese statesmen hesitate to admit such fears. A peace emissary at the time of the Opium War, for instance, stressed that China need not fear the nation across the sea. Rather, in his opinion, the real danger to China's future would come from Russia.

Having already invaded Turkistan and the Pamirs on China's frontiers, Russian ambitions now coveted Manchuria and Tibet. The completion of the Trans-Siberian Railway would enable Russia to launch invasions along the 3,500-mile Chinese border from any direction.

In 1896, emphasizing the need to conclude an Anglo-Chinese alliance, Lord Curzon stressed that China's natural enmity towards Russia made her a natural ally of Great Britain. He reasoned that it was China's desire to keep the Russian army away from Korea and its navy out of the Yellow Sea; in any event, those should form China's national objectives.

Moreover, China's interests called for the maintenance of Yarkand and Kashgar. Not only should the borders of the Pamirs be defended, but there was a need to make them defensible. Lord Curzon also expressed the view that Britain did not wish to have a common frontier with Russia at Hindukush and Karakoram. China was—and should be—placing great importance on her sovereignty over Tibet, a region which came clearly within Russian ambitions. While Britain did not intend to enter into a dispute with Russia, she did not welcome Russian designs. Should the Trans-Siberian Railway pose a threat to the territorial integrity of China, it would at the same time constitute a serious competition to Britain's Far Eastern trade.

Furthermore, he continued, the recent French advances in South Asia, menacing the Siamese-Burma borders, were viewed with alarm by China, which felt great indignation over the seizure of Tongking by France. To have France as a neighboring nation of the Indian Empire was difficult for the British Government to accept. It had, therefore, an overriding and inherent reason to establish close and sympathetic understanding between Great Britain and China in the Far East.

As was apparent in the statement of Lord Curzon, the Anglo-Chinese alliance was not only a matter of debate but became an actual subject of diplomacy.

In reply to the Chinese protest against the seizure by Britain in April, 1895 of Port Hamilton, the British Government in its conversation with the Chinese Minister in London not only alluded to the possibility of the Anglo-Chinese alliance but subsequently spared no efforts to cultivate the friendship of China. Among the steps in this direction were the following:

a. When hostilities broke out between Siam and France in 1893, the British Government, through its Minister Mac-Donald in China, proposed an alliance with China for the protection of Siam against French aggression.

b. Great Britain, during negotiations with Russia over the demarcation of the frontiers of northeastern Afghanistan in the winter of 1893, requested the cooperation of China. To realize this scheme, she was ready to make certain territorial concessions to China along the borders of Siam and Afghanistan. However, fearing that any such alliance would inevitably turn Russia and France into enemies, China politely declined any proposal that would lead her into an undesirable entanglement.

c. Great Britain's policy of cooperation whilst seeking an Anglo-Chinese alliance continued up to the time of the Sino-Japanese War.

d. As soon as China and Japan became engaged in war, the British Government promptly proclaimed a policy of "strict neutrality" towards the belligerents, but made no secret of the fact that her sympathies were on the side of China. The commander of the British Far Eastern Fleet is reported to have signaled the approach of the Japanese fleet to the Chinese naval commander. The British newspapers also showed no hesitancy in expressing strong anger and denunciation when the Japanese warship *Naniwa* sank the *Kowshing,* a British transport flying the Union Jack while transporting Chinese troops.

However, when Japan scored outstanding victories over China in battles at Pyongyang and in the Yellow Sea, British public opinion underwent a radical change. The London *Times* in its editorial stated that it was gratifying to note that on the question of Japan's demand for treaty revision the British people did not insist on Japan giving substantial evidence that she should not be placed in the same category as semicivilized countries. By ratifying the treaty, Great Britain had shown her readiness to recognize that Japan was qualified to be included among the civilized countries of the world, added the paper, and had also excluded every rational ground for complaints against British policy. Far from having antagonistic interests, the two nations had several common interests of great importance.

The paper claimed that Russia, disregarding her assurance to China not to occupy Korea, still ardently hoped to possess a major ice-free outlet to the Pacific Ocean. In the face of this grave situation, neither Great Britain nor Japan could stand idly by. Furthermore, there were reports that whatever the outcome of the Sino-Japanese War, foreign powers were preparing to interfere. It would be unthinkable, the *Times* stated, for both Japan and Great Britain to remain silent and not assist one another in the face of possible intervention.

It is easy to accept the fact that the change in British public opinion was due to the realization that it was hopeless to rely on China, and that it would be more feasible to turn to Japan. Defeated in war, China could no longer be relied upon to protect her own interests, much less British interests. Great Britain must, therefore, seek a new ally. The comments of the *Times* testify to the complete abandonment of Britain's former policy towards friendly ties with China. The paper remarked that the war had completely shattered the mystery of China, a nation of incalculable potentialities. China was actually only a vast assemblage of teeming millions, without vitality, which could only be organized by force and power from without. Thus, Britain must keep close watch and preclude other nations from performing this task to her disadvantage, the *Times* warned.

Shortly after the signing of the Shimonoseki Peace Treaty, the so-called Triple Intervention by Russia, Germany, and France arose. Although invited to participate in the intervention of the Three Powers, Great Britain, having to re-examine the entire range of Far Eastern problems from a broader viewpoint, refused. Hitherto, Great Britain, which had regarded China as a natural ally against Russia, had trusted and assisted the former for the purpose of maintaining her position in the Far East. Now that the Celestial Empire had been completely defeated in the Sino-Japanese War, Britain realized that not only would China be unable to play an important role in the Far East but that her feebleness would be a source of perpetual danger and temptations.

The paramount problems now facing the British statesmen were: (1) how to ensure the maintenance of Great Britain's commanding power position in the Far East and (2) how to protect the huge commercial interests of the British Empire in the area.

By emerging victorious in the war, Japan demonstrated her real capability as a strong nation. Accordingly, Japan should no longer be given a cold reception as "an ignored element" in the region. It was easy to assume that participation in the intervention would give rise to a storm of fierce indignation in and out of the Japanese Government, adversely affecting Britain—with her rich commercial interests in the Far East—more than any other nation. Britain also felt that to be hated by Russia on the one hand and by Japan on the other might make her position in the Far East highly untenable.

It was also recognized that during the Sino-Japanese War, Japan had followed a policy of respecting British interests. Following the *Kowshing* incident, resulting in the loss of a British transport, Japan promptly promised to pay just compensations. Moreover, during the hostilities, Japan also refrained from taking military actions in Shanghai and its vicinity. While negotiating the commercial clauses of the peace treaty with China, Japan notified Great Britain that she had no intention of monopolizing specific commercial interests. She even gave assurances of her willingness to share with Great Britain and other powers the most-favored-nation treatment with regards to commercial advantages, extracted from China under the peace treaty.

There were other reasons prompting British refusal to join the intervening powers. The effects of the Sino-Japanese War did not constitute a menace to Great Britain, whose interests were concentrated around Shanghai, as much as they did to Russia with her interests mainly located in North China. Great Britain regarded the annexation of the Liaotung Peninsula by Japan as an aid to check Russian advances in Korea. British public opinion would not have countenanced any action, such as intervention, that would serve Russian interests.

While British statesmen displayed keen perception regarding the dangers of keeping aloof, they correctly understood the fact that, in the light of the conflicting interests of the three intervening powers, no one could absolutely guarantee the maintenance of their cooperation. Even if the accord did remain unbroken throughout the duration of the intervention, Great Britain wished to reserve complete freedom of action. After a detailed scrutiny of various standpoints, Great Britain concluded that her Far Eastern interests would not be impaired by the Japanese terms of the peace treaty. She further believed that the intervention was not justified and could only be secured by military force.

In accordance with her policy of nonintervention towards Japan, the British Government also decided not to resort to any hostile action towards the other powers. Consequently the British Foreign Minister, in an official statement, notified Minister Kato that the British Government, while entertaining feelings of cordiality, regretted its inability to assist Japan, regarding a neutral policy as the most appropriate under the existing state of affairs.

Indignant over the French attitude towards the Formosa

problem, Great Britain not only refused to comply with French wishes but did not hesitate to notify Japan that she was sympathetic towards Japan's possession of Formosa.

To Great Britain, whose Far Eastern frontiers were under heavy pressures from Russia, the latter constituted a hereditary enemy. It was her Far East policy, therefore, to seek the friendship of a powerful buffer state which would contribute to her own defense. For the most part, until 1894, China played this role. With a friendly China as a barrier to Russian aggression, Great Britain had been lulled into a false sense of security. But this nation on whom Britain had placed so much reliance displayed shocking impotence in its war against Japan. This fact completely altered Great Britain's attitude towards Japan. Renouncing her former policy of assisting China and slighting Japan, she adopted energetic measures to court the friendship of Japan, whom she now regarded as the most promising and powerful nation to protect British interests against Russian encroachments. This *volte-face* on Britain's part, highly resented by the Chinese, swung China rapidly towards Russia, and laid the foundation of the Anglo-Japanese Alliance.

Sino-Russian Secret Treaty of Alliance —Russian Aggression in Manchuria—

THE MEMOIRS of Count Sergyey Yulievich Witte, the moving spirit behind the Triple Intervention, reveal that neither Tsar Alexander III—the key planner of the Trans-Siberian Railway—nor Witte had designs of using the railway as a tool to further an aggressive policy in the Far East. The Tsar had even objected to the plan of extending a branch line of the Siberian Railway from Kyakhta to Peking, not only because he considered that Vladivostok was the most ideal terminal, but because he feared that the railway to Peking might incite the whole of Europe against Russia.

After pondering over the fact that a roundabout route would bring the new railway into direct competition with the Amur Steamship Company and considering the almost insuperable technical and engineering difficulties in the way of tracking the thick forest belt and vast marshlands of the Amur region, the Tsar concluded that the most practical and shortest route would be to cut across Manchuria to Vladivostok, thereby saving a distance of 340 miles.

But while the Russian authorities were still debating the best method of gaining China's peaceful acquiescence to this bold venture, the Sino-Japanese War erupted, resulting in the concession of Liaotung Peninsula. This new state of affairs in an area hitherto considered by Russia to be her sphere of influence made Korea's independence seem only nominal and constituted a grave hindrance to the Tsar's ambitions in the Far East. Absolutely convinced that Japan must be driven out of the Liaotung Peninsula, Russia readily agreed to the German suggestion to stage the Triple Intervention.

For Russia the fruits of this forceful intervention were so satisfying that they provided a definite impetus for her to execute a complete change of policy, from one of clouded ambitions to that of undisguised aggression. Under the terms of the Treaty of Shimonoseki, China had to pay an indemnity to Japan.

Posing once again as China's benefactor, Count Witte negotiated with the Chinese Minister in Russia during the period of the intervention to extend a Russo-French loan of 400 million francs at 4 per cent interest, payable in 36 years and guaranteed by the Russian Government (June, 1895). After extending this loan to China, Count Witte proceeded to establish the Russo-Chinese Bank, founded largely on French capital and capitalized at 6 million rubles. The statute of the said bank (Article XIV) defined its aims as the promotion of commercial ties with the countries of Asia.

But it is undeniable that the real objective of this financial organ was to reap economic advantage from the very close relations which now existed between Russia and China, arising from the intervention and the new Russian-guaranteed loan.

In May, 1896, in response to the personal insistence of the Tsar, it was decided to despatch the Viceroy Li Hung-chang to Moscow to attend the coronation, at which time the Viceroy was to express Chinese gratitude to Russia for her friendly role in the Triple Intervention and for the extension of the loan. Count Witte, who was then Minister of Finance, saw the occasion of the visit to be a golden opportunity to negotiate an agreement which would permit the construction of the railway across northern Manchuria to Vladivostok. In view of Foreign Minister Lobanoff's scant knowledge of the Far Eastern situation, Count Witte sought and received the Tsar's approval to conduct this extremely delicate negotiation. At that time, Viceroy Li Hung-chang was known to be an ardent Russophile, and regarded Japan as an inveterate enemy and Britain as treacherous.

On the other hand, Russia and France were considered by the Viceroy to be more powerful than Japan and Great Britain, and in addition had rendered valuable assistance to China, politically and economically. With each successive act in the intriguing Sino-Russian drama, Russia's grandiose dream of a Far Eastern empire began to gradually unfold. The latest act—the Sino-Russian Secret Treaty of Alliance concluded by Viceroy Li Hung-chang and Prince Lobanoff-Rostoffsky on May 22, 1896, during Li's stay in Moscow—was still another step in the same direction.

The contents of this treaty of alliance, wrapped in secrecy, were long a mystery to the puzzled outside world. The outline only became clear through the memoirs of Count Witte and M. A. Gerard, who was French Minister in China, and in 1922 China was compelled to publish the entire text of the treaty at the Washington Conference.

Apprehensive that the Viceroy might become a victim of foreign conspiracy and clandestine influences during his overseas tour, Count Witte sent Uftomsky specially to Suez to have the Viceroy transferred to a Russian vessel. As the Viceroy would first set foot on Russian soil at Odessa, Count Witte prepared a military escort designed to satisfy the pride of the Viceroy and at the same time to present an inspiring show of Russia's military grandeur.

It was with the greatest circumspection that Count Witte set the stage for the negotiations, concealing every trace of impatience from the Chinese officials and paying utmost attention not to hurt their sense of self-respect even to the slightest degree. By relating recent acts of Russian assistance, the Count did not forget to avow Russia's friendship for China, and the consequent benefits which the latter had derived.

Impressing upon Li the importance of Russia's proclaiming a policy of respecting China's territorial integrity, Count Witte clearly stated that once such a declaration to respect China's territorial integrity was made by Russia, it would be permanent and binding.

In his cunning approach to the question of constructing the Trans-Siberian Railway, Count Witte, while reiterating the importance of maintaining friendly relations between China and Russia, related an instance in which the existence of such a railway might have had far-reaching consequences for China. Stating that during the Sino-Japanese War a Russian detachment had been ordered to move to Kirin from Vladivostok, but was unable to do so before the war terminated on account of the lack of rail facilities, Count Witte laid great stress on the necessity of constructing the railroad that would traverse the shortest distance through northern Manchuria and Mongolia to Vladivostok and would enable Russia to preserve the territory of the Chinese Empire.

The Count also pointed out that the railway would economically develop the region through which it would pass, and was not likely to meet with any objections from Japan. Li at first was not favorably disposed to the idea, but fears of possible Japanese aggression in Manchuria and his profound sense of owing a debt of gratitude to Russia finally induced him to consent. Thus, Russia acquired the right to construct the railway across northern Manchuria to Vladivostok, and succeeded in persuading China to conclude the secret treaty of defensive alliance aimed at checking Japanese invasion of Chinese territory or Russian possessions in the Far East. The Tsar was informed of the negotiations by Lobanoff who had personally drawn up the text of the treaty itself.

There is an interesting episode to this treaty of alliance. After the provisions of the treaty had been drafted, Count Witte was extremely astonished to discover that the words *"par le Japon"* had been omitted from the text.

By inserting the words "third powers," the treaty became applicable in a much more general sense. Count Witte clearly realized that there was a glaring difference between concluding an offensive and defensive alliance with China directed only against Japan and one that was directed towards the other powers generally. Not only was it out of the question to conclude such an alliance with China against Great Britain, France, and other European powers, but it was fraught with great dangers. Should such a treaty become effective, there was no denying the fact that these powers concerned would at once regard Russia with hostility.

For these reasons, Count Witte immediately requested the Tsar to restore the original provisions of the treaty. However, on the day of the signing of the treaty—May 22, 1896— despite all his precautions, the Count was stunned to see that the treaty had not been altered. His attention drawn to this point, the embarrassed Lobanoff admitted that he had committed a grave blunder. He had honestly forgotten to inform his secretary to make the necessary alterations. Suddenly taking out his watch, the seemingly unruffled Lobanoff abruptly declared:

"Gentlemen, it is already past 12 o'clock. Cold dishes are most unappetizing. Let us leave the transaction of our business until after the luncheon." When the officials of both nations reassembled for the signing ceremony, Li Hung-chang, on behalf of China, and Count Witte and Prince Lobanoff-Rostoffsky, on behalf of Russia, formally affixed their signatures to fresh copies of the Sino-Russian Secret Treaty of Alliance which had, in the meantime, been appropriately amended by the secretary.

The Li-Lobanoff Secret Treaty of Alliance contained six provisions, as follows:

Article I: Russia and China agreed to mutually render assistance with all available land and sea forces in case of Japanese aggression against Russian territory in Eastern Asia, China and Korea;

Article II: Neither party should conclude a peace treaty without the consent of the other party;

Article III: All Chinese ports should, in case of necessity during military operations, be open to Russian vessels, and every facility should be provided by the Chinese authorities;

Article IV: To facilitate the movement of Russian land forces to threatened positions, the Chinese Government consented to the construction of a railway across Kirin and Heilungkiang Provinces, but the junction of this railway and the Chinese railway should not serve as a pretext for encroachment on Chinese territory or infringement against the Emperor of China; the construction and exploitation of the railway should be accorded to the Russo-Chinese Bank upon terms mutually agreeable to the Chinese Minister in Russia and the said Bank;

Article V: Russia should be free to use the said railway for transporting troops and provisions in time of war and peace;

Article VI: From the date of confirmation of Article IV, the Treaty of Alliance should be in force for a period of fifteen years.

Following the conclusion of the Sino-Russian Secret Treaty, Russia lost no time in translating into action the railway provision stipulated in Article IV, and on September 8, 1896 an agreement on the Chinese Eastern Railway across northern

Manchuria was concluded. Thus, Russia succeeded completely in furthering her aggressive policy in East Asia by concluding the Sino-Russian Secret Treaty and acquiring the right to construct the Chinese Eastern Railway.

Count Witte proudly proclaimed that the Russo-Chinese Alliance had a double significance. One was the acquisition of the right to construct the Trans-Siberian Railway along a straight course to Vladivostok without circumventing the Amur River and the other was the establishment of solid friendly relations with the Celestial Empire. Echoing similar sentiments, Prince Lobanoff declared that "Russian diplomacy has achieved two major objectives which Russia had been pursuing in the Far East. First, the exclusion of Japan from the continent and, secondly, the completion of the Trans-Siberian Railway through Chinese territory."

Russian activities were not confined to Manchuria, but included Korea as well. Before the Sino-Japanese War, Waeber, the Russian Minister to Korea, succeeded in winning the active sympathy of the Queen and her supporters in the Korean Court. In addition, he managed to conciliate the Koreans who were discontented with Yuan Shih-kai. Although Japan replaced China after the war as the dominant power, Russia continued to exercise great influence in Korea. Russian success in the Triple Intervention drove Japan into a very difficult situation in the Peninsula.

Meanwhile, Minister Goro Miura's alleged implication in the coup d'etat of October 8, 1895 was a severe setback for Japanese influence in the Korean Court. On February 10, 1896, the Russian army suddenly landed at Inchon and marched on Seoul in an effort to thwart Japan from assumming control of affairs in Korea. Next morning at daybreak the King, with the seal of state, the Crown Prince, Princess, and court ladies escaped from the palace and sought refuge in the Russian Legation. While this affair boosted Russian prestige in Korea, for Japan it was a severe setback that she could ill afford.

Decisively manipulating her strings of influence, Russia not only gained mining concessions on the coast of Tumeng-king on April 22, 1897, but lumbering rights along the northern frontier on August 28, 1897. Furthermore, under a secret agreement reached between Russia and Korea during the coronation of Tsar Nicholas II, the latter was obliged to engage Russian military and financial advisers. The Russian army was also assigned to give military training to Korean soldiers since June, 1896. In July, 1897, three Russian officers and ten noncommissioned officers arrived in Seoul to train the Korean soldiers. On September 6, 1897, they were employed for a period of three years to train approximately 3,000 men for the Imperial Guards and five infantry battalions.

Under these circumstances, Russia, laying her hands on Korean finance, established the Russo-Korean Bank, to which a Russian named Alexieff was appointed as a financial adviser and general commissioner of Korean customs. Inspired by these successes, the Russians displayed an undisguised ambition to take possession of the strategic harbor of Mosampo in southernmost Korea. These Russian designs were supported by her ally, France. The two countries pursued a common policy in meeting every major development in the Far East, as evidenced by the fact that France was a party to the Triple Intervention of 1895, provided funds for the Russian loan to China and for the Russo-Chinese Bank, and was an active participant in all enterprises.

Germany, for her part, also upheld Russia's Far Eastern policy by joining the *Dreibund's* Triple Intervention. On April 26, 1895, three days after informing Japan of the proclamation of the Three Powers, the Kaiser, while stressing Russia's mission of conquering the Yellow Race, promised the Tsar that his country would not hamper Russia's consolidation of a rear base and her policy in East Asia. The Tsar also accepted the Kaiser's European motto of *"Völker Europas, wahrt Eure heiligen Güter."*

This policy was clearly defined in the statement relating to German policy towards Russia which the Kaiser transmitted to Herr Rotenhan, Vice Minister for Foreign Affairs, on July 30, 1895. The statement of policy urged Germany to keep the Russians so preoccupied in the Far East that they would be unable to engage in secret maneuvers in Europe, particularly in eastern Europe. The Kaiser hoped that Russia, as the representative of the Orthodox Church and of Western civilization as well as the Defender of the Holy Cross, would counter the growing threat posed by Japan in China by taking full advantage of the power of the Orthodox Church and of Moscow.

A similar policy was adopted by Prince Bismarck. In case Russia committed herself in the Far East, the German Emperor was prepared to eliminate any major threat to Russia's flank in exchange for certain concessions, such as the reduction of Russian forces along the German frontier and support of Germany if she should attempt to acquire territory or at least a coaling station in China.

This German policy of encouraging Russian expansionism in the Far East, excepting for brief periods of interruption at the time of the Russian loan to China and the Boxer rebellion, continued up until the Russo-Japanese War.

The year 1898 was a significant turning point not only in the history of East Asia, but of world diplomacy. Discovering that her past policy of "glorious isolation" was no longer tenable, Great Britain made conciliatory moves towards Russia, but met with no success. A similar effort to woo Germany's cooperation also ended in failure. As a last resort, Great Britain in 1898 turned to Japan, hinting at a possible alliance. Events moved rapidly after Germany's lease of Kiaochow Bay. Russia gained her right to lease Kwantung Province, France the Kwangchow Bay area, and Britain both Weihaiwei and Kowloon. In this stage of virtual disintegration of China, it was clearly apparent that the most dominant position in this Far Eastern crisis was occupied by Russia.

Despite the extreme complexities, 1898 marked one of the most interesting periods of Russia's Far Eastern policy. As stated earlier, the original Russian project to lay the Trans-Siberian Railway across North Manchuria, in the view of Count Witte, was not rooted in political, strategic, or aggressive intentions, but was based on economic and technical advantages. Russian statesmen of the time had no definite national policy towards the Far East. Their judgments were rather based on personal views regarding Japan and China.

Even Tsars Alexander III and Nicholas II, ignorant of the true state of affairs in the Far East, were apt to be dangerously swayed by the views of adventurous Russian statesmen. At the same time, there was a sad lack in Russia of a group of astute politicians who could make farsighted recommendations to the Tsar.

Contrary to the practices of a constitutional government in which the cabinet formulated important foreign policies, in Russia each Cabinet member acted either independently according to his own judgment or according to the dictates of the Tsar. Occasionally, the Tsar himself would summon the council in the imperial presence to discuss vital state problems, but these were held so far apart that they did not contribute to mutual understanding among the members of the Cabinet. It is important to remember the existence of this state of affairs when seriously attempting to understand the development of Russian Far Eastern policy following the Triple Intervention and up until the outbreak of the Russo-Japanese War.

This unique aspect of the Russian governmental machinery enabled Count Witte to achieve complete success in negotiating the Triple Intervention, the Sino-Russian Secret Treaty of Alliance, and the rights to the Chinese Eastern Railways. Simultaneously this factor of success also later contributed to the successive failures of Russian policy.

In his book *Recollections of a Foreign Minister,* Iswalsky, Russian Minister for Foreign Affairs, recounted that Count Witte occupied a leading position in the Cabinet, not because of his de jure, but rather de facto actions. Iswalsky also admits that Count Witte behaved as though he constituted a state within the Russian Empire, dabbling not only in the financial affairs of the country but in various national enterprises. The reins of power which he grasped, he held and organized more firmly and effectively than other nominal administrative organs of the Government. This was not only a serious governmental loss, but this personal machinery was able to operate efficiently only under the guiding hands of Count Witte.

With these powers concentrated in his hands, the Count was able to exert far more influence on the course of Russia's Far Eastern policy than any other Cabinet Minister. However, this unique power which Count Witte was able to wield depended on the whims of the Tsar. Thus, during the initial stages of Russia's Far Eastern policy he was able to achieve great successes, but as soon as he fell into disfavor with the Emperor the reins of power slipped from his grasp. Indescribable confusion set in as a group of adventurous statesmen led by Admiral Abaza and Bezobrazoff gained the Tsar's confidence.

The controlling power of Count Witte over Russia's Far Eastern policy was secure until 1898, during which time the relations between Russia and China had grown in intimacy. On the other hand, in Japan there was a tendency towards Russophobia but not anti-Russianism. Had Russian policy been confined to the pacific penetration advocated by Count Witte as a course of Russian strategy, the Russo-Japanese War might well have been avoided.

With the lease of the Liaotung Peninsula in 1898, whence Japan had been ousted in 1895, the true face of Witte's pacific penetration was unmasked.

The crisis in the Far East originated with Germany's seizure of Kiaochow Bay on the pretext of suppressing a disorder caused by the murder of two German missionaries in Shantung in November, 1897. For many years prior to this event,

Germany had been constantly surveying the Chinese coast for an ideal spot to establish a naval base, or at least a coaling station. On the basis of the report submitted by the German Minister in China, the German Government decided to acquire the said Kiaochow Bay.

Accompanied by Hohenlohe, German Prime Minister, and Bülow, Foreign Minister, the Kaiser visited the Tsar on August 7, 1897, spending eleven days in the Russian capital. The primary purpose of the Kaiser's visit was to get the Tsar's prior approval to the German acquisition of Kiaochow Bay. When questioned about his reaction to the German intent, the Tsar replied that his Government was only interested in a guarantee of anchorage in the said Bay until the formal Russian acquisition of a port already marked for occupation north of Kiaochow.

Since there existed no harbor accommodation for German vessels, the Kaiser asked the Tsar if there would be any objection to the procedure of making prior arrangements with the Russian naval authority for German anchorage at the port. Voicing his willingness to entertain the Kaiser's views, the Tsar intimated that Russia not only had no intention of maintaining Kiaochow Bay to the end, but preferred the port to come under German control rather than fall into British hands.

As soon as the German Government reached its decision on the occupation of the port, the Kaiser transmitted his intention to the Tsar, who on November 7 replied by telegram that Russia was not in a position to approve or disapprove the German decision, having had only temporary possession of the area from 1895 to 1896.

Although this reply finally prompted the German Government to take possession of Kiaochow Bay, the Russian Minister of Foreign Affairs, Count Muraviev, nevertheless lodged a strong protest with the German Government, claiming that Russia had received anchorage rights *("priorité de mouiller")* from the Chinese Government in 1895.

While Russia did accept the Chinese Government's request to despatch warships to the area to observe German movements, she had no desire to confront Germany in view of the assurances given by the Tsar to the Kaiser and the realization that she might have to rely on German support for her Far Eastern policy. Thus, not only did Count Muraviev himself fail to honor his pledge to China, but early in November drafted a memorandum in which he pointed out that the German occupation of Kiaochow Bay offered Russia a signal opportunity to secure the Chinese ports of Port Arthur and Talien as bases for Russia's Pacific Fleet. Muraviev distributed this memorandum among influential members of the Cabinet, including Count Witte.

An important Cabinet meeting presided over by the Tsar was summoned to discuss the grave situation. Emphasizing that it was imperative for Russia to hold ports along the coast of the Pacific Ocean, Count Muraviev declared that circumstances now favored Russian occupation of Port Arthur and Talien.

This bold suggestion met with strong opposition from both Count Witte and Tiltoff, Minister of the Navy, who pointed to the grave danger that might arise in Russia's relations with Japan and Great Britain. Witte outlined his views to his Cabinet colleagues as follows:

"We have hitherto objected to such acts of occupation in violation of China's territorial integrity. This attitude was a contributory factor in forcing Japan to renounce her claims to Liaotung Peninsula. Moreover, we concluded a Secret Treaty of Alliance with China aimed at circumscribing Japan. This treaty placed Russia under an obligation to defend China against any Japanese move to seize Chinese territory. After assuming such a solemn undertaking, it would be unjust and dishonorable to act in a treacherous manner."

He was adamantly opposed to Count Muraviev's proposal, on grounds that it was in Russia's interest to maintain and develop good relations with China.

For his part, the Minister of the Navy, Tiltoff, supported Count Witte's assertion by declaring that it was more advantageous for the Russian Navy to acquire a port nearer to the waters of the Pacific, possibly along the coast of Korea, rather than Port Arthur and Talien which were unsatisfactory.

The Minister of the Army, Wannovsky, on the other hand, vigorously supported Count Muraviev.

In view of the conflicting opinions, Tsar Nicholas II refrained from expressing his views in favor of the Minister of Foreign Affairs, but a few days later when he granted a private audience to the Minister of Finance he openly admitted that he had already made up his mind to occupy both Port Arthur and Talien. The Tsar gave the following reason for having decided to order his troops to be ferried by transports to accomplish this mission: "At the end of the conference, Muraviev had informed him that a British fleet was maneuvering off Port Arthur and Talien, prepared to seize these ports if Russia did not occupy them forthwith."

From his conversations with the British Ambassador, Count Witte was able to confirm later that the foregoing information was totally unfounded. Thereupon, he made representations to the Kaiser through the German Ambassador in Moscow, urging German withdrawal from Kiaochow Bay in the hope that this would deprive Russia of any pretense for occupying Port Arthur. This move not only ended in a fiasco, but lowered Count Witte's prestige in the eyes of the Tsar and worsened his relations with Muraviev.

In early December, 1897, the Russian fleet occupied Port Arthur and Talien. As if to confirm the adoption of the aggressive policy advocated by Wannovsky, General Kuropatkin was appointed Minister of War in January, 1898. Russian demands were no longer confined to Port Arthur and Talien, but extended to the whole of the southernmost section of the peninsula. Russian military operations, launched on March 15, completely cleared Port Arthur of Chinese troops by the morning of March 16. This sudden occupation included not only the city with its gun emplacements, but also Talien.

China suffered not only deep humiliation and deprivation of her territorial sovereignty, but was forced to sign on March 27, 1898, a treaty leasing Kwantung Province to her erstwhile ally. Despite the adamant stand of the Empress Dowager, Russia succeeded in legalizing the lease by bribing Viceroy Li Hung-chang with half a million rubles and Chang Yin-heng with a quarter of a million rubles.

The treaty in question gave Russia the lease of Port Arthur and Talien, including adjacent waters, for a period of twenty-five years.

Under this agreement, China transferred all authority relating to army and navy commands as well as supreme administrative power within the said territory and waters (Articles I–IV); established a neutral zone along the northern extremity of the territory (Article V); closed Port Arthur as a naval base to all shipping except that of Russia and China, and designated Talienwan as a trading port, excepting for sectors to be used for military purposes (Article VI); accorded Russia the right to construct military facilities on the ceded territory (Article VII); and extended the concession granted to the Chinese Eastern Railway Company in 1896, permitting Russia, if necessary, the right to construct a connecting line from the main line of the said railway either to Talienwan or to any other convenient point along the coast of Yingkou and the Yalu River (Article VIII).

A supplementary treaty of May 5, 1898, demarcated the ceded territory and its neutral zone (Articles I and II). China received Russia's concurrence to restrict the terminus of the branch line of the Chinese Eastern Railway in Liaotung Peninsula to Port Arthur and Talien, and it was agreed that railway rights in the area along the said branch line would not be transferred to any national not of the two countries concerned (Article III). Furthermore, the Chinese Government consented not to concede the neutral zone, permit its use or allow trade to be conducted there by nationals other than those of Russia (Article IV). Road and mining privileges also could not be transferred without Russian concurrence (Article V).

A formal agreement for the construction of a new South Manchurian branch of the Chinese Eastern Railway was signed on July 6, 1898, by Russia (i.e. the Chinese Eastern Railway Company) and the Government of China. This agreement was based on the provisions of the agreement of 1896 for the construction and operation of the Chinese Eastern Railway.

The foregoing concessions wrested from China from March to July, 1898, are some of the outstanding achievements of Russia's subtle Far Eastern policy. All powers were subsequently notified by Russia that the character of the treaty of March 27 was a direct and natural result of the friendly relations existing between two neighboring empires. Moreover, their efforts should be broadly directed towards maintaining the peace and order of neighboring territories, and Russia promised to respect China's sovereignty and the commercial interests of the powers.

Needless to say, the results were not actually a direct outcome of either Russo-Chinese amity or the Russo-Chinese Treaty of Alliance. China had entertained no desire to accept the Russian demands.

During the process of negotiating the treaty in 1896, Viceroy Li Hung-chang had repeatedly informed Count Witte that "in Russia's own interest, it was advisable not to extend further southward the Trans-Siberian Railway to Vladivostok. The people of this region generally dislike the white race, fearing that the latter would visit misfortune upon them. Thus, any Russian advance into this region would undoubtedly lead to political instability and would prove calamitous to both Russia and China."

At the time of the German occupation of Kiaochow Bay,

Russia, still retaining the confidence of the Chinese, was requested by Viceroy Li Hung-chang through the Russian Minister to China to use her good offices in getting the German warships to withdraw from Kiaochow.

When the Japanese Minister to Peking, Yano, called on the Russian Minister on the morning of November 18, 1897, the latter evinced deep dissatisfaction with Germany's behavior and was convinced that the Russian Government would lodge a protest against the German action. As previously stated, the Russian Minister for Foreign Affairs, Count Muraviev, did in fact protest to the German Ambassador in Moscow.

With this indication of Russian support, China naturally began to rely on the Russians. Shortly thereafter, however, there was a complete shift in the attitude of the Tsar and the Russian Government. When Russia displayed no disposition to resist German occupation of Kiaochow Bay, but rather regarded the German move as an opportunity to seize Port Arthur and Talienwan, a group of influential figures within the Chinese Government began advocating a theory of relying on Japan and Great Britain to counter the Russo-German designs.

This theory received added momentum when two leaders from the south, Chan Chih-tung and Liu Kun-i, gained the support of even Weng Tung-he who hoped, perchance, that after sounding out both the Japanese and British Governments it would be possible to form a triple alliance.

Seeing no material advantage in allying herself with such powerless nations—Japan and particularly China—Great Britain turned a deaf ear to Chinese solicitations. Great Britain, it should be noted, in principle did not object to German occupation of Kiaochow Bay, but feared that this action might precipitate similar moves by other powers. The German Ambassador was told by Lord Salisbury that Germany's method of attaining her objective, rather than the objective itself, had created an unfavorable impression. In this respect, he added, Russia had deported herself with extraordinary skill.

In an attempt to gain British cooperation, Yano, the Japanese Minister in Peking, approached MacDonald, the British Minister, with the suggestion that the latter should mediate in the prolonged negotiations on Kiaochow Bay which were a source of concern to Japan. Yano's attempt met with dismal failure when MacDonald revealed Britain's discontent over the fact that the Chinese Government had already been in touch with the Russian Government over the issue and the local Chinese authorities in Swatow had taken an Englishman into custody. Far from being in a mood to assist the Chinese Government, there was growing pressure in Britain to take disciplinary action. There now appeared to be no hope of Japan cooperating with Britain in encouraging China to oppose Germany's occupation of Kiaochow Bay.

Accordingly, the Japanese Government on November 24, 1897, cabled the following instructions to Minister Yano:

"In view of the obscure attitude of the powers, the Japanese Government believes that the time is not yet ripe to formulate any definite policy. On the other hand, since it is obvious that peace in the Orient is most advantageous to both Japan and China, every effort should be bent on halting China from resorting to arms."

Betrayed by Russia and disappointed in the passive attitude of both Japan and Great Britain, China had no other course but to submit to German demands.

Japanese Policy towards Manchuria and Korea

IN THE years immediately preceding the Sino-Japanese War, Japan was confronted with the crucial problem of deciding which of the contending powers she would support—Russia and France or Great Britain—as they scrambled for hegemony in the Far East. During the early stages of the war,

Great Britain was suspected of having allied herself on the side of China while Russia was believed to be friendly towards Japan.

However, as the tide of war turned decisively in Japan's favor, Great Britain immediately turned her back on China and adopted a pro-Japan policy. Russia, on the other hand, regarded Japan's victory on the continent with such resentful envy that a sudden attack against the flanks of the Japanese army on the mainland could not be positively ruled out.

From the bitter lessons of the Triple Intervention, Japan was fully alive to the fact that, in the maintenance of her position, a military victory in the field was not enough, that she would have to prepare to win diplomatic victories as well. It was undeniable that the sphere of Japan's future expansion did exist in Manchuria and particularly in Korea. Hence, Japan could not allow Russian advances—military, political or economic—in these areas to go unchallenged.

To make her position invulnerable, two courses were open to Japan: she could either reach a compromise understanding on basic principles with Russia, or seek British cooperation to stem any further Russian expansionism. In other words, a Russo-Japanese rapprochement or an Anglo-Japanese alliance.

Although this policy of compromise towards Russia evoked little public enthusiasm, it nevertheless became Japan's foreign policy because of the support of Prime Minister Hirobumi Ito and influential elder statesmen who were of the opinion that it was easier and more effective to conclude a Russo-Japanese agreement than to finalize an Anglo-Japanese alliance.

They contended, firstly, that Great Britain, adhering to her policy of glorious isolation, was not prepared to conclude an alliance with Japan. Secondly, even if she did succeed in entering into such an alliance with Great Britain, this very act might endanger Japan's position in the Far East, even to the extent of provoking the Russians into hostilities with

Japan, an eventuality for which Japan was ill prepared. Count Munemitsu Mutsu, who dismissed the theory of an Anglo-Japanese alliance as mere idle talk unless Japan's national power was greatly augmented, made the following comment in an editorial appearing in the *Sekai no Nippon* (Japan in the World) of August, 1896:

"While the Anglo-Japanese alliance may sound beautiful, what the people of our time expect of it surpasses expectations. Great Britain, it is clear, cannot be expected to play the role of Don Quixote, mindful only of saving others. In recompense for the assurance of Japan's security, she expects the same measure of guarantee for her own security. If Japan is unable to give a similar assurance, Great Britain cannot be expected to be counted as Japan's ally. I very much doubt whether the Japanese advocates of such an alliance can categorically state that Japan's power in existing conditions is capable of ensuring the unlimited defence of Great Britain. . . . While it is not denied that Great Britain is seeking rapprochement with Japan, it is also a fact that she is trying to find some means whereby she can uphold her status in the Far East. Insofar as I am informed, Great Britain, although recognizing Japan's capacity for self-defense, is fully acquainted with her inability to despatch an allied force to fight on the continent as well as her inability to send a fleet to waters beyond Singapore. The Anglo-Japanese alliance would be meaningless, if because of Japan's incapacity to act externally, the responsibility of defense fell only on the shoulders of Great Britain, unilaterally obligated to defend Japan. This is the reason why Britain calls Italy her ally, but is unable to classify Japan in this category."

In these circumstances, despite the manifold difficulties in the way of an Anglo-Japanese alliance, a basis for negotiations with Russia was not found wanting. Japan had great commercial, political, and strategic interests in Korea, and believed that her future destiny hinged on her advance and expansion in the peninsula.

In Manchuria, Japan's economic interests were still insignificant. Although Russian penetration in Manchuria undoubtedly constituted a grave menace to Japan, the overriding concern was to keep the Russians from seizing a predominant position in Korea. In other words, there was a tendency in Japan to tolerate the Russian presence in Manchuria as an inevitable consequence of the completion of the Trans-Siberian Railway.

It is not surprising that an entirely opposite view was taken by Russia. Not only had she invested large sums of money in Manchuria, but the territory also fulfilled her long years of craving to possess an ice-free outlet at Port Arthur. Thus, Russia attached far more importance to her control of the strategic Manchurian base than any other territory in Asia, both economically and politically. It constituted a cornerstone of her Far East policy. Korea, where Russian investments were negligible, was only of strategic and political importance.

In the light of these circumstances, the Japanese Government was convinced that a compromise was possible with Russia on the basis of the so-called Exchange Policy, that is, the recognition of Manchuria as Russia's sphere of influence in exchange for Korea. This policy of exchanging spheres of influence became, in effect, Japan's golden rule for reaching a peaceful solution with Russia, supported as it was by such powerful leaders as Marquis Aritomo Yamagata, Prince Hirobumi Ito, and statesmen below the rank of *genro,* including prominent diplomats Tokujiro Nishi, Minister of Foreign Affairs, Jutaro Komura, Vice Minister of Foreign Affairs, and Tadasu Hayashi, Minister to Korea.

The Cabinet decision to send Prince Ito to Moscow shortly after the Triple Intervention to hold negotiations on the Korean problem had to be postponed by the coronation of Tsar Nicolas II. However, consultations between Japan and Korea were opened in Seoul between Komura and Waeber, Russian Minister to Korea, and in Moscow between Marshal

Yamagata and Lobanoff, Russian Minister of Foreign Affairs. As an outcome of these conversations, the Waeber-Komura Memorandum was signed in Seoul on May 14, 1896 and the Yamagata-Lobanoff Protocol was initialed in Moscow on May 28, both being of a similar nature. The contents of the latter agreement were as follows:

ARTICLE I

The two powers shall counsel the Korean Government to establish a sound financial system. Should foreign loans become necessary, the two powers shall upon mutual agreement render financial assistance.

ARTICLE II

Both Japan and Russia shall entrust to the Government of Korea—within the limits of the financial and economic resources of the country—the establishment and maintenance of military and police forces composed of Korean nationals.

ARTICLE III

Japan retains the right to continue to administer the telegraphic lines which are actually in her possession, while Russia reserves the right to establish a telegraphic line from Seoul to her frontier. The two powers agree to permit the Korean Government to purchase the said telegraphic lines.

ARTICLE IV

The foregoing clauses being basic principles, should the necessity arise to conduct negotiations on other particulars, the representatives of the two Governments concerned shall arrive at an amicable understanding.

Under the Yamagata-Lobanoff Protocol, Russia not only acquired the right to establish telegraphic lines, but the right to station the same number of troops as Japan at every seaport as well as Seoul. For Japan to have agreed that the two countries would act in concert to render financial assistance to Korea virtually amounted to Japan's ceding a part of her vested rights in the absence of Russian demands. Subsequently, Russia assumed almost complete control over Korea's military and financial affairs.

Highly dissatisfied with the state of affairs in Korea, the Japanese Government made overtures to Russia through its Chargé d'Affaires Motono at St. Petersburg, attempting to ascertain whether there was an intended desire to reach a friendly understanding with Japan over the Korean issue. Aside from a very vague assurance of goodwill, Japan failed to receive any satisfactory reply from the authoritarian Russian Government.

With the objective of forestalling the anticipated vigorous protestations from Japan against the lease of Port Arthur and Talien, the Russian Government made a gesture of goodwill towards Japan by voluntarily withdrawing her military instructors and financial advisers from Korea. In another surprise move, Russia proposed on March 17, 1898 a Russo-Japanese understanding on Korea in which the two parties would pledge not to interfere in the internal affairs of Korea. Simultaneously, Russia made it unmistakably clear that, despite all obstacles, she intended to lease Port Arthur and Talien. The Japanese Government replied on March 19, 1898, as follows:

"Regarding the Russian Government's proposal for an agreement of self-restraint (confirmation of Korea's autonomy and noninterference in its internal affairs), the Imperial Government is not averse to the conclusion of such an accord. . . . However, recognizing that Korea might be faced with the need to seek counsel and assistance of foreign states, Japan is of the view that, being a neighboring state with special interests and relations, it is only proper that she should bear these obligations. Hence, in the event the Russian Government concurs with these views, the Imperial Government would recognize Manchuria and its coastline as being outside of its sphere of interests."

According to the report of the Russian Minister to Japan, Rosen, the lease of Port Arthur and Talien aroused great public indignation against Russia in Japan. The Japanese Government, maintaining a realistic and calm attitude, attributed Russian activity as having been directed towards the acquisition of an ice-free port along the peninsular coast. With the possession of such a port in Manchuria, Japan considered that it was now opportune to attempt a settlement of the only bone of contention existing between the two powers: the problem of Korea.

The Japanese Minister for Foreign Affairs, Tokujiro Nishi, upon being informed of Russia's lease of the Liaotung Peninsula, not only acknowledged this notification, but hinted to Rosen that the Japanese Government desired to conclude an agreement whereby the two countries would abstain from interfering with each other's policies, that of Russia's in Manchuria and that of Japan's in Korea, on which basis they would reach a complete and friendly understanding.

The Russian Government's reaction to Japan's proposal, while expressing utmost satisfaction over the statement that Japan considered Manchuria and its littoral as being outside of her sphere of interests, took exception to the Japanese proposal on Korea. When Rosen read the above reply to Nishi, the latter could only smile ironically and utter disappointedly that he had no comment to make. It was also quite apparent that he was helpless to do anything. Thus, the problem of Korea had to be left in abeyance for the time being.

Nonetheless, Russia took steps to appease Japanese public opinion, irritated by the lease of Port Arthur and Talien, in order to preclude a collision. In conformity with Article IV of the Yamagata-Lobanoff Protocol, the Nishi-Rosen Protocol of April 25, 1898 was concluded, the essential points of which were as follows:

ARTICLE I

Japan and Russia confirm the sovereignty and complete independence of Korea, and agree to abstain from interfering in the internal affairs of that country.

ARTICLE II

Japan and Russia, in the event Korea should request either Japan or Russia for counsel and assistance, shall not take any measure regarding the appointment of military instructors or financial advisers without having first arrived at a mutual understanding on the subject.

ARTICLE III

Recognizing Japan's predominant and developing commercial and industrial enterprises in Korea, as well as the large number of her nationals residing in that country, the Imperial Russian Government agrees not to obstruct the development of the commercial and industrial relations between Japan and Korea.

Aptly described by Rosen as "lame and pointless," this protocol did not concern itself with the fundamental issues, but Japan under conditions that prevailed at the time could not expect to secure more favorable stipulations. The author of Count Takaaki Kato's biography described the situation in these words:

"The theory of an Anglo-Japanese alliance found wide support among people outside of government circles, but those inside the government did not declare their support outwardly. In the first place, the Genros were either Russophobes or Russophiles, with Prime Minister Ito evincing fear of Russia. Members of the cabinet hesitated to adopt an anti-Russian and pro-British policy. In addition, Nishi, Minister of Foreign Affairs, and the 'brains' at Kasumigaseki also argued against this policy as being premature. The disintegrating stage of Japanese diplomacy was supported, as it were, by the four shaky pillars: political controversy, financial difficulty, pro-Russianism of the Genros, and Prince Ito's policy of 'safety first.' "

A letter which Tokujiro Nishi, Minister of Foreign Affairs, addressed to Count Kato on February 18, 1898, is quite revealing in this connection. He wrote pessimistically:

"When pausing to consider the state of domestic affairs, I find that everything is going awry, politically and economically. In these circumstances, I have very little actual strength to divert abroad."

The unstable domestic conditions in Japan prevented the country from taking any firm foreign policy in either direction. Confronted by Russia's arrogant and aggressive policy, not to speak of her insincerity towards Japan, the nation began to drift away from Russia and draw closer to Great Britain.

Anglo-Japanese Rapprochement
—Change in British Policy towards China—

THE IDEA of the Anglo-Japanese Alliance itself was of long standing. The day the Rosebery Cabinet relinquished the reins of government (June 23, 1895), the British Minister for Foreign Affairs, Lord Kimberley, during the course of his meeting with the Japanese Minister in London, Takaaki Kato, expressed his firm belief that Great Britain and Japan shared vital interests. Stressing the need for Japan to augment her military forces, especially her naval power, the British Minister discounted any grounds for jealousy between the two powers which geographically were so widely separated.

This sharing of similar interests, he emphasized with genuine feelings of deep sincerity, should henceforward link both Great Britain and Japan in close association and relations of friendship. With such an understanding, Lord Kimberley concluded, in an event of an emergency each could render assistance to the other.

At the same time in Japan, Tadasu Hayashi, Japanese Foreign Minister at the time of the Triple Intervention, in an article appearing in the *Jiji Shimpo* of May 28, 1895, under the title "Japan Should Define Her Foreign Policy," emphatically stressed the necessity of concluding an Anglo-Japanese alliance. On June 21 the *Jiji Shimpo* editorially endorsed Count Hayashi's views. Moreover, the Japanese Minister to Russia, Nishi, in his report on the course of the Triple Intervention in May, 1895, also stressed the necessity for Japan's future cooperation with Great Britain.

One of the first British statesmen to propose the idea of an Anglo-Japanese alliance was Sir Ellis Ashmead-Bartlett. In the House of Commons on March 1, 1898, while questioning how Great Britain intended to maintain her position in the event of German participation in the Russo-French alliance in the Far East, he put forth his views that only Japanese assistance could help Britain in preserving her status in the Northern Pacific region and in thwarting Russian aggrandizement in China. The British Government could, if it so chose, use the power of Japan to control the whole China question and the Northern Pacific.

Another significant development in the relations between Great Britain and Japan occurred on March 17, 1898, when Joseph Chamberlain, Secretary of State for the Colonies in the Salisbury Cabinet, touched on the Far Eastern question during a banquet at which Minister Takaaki Kato was present. In the course of his conversation Chamberlain directed Kato's attention to the urgency of Japan entering into negotiations with Great Britain for the conclusion of an Anglo-Japanese alliance. "Once the northern regions of China fall under Russian dominance," warned Chamberlain, "regardless of the arguments of some Englishmen of the day to the contrary, such a development will create conditions contributing to the eventual dismemberment of the Chinese Empire. However, it is Great Britain's intention to forestall such an eventuality, desiring as she does the unbridled security of the celestial empire." He explained his belief that Japan's position, too, could not be otherwise. In other words, Great Britain and Japan not only shared interests in common, but were similarly placed. Thus, it was rather surprising to Chamberlain that Japan had not hitherto made any positive approaches to the British Government.

To this latter statement, Minister Kato replied that the Japanese Government might also entertain the same feeling of astonishment at Britain's negative stand.

Chamberlain lost no time in pointing out to Kato that this silence of both sides served no practical purpose. The need was rather for both parties to hold heart-to-heart discussions in an effort to try to understand each other. "I cannot positively state that the British Government will give her approval on this matter, but I can assure you," Chamberlain confided to Kato, "there is no room for doubt that she will favorably consider and amicably respond to any overtures made by Japan." Chamberlain added that whatever the outcome of the negotiations between the two countries, if it was Japan's wish, the British Government saw no difficulty in keeping the matter secret.

Minister Kato lost no time in reporting the Kato-Chamberlain conversation to Count Okuma, Minister of Foreign Affairs, and in the place of the pending Russo-Japanese rapprochement, urged the advisability of holding Anglo-Japanese negotiations. "Frankly speaking," he pointed out, "the Japanese Government appears to be coping with the present situation in two ways—showing undue concern towards Russia and cold-shouldering Great Britain almost to the extent of total neglect."

Kato seriously questioned the wisdom of Japan following such a policy, believing that it would be in Japan's interests to negotiate secretly with Britain even while conducting talks with Russia concerning Korea. "I am of the opinion," he continued, "that Great Britain will not only support Japanese expansion in the Korean Peninsula, but would even welcome such an advance by Japan as it would conveniently halt Russia's southward thrust. Even in ordinary times, Japan and Great Britain share many common interests. It is, therefore, quite natural that these two countries should make common cause. Unlike the expedient nature of the negotiations with Russia, an understanding with Britain for the maintenance of continuing friendly relations would, in view of the important role which the British navy will undoubtedly play in both the Eastern and Western waters in the years to come, be in Japan's best interests."

Unable to come to any decision on the Chamberlain proposal and fearing a mounting demand for such an alliance, the Ito Cabinet adopted an attitude of active indifference. Thus, the clamor for the alliance was silenced.

Difficulties in the way of accelerating such an alliance also existed in England. Without the assurance of German friendship, it was precarious for England to pit herself against Russia and France in the Far East. Admittedly Japan's strength was growing, but it was not of a world nature, being confined to the Far East. Was it wise for Great Britain, having entered into such an alliance with a Far Eastern power, to find herself engaged single-handedly against Russia in another part of the world? British stakes in the Far East being predominantly commercial, peace was an essential ingredient. Was there not a danger that the alliance with Japan might unnecessarily touch off the powder keg of war, destroying the peace that was so indispensable to British commerce? In addition, there was prejudice in the British royal circles against the non-Christian yellow race.

Consequently, it was only after Japan realized the futility of compromising with Russia, and Great Britain herself failed either to reach a settlement with Russia or to conclude an alliance with Germany that the two principal powers began to seriously consider an alliance.

In order to grasp the real significance and value of the Anglo-Japanese alliance, it is of utmost importance to review the transformation of Great Britain's Far Eastern policy. For over half a century, Great Britain had been successfully maintaining her national prestige in China, developing her vast commercial interests and giving the lead to the policies of the Western powers towards China.

However, following the Sino-Japanese War and the consequent diplomatic rivalries, England's position became more and more disadvantageous. On the other hand, as the three powers which had intervened in China rapidly began to expand their influence, China's attitude towards them became more conciliatory. Taking advantage of this change in attitude and with the assistance of the Chinese, the tripartite interventionists—Russia, France, and Germany—seized every opportunity, both large and small, to jeopardize Britain's position in the Far East.

In light of the fact that she was being forced into a position of isolation and incapability of forestalling the encroachments of the intervention powers, particularly Russia, Great Britain was obliged to adopt a "policy of compensation." To counter the Russo-French loan of 1895, Great Britain, in cooperation with the Deutsche-Asiatische Bank, extended two loans to the Chinese Government in 1896 and 1898 through the Hong Kong and Shanghai Bank.

To cope with the lease of Kiaochow Bay to Germany and Kwantung Province to Russia, Britain—in order to keep the balance of power in the Far East—obtained the lease of Weihaiwei "for so long a period as Port Arthur shall remain in the occupation of Russia." When the French leased Kwangchow-wan, she countered this move by securing the lease of Kowloon, a peninsula on the mainland adjacent to Hong Kong.

In addition to these rights, Britain also exacted from China the declaration affirming the nontransference of the Yangtze Basin, declaration regarding the inspectorship of the customs, opening up of inland ports, designation of several treaty ports, and rights concerning railways and mining.

But this British policy of compensation in China was not a substantive policy, for she had no real desire to vie for spheres of influence which would eventually lead to the dismemberment of China. British interests in the Far East being largely commercial, she not only urged the "open door" but desired the maintenance of China's independence and sovereignty.

Having failed in her attempts to block the demands of the powers against China, the British Government had no other alternative but to adopt the policy of compensation. However, every compensation she had received signified not success, but rather failure of British diplomacy. As a result, her commercial interests were gravely threatened; her prestige in the Far East damaged.

This state of affairs was admittedly humiliating to Great Britain which had hitherto been single-handedly undertaking the task of developing China and had been exercising decisive influence among the powers. To the people at home in England, it was a shocking development. In their view, the mainland powers were unitedly scheming to attack the trading supremacy of Great Britain, and the promises of these powers could not be relied upon. The British feared that if Russia, Germany, and France occupied portions of China, then proceeded to partition the whole of the country, they would set up an exclusionist system which would constitute a serious barrier to Britain's trade.

They also imagined that Russia, in occupation of Manchuria, would build up such a powerful military force that by the time it had locked the "open door," Great Britain would be in no position to offer any effective resistance. While it might take many years to annex Manchuria, once this was accomplished, she would be in a position to move southwards into Chihli Province. Even so mild a statesman as Count Witte had told the British Ambassador that Chihli, Shansi, Shensi, and Kansu were within Russia's spheres of influence, declaring at the same time that the Russian Government was planning to extend the branch line of the Trans-Siberian Railway up to Lanchow. Between this region and the Yangtze, there were no formidable natural barriers. Thus, it was only a matter of time before Russia controlled the whole expanse of China.

The British position in the Far East concerned not merely the interests of Britain herself, but was directly related to the very destiny of the British Empire. Unless the independence and integrity of China could be assured, not only would Britain lose her markets in China, but the continued possession of her colonies, Hong Kong, Malaya, and Burma, could prove exceedingly difficult. A Russian attack on India was no longer in the realm of impossibility.

Under these depressing circumstances, British public opinion strongly urged the Government to take drastic measures. For its part, the Government, reaffirming the Open Door policy, did not hesitate to declare that it would not countenance a relation of absolute preponderance of any one country towards Peking.

In the early stages of the Far Eastern turmoil, Great Britain viewed the situation rather optimistically—at least outwardly. During his speech delivered at Guildhall on November 9, 1895, Lord Salisbury called on the British people not to be unduly alarmed over the situation in the Far East, enjoining them to trust the Government. Whatever might happen in the region, be it in the direction of war or trade, Britain should be able to meet any challenges at competition.

Then in 1898, following Germany's lease of Kiaochow Bay and Russia's lease of Kwantung Province, the Chancellor of the Exchequer Balfour stated that after several months of intensive diplomatic activities, the British position, commercially and strategically, was increasingly powerful. Britain should, therefore, look to the future with confidence and with feelings of reassurance. A few months later, Balfour stated that insofar as the Open Door policy was concerned, the door had never in a real sense been closed.

The Prime Minister also assured his audience at Albert Hall that "all newcomers shall retain their property, that despite delirious outcries of isolation, we have adequate strength to fulfil our obligations." The British Government, embarking on a policy of patience and watchfulness, exerted every effort to avoid unnecessarily disturbing the peace of the Far East and refrained from any untimely action.

The year 1898 marked an important turning point in Russia's Far Eastern policy and for Britain, too, it was a year of decision, a decision to abandon her traditional policy of so-called glorious isolation. It was not only in the Far East, but in other parts of the world that British statesmen in 1898 began to recognize the impending threat to this policy. In the years which followed the Triple Intervention of 1895, British isolationism had been the target of scornful attacks in the foreign press.

In place of this traditional policy of glorious isolation, certain influential members of the British Cabinet began campaigning for a policy of alliances.

Three alternatives were open to Britain in the Far East: (1) to ally herself with Japan; (2) to ally herself with Germany and win the adherence of either Japan or the United States to the alliance; and (3) to reach a friendly understanding with Russia.

It was the third alternative which Britain initially attempted to attain—a satisfactory understanding with Russia. Edward Grey asserted: "Russia and Britain will confront each other in the Far East, but this need not necessarily lead to mutual enmity." The British attitude was that there was adequate room in China to accommodate both Great Britain and Russia. As long as Russia did not entertain territorial designs or place commercial obstacles in Britain's way, there would be no serious opposition on Britain's part to Russia managing affairs in Manchuria and acquiring an ice-free port in the Pacific.

Touching upon this point in Bristol on February 5, 1896, Arthur J. Balfour stated that the British Government had no objection to Russia's intention to seek an outlet to the Pacific. The same theme was reiterated later by both Curzon and Lansdowne. In furtherance of this policy, Britain also did not oppose the construction of the Chinese Eastern Railway by Russia, as is clear from the statement made to the House of Commons by Balfour that Britain as well as commerce in general would benefit in a large measure from the construction of the railway, regardless of the conditions or the country which undertook its construction.

A great number of British statesmen also considered an understanding between Great Britain and Russia to be more advantageous than an alliance with Germany. Herbert Henry Asquith admitted that "it was becoming increasingly difficult to harmonize German activities in China and Britain's declared policy. In fact, Germany could offer nothing to such an alliance."

On January 17, 1889, O'Conor, the British Ambassador to Russia, was instructed to sound out the views of Count Witte as to the possibility of Great Britain and Russia cooperating with each other in China. The Ambassador's proposal, made on January 19, to Foreign Minister Count Muraviev, was received with unexpected cordiality. On this occasion, the Ambassador emphasized the importance of this understanding—if it was to be effective and permanent—being expanded to cover the entire range of mutual interests, instead of being limited to important questions concerning the Far East.

Without making any official commitments, Lord Salisbury cited the example of Russia having greater interests than Great Britain in the Black Sea region in relation to Turkey and the area of the Euphrates Valley down to Baghdad, whereas British interests outweighed those of Russia in Turkish Africa and Arabia and the Euphrates Valley beyond Baghdad. The same, he remarked, could be said of China, citing the Yellow River Valley and the region to the north, and the area of the Yangtze Valley. He made it unmistakably clear, however, that the prerequisite to this understanding was not the partition of territory, but the partition of preponderance, including the observance of existing treaties and noninfringement of territorial sovereignty.

Although this proposal was first received with more than usual interest by the Russian Government, it feared that any premature move in relation to Turkey might lose the friendship of both Germany and France. Hinting that the question of China should be accorded priority, the Russian Government voiced its desire to participate in the Anglo-German loan which was then under negotiation.

The British Government seemingly did not at first object to this Russian proposal and succeeded, in connection with the declaration of nonalienation of the Yangtze Basin, in acquiring several political and commercial rights, for inspectorship of the customs and opening of inland ports. Nevertheless, after repeated negotiations, it excluded Russia from the Anglo-German loan, charging her with insincerity and ambiguity towards the British proposals.

Deeply dissatisfied with the British gains in China, Russia vigorously protested against the loan. On February 19, Russia followed this with a notification to the British Government that she intended to lease Port Arthur and Talien, which aroused fears in Britain that they would be fortified. Negotiations between the two powers collapsed when it became abundantly apparent that their aims in China were entirely opposite.

The next alternative for Great Britain was to move in the direction of concluding the Anglo-German alliance. Just before the Anglo-Russian negotiations ended in a deadlock, Joseph Chamberlain, Secretary of State for the Colonies, opened the way for negotiations with Hatzfeldt, the German Minister in London, on the conclusion of the Anglo-German alliance towards the end of February, 1898. During the course of these negotiations, the Kaiser and his Foreign Minister Bülow evinced their reluctance to risk the enmity of Russia and to fight to safeguard Great Britain's interests in the Far East. Not only did the discussions between the two countries make no headway, but even the Anglo-German special agreement concerning the Far East received scant, if any, attention.

It is true that Germany's interests in the Far East were also commercial, but she had other vital interests which prevented her from participating in an alliance with Britain. Moreover, German interests in Europe were a hundredfold more important than her interests in Asia.

It was quite natural for Germany to shun any proposal that would make Russia and France antagonistic, merely for the sake of her interests in Asia. In order to relieve Russian pressure on her eastern frontiers, did not Germany actually encourage Russian entanglement in the Far East?

Having failed to attain any agreement, general or specific, with either Russia or Germany, Great Britain was left with the only other alternative, that is, the conclusion of an alliance with Japan, the only powerful nation in the Far East. It was thus with unusual seriousness that Britain embarked upon her policy of achieving this alliance with Japan.

CHAPTER **3**

Anglo-German-Japanese
Rapprochement
1895-1901

1

In the years following 1895 the ambitions of the Western powers towards China became increasingly pronounced. As a result of her crippling defeat in the Sino-Japanese War, China was obliged to transfer a number of mining and railway rights to the Western powers, including recognition of land concessions, and to issue humiliating declarations on the nonalienation of territory.

In the wake of the widespread antiforeign agitations which followed, the so-called Boxer Uprising erupted violently in 1900, in which the climax was reached with the murder of the German Minister Baron von Ketteler in Peking. The attention of the entire world was soon focused on the problem of China, making international intervention on a large scale inescapable.

In these circumstances, Germany, abandoning her calm and calculating policy, began to pursue an undisguised authoritarian policy decidedly more marked than during the Triple Intervention. On receiving the report of the slaying of Ketteler, the Kaiser was so enraged that he ordered the launching of a methodical attack and the leveling to the ground of Peking—a mission which the German Minister had to bear foremost in mind.

However, the German Minister for Foreign Affairs, Prince von Bülow, sounded a note of caution against the Kaiser's rash course of action. He warned that if Germany displayed unusual zeal for the suppression of the Boxer atrocities, the rest of the Western powers might unite at the expense of German sacrifices. Great Britain was already showing signs of inducing Germany to resist Russia. Moreover, in France the revenge-seekers would undoubtedly exploit the situation.

Brushing aside Bülow's counsel, the Kaiser excitedly declared that compared to the enormity of the crime—the attack against the German Legation—everything else paled into insignificance. The recklessness of the Kaiser's attitude was also evidenced in his speech delivered to the expeditionary force to China, his attempt to appoint General Waldersee as commander of the international expeditionary force, and his unjust bargaining and oppressive attitude during this period. General Waldersee arrived in China in the middle of October, but there was little that remained to be done militarily. Thus, the importance of his exalted position sharply contrasted with the unimportance of the tasks that actually confronted him.

Certain countries wanted to recall their armies, while Russia desired the dissolution of the international force and the evacuation of Peking. Under these conditions, it became apparent that Germany's basic problems in China would have to find their solutions in Berlin.

It was not long before Germany was drawn into a major clash of interests between Great Britain and Russia. Taking advantage of the disturbed conditions in China, Russia had already taken decisive military action for the occupation of Manchuria in July, 1900. Great Britain, on the other hand, was hurriedly consolidating her hold in China's most fertile region along the Yangtze River—a sphere of British influence since 1898. Charging that Britain was attempting to claim the lion's share, Russia had advocated the idea of neutralizing the Yangtze Basin to the German Government through her Ambassador in Berlin in December, 1897. Germany, however, had failed to respond to the Russian probe.

Disappointed by the negative German reaction, Russia turned to France, querying her on the need to check the advance of British influence. Together with France, Germany, favoring an Open Door policy for all trading nations, opposed Britain's policy along the Yangtze River. Without injuring Russian interests in Manchuria, she envisaged the same triumvirate of Russia, France, and Germany—which opposed Japan after the Sino-Japanese War—countering Great Britain. But the Russian approach for a joint intervention against Great Britain was turned down by Bülow on grounds that from the German point of view the success of such a venture was improbable.

That Great Britain and Russia would exclude Germany in eventually partitioning their spheres of influence through direct negotiations affecting the destiny of China was anticipated. This was evidenced by the Anglo-Russian Agreement of April 28, 1899. By this agreement, Russia pledged not to seek any railway rights for its citizens in the Yangtze River region while Great Britain pledged to respect Russia's exclusive railway rights north of the Great Wall.

The fact should not go unnoticed that Baron von Holstein, who had earlier thought that there was no prospect of an Anglo-Russian understanding, did attempt fruitlessly to forestall such an agreement. On July 27, 1900, he wrote that it was clear that Great Britain would make further concessions to Russia in the Far East in exchange for British interests in the Yangtze basin. If only for this reason, Holstein continued, Germany had no interests in the Anglo-Russian agreement.

In Holstein's view, the only way to impede the progress of the agreement was to approach Russia on individual issues, avoiding the general problem. His scheme in this regard met with some success. In other words, by making overtures to France and Russia, Germany hoped to prevent the exclusive surveillance of Chinese vessels by the British fleet on the

Yangtze River, which Great Britain was unquestionably exercising early in August for the purpose of acquiring a privileged status along the river. German moves in this direction and the prospects that even America might participate in the group of competing countries ranged against Britain's Yangtze policy profoundly influenced Great Britain, compelling her to make concessions.

On August 22, 1900, the Kaiser, meeting the Prince of Wales and Ambassador Lascelles at Wilhelmshohe, pointed out that two possibilities were open to Great Britain in the pursuance of her policy regarding the Yangtze region. One was for Britain to maintain absolute paramountcy, in which case she would have to rely solely on her own defensive strength. In view of the United States, this policy could not be easily executed. The other policy—and the one favored by Germany—would be for Britain to proclaim free trade and equal opportunity. In the latter case, both Great Britain and Germany would be able to combine themselves against other countries not in sympathy with this principle.

Both the Prince of Wales and Ambassador Lascelles, expressing support for the second alternative, promised to do their utmost to secure Lord Salisbury's concurrence. It was a sombre Lord Salisbury who, shortly thereafter, declared that Great Britain had never pursued in China any policy other than that of equal opportunity.

2

THE way was thus opened for future negotiations between Great Britain and Germany leading ultimately to the conclusion of a new agreement. At first Bülow, in order to ensure the principle of free trade along the Yangtze River, hoped to have the nations with preponderant commercial interests in China, such as Great Britain, America, France, and Japan, also affiliated in an agreement.

To allay British suspicions, the German Ambassador in London, Hatzfeldt, suggested separate negotiations with Great Britain, to be followed by parleys with other interested countries. He further hoped to realize his long cherished desire of increasing the bonds of friendship between Great Britain and Germany as far as possible.

In this connection, it should not be overlooked that Great Britain and Germany instituted the negotiations with entirely different objectives in mind, giving rise to grave inconsistencies in the results of the accord. Great Britain, although under heavy world pressure to forego her fundamental scheme of developing a special position along the Yangtze Basin, was determined to exact a high price for her concessions to Germany—a price which would, in effect, place Germany under an obligation to adopt an anti-Russian policy.

Consequently, in the course of the negotiations, the question arose of the ejection from Chihli Province of Russia, which had strategically occupied the railways linking Taku and Tientsin as well as Tientsin and Peking, both of which had been constructed with British capital. Wishing to avoid becoming enmeshed in Anglo-Russian rivalry, Germany, under the pretext of military exigency, informed the British Government that during the German military action under Commander-in-Chief General Waldersee it was necessary for the Russian army to be in occupation of these railways.

Later, on September 25, 1900, with the aim of curbing Russian advances in Manchuria, Salisbury insisted that the understanding ensuring equal opportunity in the Yangtze Basin should be extended to all ports and harbors in China. Hatzfeldt, objecting to the British design of pitting Germany as a buffer against Russian ambitions, promptly assailed the British idea.

Upon receiving Hatzfeldt's protest, Salisbury replied that the British Government had no intention of injuring Russian interests in the hinterlands of Manchuria. Adding that the coastal harbors in that area were already opened as treaty ports, Salisbury even expressed Britain's willingness to exclude certain harbors along the Amur River to which the Russian Government attached special importance.

A few days later, Salisbury hit upon a formula, under which Great Britain and Russia would both be obliged to maintain free ports in the territory of China south of latitude 38°. This formula would exclude from the agreement such ports as those along the Amur River, Port Arthur, and even a part of Chihli Province. Extremely satisfied with the nature of the British proposal, Germany energetically pressed for the early conclusion of the agreement—which, in her view, would at the same time bar any compromise between Great Britain and Russia that would preserve Manchuria for Russia and the Yangtze Basin for Britain.

During the course of these negotiations, Great Britain and Germany engaged in an argument in which the latter resented the former's design of engendering hostility towards Russia. The essential points of the German draft of the Anglo-German Agreement of September 22 concerning the Yangtze Basin were based on the permanent common interests of the two powers to preserve the principle of the Open Door along the Yangtze River.

Furthermore, they should not only act in concert to uphold this principle, but pledge not to make use of the present complication to obtain territorial advantages in China. However, should any other power attempt to obtain such territorial advantages, Great Britain and Germany would hold prior consultations in case it became necessary to acquire corresponding territorial rights in order to preserve the balance of power.

For his part, Salisbury submitted a new proposal to strengthen the agreement by attaching the following clause to the last part of the draft agreement: "and will oppose in such manner as may be agreed upon between the two powers, any attempt on the part of any other power to obtain territorial advantages in a similar manner."

Both Hatzfeldt and Bülow were quick to discern in the British amendment a dagger pointed at Russia. By attaching this amendment, the treaty took on the characteristic features of an Anglo-German alliance, ready to cope with individual issues and aimed at common action against other powers, not unlike the Anglo-Portuguese colonial agreement of 1898. In any case, this was the British position. Germany, on the contrary, did not—insofar as it affected Russian interests—find such an idea palatable.

But the two powers were in accord in their desire to reach an agreement. As an alternative to the insertion advanced by Salisbury, Bülow proposed on October 3, 1900, the following insertion: "and will direct their policy towards maintaining undiminished the territorial condition of the Chinese Empire."

It must be said that the adoption of such a stipulation might well have been very dangerous. The object and measures embodied in the stipulation were too general, undefinable, and obscure. On the other hand, obligating German policy to follow a set course would have been tantamount to British admission that Germany really had no intention of pursuing such a course.

While Britain endeavored to have the German insertion clearly define Manchuria as an integral part of Chinese territory, Germany was inclined to assign Manchuria to Russia.

Upon reading the despatch from General Waldersee that Russia intended to seize the British-leased railway to Peking, the Kaiser made the following annotation in the margin:

"Suum cuique." (To each his own).

"Manchuria to Russia, the railways to Britain. If Russia is not content with this, she must vie with Britain."

It will be recalled that in the early stages of the negotiations, Hatzfeldt made no secret of his intent not to drive the Russians out of Manchuria. Bülow also appeared to understand that the territorial condition of China meant the virtual maintenance of the status quo. Though Russian-occupied

Manchuria was considered a part of this understanding, the fact remains that the transfer of Manchuria to Russia had not yet been effectively executed under treaty provisions between China and Russia.

An entirely different interpretation from that of Bülow was held by Great Britain, which could regard Manchuria as part of the Chinese territorial condition, the integrity of which both Britain and Germany should endeavor to preserve. When Salisbury learned of the draft amendment drawn up by Bülow, he could not conceal his disappointment and dissatisfaction, particularly in view of the possibility of misunderstanding arising in the future as a result of the inefficacious stipulation that Bülow had substituted. Notwithstanding, Salisbury ignored the matter, demanding only that a new clause be inserted, regulating the maintenance of all the vested rights of both Great Britain and Germany based on effective treaties in China. This move was aimed at recovering the railways in Chihli Province which had been occupied by the Russian army with General Waldersee's tacit approval.

In view of Britain's naval supremacy along the Yangtze River, Bülow did not hesitate to meet the British requests regarding her railways and accordingly instructed General Waldersee. Although Salisbury's demands for the preservation of all treaties with China appeared simple enough, he had these demands confirmed and inserted in the preamble of the agreement.

Salisbury also proposed that the protection of free trade by both powers should be extended to the entire area "over which they have influence," the aim of which seemed to be based on the British machination to enlarge the application of the provision of the agreement to the area north of latitude 38°. But Bülow desired to amend the British proposal to read "as far as they can exercise influence," and hoped to refrain from discussing the real extent of that influence.

Thus, Great Britain and Germany finally arrived at a fundamental understanding on the draft of the agreement. The exchange of official documents on the Anglo-German Yangtze Agreement between Salisbury and Hatzfeldt took place in London on October 16, 1900.

Under the agreement reached between Great Britain and Germany, the two powers agreed to uphold the principles of the Open Door and territorial integrity in China and "to discuss common actions" in case another power made use of the complications in China for the purpose of obtaining territorial advantages, and also to invite other interested powers to accept these principles.

The text of the agreement was as follows:

Her Britannic Majesty's Government and the Imperial German Government, being desirous to maintain their interests in China and their rights under existing Treaties, have agreed to observe the following principles in regard to their mutual policy in China:

1. It is a matter of joint and permanent international interest that the ports on the rivers and littoral of China should remain free and open to trade and to every other legitimate form of economic activity for the nationals of all countries without distinction; and the two Governments agree on their part to uphold the same for all Chinese territory as far as they can exercise influence.

2. Her Britannic Majesty's Government and the Imperial German Government will not, on their part, make use of the present complications to obtain for themselves any territorial advantages in Chinese dominons, and will direct their policy towards maintaining undiminished the territorial condition of the Chinese Empire.

3. In case of another Power making use of the complications in China in order to obtain under any form whatever such territorial advantages the two Contracting Parties reserve to themselves to come to a preliminary understanding as to the eventual steps to be taken for the protection of their own interests in China.

4. The two Governments will communicate this Agreement to the other Powers interested, and especially to Austria-Hungary, France, Italy, Japan, Russia, and the United States of America, and will invite them to accept the principles recorded in it.

3

O<small>N</small> October 24, 1900, J. B. Whitehead, British Chargé d'Affaires, and Weder, German Minister to Japan, notified the Japanese Government of the text of the Anglo-German agreement and inquired whether the principles contained in the said agreement were acceptable to Japan. But Kato, Japanese Minister for Foreign Affairs, having already been informed on the previous day of the conclusion of the agreement by both Ministers Hayashi in London and Inouye in Germany, had sent the following telegraphic instructions to the two Ministers:

"The Japanese Government desires immediate confirmation of its presumption that a third party accepting the principle contained in Article IV would enjoy the right to accede to Article III of the agreement."

Upon acknowledgment by both the German and British Governments that the Japanese Government's presumption was correct, the Japanese Government decided to participate in the Anglo-German Agreement. However, on October 29, 1900, Japan took the occasion of its participation to notify the Governments of both Great Britain and Germany in the following vein:

"Having accepted the assurances of the two contracting powers that Japan—in lieu of the signatory powers—would enjoy the same status as that of the Entente Powers, the Imperial Japanese Government has the pleasure to notify your Governments that in participating in the said agreement it unhesitatingly assures you of its acceptance of the principles contained in this agreement."

While three nations—Austria, Italy, and Japan—accepted all the principles of the agreement, the United States accepted only the first two articles, and was noncommittal on the third article. Russia and France, on the other hand, generally approved the second article. That the Anglo-German Agreement unfavorably impressed the Russian Government was quite apparent in the latter's statements to both the British and German Governments that she could accept the principles only insofar as these were compatible with her own interpretations.

4

As was clearly stated earlier, neither of the signatories to the Anglo-German Agreement was able to achieve all the hoped-for objectives. Not only did Germany fail to realize her hopes of concluding an understanding concerning the Yangtze River Basin, but she was obliged to accept a far more general understanding on China, as desired by Great Britain. The British Government's fundamental and extensive demand, designed to frustrate Russian encroachments, relied heavily on acquiring German assistance, which in turn depended solely on Germany's own intentions and interpretation of the agreement. However, no such intentions were entertained by the German Government.

During the course of the negotiations on the agreement, it should have already been crystal clear to Great Britain that Germany had no designs to evict Russia from Manchuria. Such being the case, the charge of breach of faith on the part of Germany for later withholding assistance is not wholly tenable. Having accepted Article II of the Agreement, which both parties knew could be and to a certain extent would be interpreted to suit the convenience of either of the contracting parties, neither of the two powers could entirely escape the onus of having acted in a manner analogous to bad faith.

It should be admitted that Bülow's conduct in providing such an ambiguous stipulation—in order to please the British —was not less irresponsible than Salisbury's gullibility in acquiescing to Article II without due deliberation, well aware that it was phrased in only vague terms.

It is, therefore, hardly surprising that difference of opinions should have arisen between Great Britain and Germany regarding the interpretation of the Agreement. Within several weeks of the signing of the Agreement, early in November, 1900, Russian General Lenewitsch occupied the south bank of the Yellow River near Tientsin. Deeply perturbed by this Russian action, the British Government on January 28, 1901 sought the views of the German Government on whether any violation of the Anglo-German Agreement had been committed. In reply Bülow stated that, since Russia had made no sovereign demands and had constructed no military establishments in the occupied area according to information available to him, he did not consider that there had been a violation of the Agreement. Subsequently, an even more bitter dispute over the interpretation of the Agreement relating to the Manchurian question ensued.

The immense economic potentials which Russia had thus acquired in North China caused great consternation in Great Britain. Determined to crush the Russo-Chinese secret treaty on Manchuria, the British Government called on the German as well as the Japanese Government to act under the provisions of the Anglo-German Agreement. But Bülow replied on February 21 that Germany had no obligation under the Anglo-German Agreement to take any military action to nullify Russia's de facto annexation of Manchuria.

Moreover, on the following day, Bülow intimated to Japanese Minister Inouye that Germany, because of her insignificant interests in Manchuria, deemed it appropriate to adopt a wait-and-see policy, taking no initiative until after considering the actions pursued by other nations with larger interests in the area. In a speech to the German Diet on

March 15, Bülow reaffirmed Germany's view that the Anglo-German Agreement, as was clear from its wording, did not apply to Manchuria, and that furthermore Germany possessed no fundamental interest there.

Thereupon, the Japanese Government despatched telegraphic instructions to Minister Hayashi in London to transmit an aide memoire to the British Government to ascertain the German view. In a British aide memoire, the Assistant Secretary for Foreign Affairs Bertie pointed out that "according to the British Government's view, Article II of the Anglo-German Agreement could be applicable to the Manchurian provinces, but it was not in a responsible position to speak for the views of other governments as to their interpretations of that article."

Quickly reacting to the British Government's view, the German Assistant Secretary for Foreign Affairs informed Minister Inouye that he was astonished to learn, according to information from London, that the British Government had replied affirmatively to the query of the Japanese Government on the question of the inclusion of Manchuria in the Anglo-German Agreement. He recalled that the British Government first proposed to insert a stipulation in the agreement to the effect that Manchuria would be excluded, and that during the negotiations agreed to substitute the insertion with the wording "as far as they can exercise influence" in compliance with the suggestion of the German Government.

It is thereby apparent that Germany and Britain were sharply divided on the interpretation of Article II of the Agreement. Since Great Britain declined to assume any responsibility for the German interpretation of the Agreement, Japan was, to say the least, extremely perplexed. The authorities of the Japanese Ministry of Foreign Affairs took the stand that Germany was misinterpreting the Agreement by her assertion that Manchuria was out of its sphere and beyond the "exercise of influence."

On the other hand, in light of the circumstances surrounding the materialization of the Agreement, Germany's interpretation could not be labeled as completely "unjust." The fact remains that Great Britain, by expressing her view that she was unable to assume responsibility for the interpretation of other nations regarding the Agreement, had demonstrated a lack of confidence in the infallibility of her own interpretation. Hence, there were sufficient grounds from the very outset for these varying interpretations.

5

THERE was now an impelling need to resolve the two interpretations of the Anglo-German Agreement by both Great Britain and Germany. In conformity with the wording of the Agreement, it was possible for Great Britain to request the German Government's diplomatic support insofar as the denunciation of the Russo-Chinese secret pact on Manchuria was concerned. But Lord Lansdowne, who had replaced Lord Salisbury as the guiding hand of British diplomacy since the autumn of 1900, was uncertain as to the advisability of citing the Agreement in view of the progress of the negotiations.

However, on February 7, 1901, when notifying Baron von Eckardstein, then First Secretary of the German Embassy in London, of the British intention to denounce the secret pact on Manchuria, Lansdowne at least appealed, without directly referring to the said pact, for serious consideration of the political implications of the pending German decision. Moreover, in his conversation with Ambassador Hatzfeldt on March 22, Lord Lansdowne not only acknowledged that Manchuria was clearly excluded from the Anglo-German Agreement during the course of negotiations, but that the Agreement did not obligate either of the two contracting parties to enforce respect for the principles of the Agreement upon third parties.

When questioned about the agreement in the House of Lords on March 28, Lord Lansdowne explained that Article I, in view of its reservations, was not concerned with Manchuria, but that Article II, in the British view, should be applied to the whole of China, including Manchuria, as it contained no such reservations.

On the one hand, while not desiring to be accused openly as an abrogator of the Agreement, Bülow, at the same time, was anxious to avoid the danger of being involved in a war with Russia over the Manchurian question. Bülow felt, however, that he should find some means of satisfying Great Britain, stemming not from any German obligation under the questionable Agreement but based on higher political considerations which had led to the conclusion of the Agreement —that is, the German objective of hampering any direct compromise between Great Britain and Russia. He proposed to Great Britain the issuance of a statement declaring that the Chinese Empire should not conclude any individual treaty with the other powers until the former had carried out the peace terms of the Boxer Uprising, especially the payment of indemnities.

Lord Lansdowne expressed his satisfaction with Bülow's proposal on February 12, and, within a few days, Great Britain and Japan warned the Chinese Empire against ratification of the Russo-Chinese secret agreement on Manchuria. Germany followed with a warning to China not to conclude any agreement with either territorial or financial implications before fulfilling her obligations to all the powers concerned.

In the same statement made in the House of Lords on March 28, Lord Lansdowne, commenting on the British view regarding the differences of interpretations of the Anglo-German Agreement, declared that Germany acted in a practical manner which was in harmony with the views of Great Britain. He also warned the Chinese Empire against concluding any special agreement with the other powers.

Phrasing his words in diplomatic language, he stated euphemistically that it was certainly not important whether Germany arrived at this conclusion on the basis of the Anglo-German Agreement or of general political considerations.

In light of the intricacies of the Far Eastern situation, Russia, around February and March, 1901, adopted a threatening attitude towards China, demanding ratification of the secret agreement on Manchuria. But early in April the rising tide of unfavorable circumstances finally drove Russia to abandon her plan, and on April 5 she issued a statement to this effect in the *Official Gazette*. For having played a leading role in foiling Russia's design, Germany became the target of Russia's violent indignation.

As for Germany, which was pursuing the policy of the free hand, her attitude at times found disfavor with and at other times pleased each of the three powers with whom she had to contend in the Far East: Great Britain, Russia, and Japan. While incurring Britain's displeasure by insisting that the Anglo-German Agreement should not be applied to Manchuria, Germany showed herself favorably disposed in the defense of the latter's railway rights in North China. Though she provoked Japan's antipathy by the Triple Intervention, Germany not only assured Japan that she had no secret treaty with Russia, but pledged a policy of friendly neutrality in the event Japan became engaged in a war with Russia. With regards to Russia, while evincing no objection to Russian designs of permanently or temporarily occupying Manchuria, even to the extent of establishing a protectorate in that region, Germany did, in effect, cooperate with Great Britain and Japan in thwarting the Russo-Chinese secret agreement which would have legitimatized the occupation of Manchuria.

Consequently, neither Great Britain, Japan, nor Russia was wholly satisfied with German policy, but at the same time they could not, owing to their respective circumstances, openly express their displeasure towards Germany because of the substantial assistance and advantages each derived from such a policy. But behind this German policy of dividing the three powers lay hidden dangers that these very powers, realizing the disadvantages of being the objects of German manipulation, might attempt to sink their differences in order to encircle Germany from the back. Germany's policy of the free hand was always fraught with this danger.

On the delicate question of interpretation of Article II of the Anglo-German Agreement, Great Britain displayed exceptional forbearance in order to facilitate the more important negotiations for an Anglo-German alliance which were initiated by Chamberlain in 1898 and continued until the end of 1901. The question of the alliance remained a live issue. Although it is not necessarily correct to say that this agreement led to the breakdown of the negotiations for an Anglo-German alliance, there is no room for doubt that it was a complicating factor.

CHAPTER **4**

First Anglo-Japanese Alliance
1898-1902

~~~~~~

ALTHOUGH the idea of an Anglo-Japanese alliance had long existed, it was not until the British occupation of Weihaiwei that cooperation between the two powers assumed a more positive form. Recognizing Japan's preferential rights in Weihaiwei, Great Britain signified her intention to support Japan if the latter were determined to lease the territory. However, this British policy was based on the contemplated withdrawal from the area by Japan and a desire to restore the balance of power in Chihli-wan, which had been undermined by the Russian occupation of Port Arthur and Talien.

The British Minister in Japan, Sir Ernest Satow, accordingly called on Tokusaburo Nishi, Minister of Foreign Affairs, on March 20, 1898 to notify the Japanese Government of the British decision to lease Weihaiwei—following the evacuation of the place by the Japanese forces—under terms identical with the Russian lease of Port Arthur. Whereas her interests lay predominantly along the Yangtze River in South China, Britain could not remain indifferent to the powerful influence which Russia exercised over the Chinese Government. The British Minister's questioning of Foreign Minister Nishi on the attitude of the Japanese Government towards the British proposal was marked with feelings of deep friendship.

Subsequently on the 22nd of March, Foreign Minister

Nishi in his reply to the British Government stated that while the Imperial Japanese Government desired to see China in possession of Weihaiwei in the future, in the prevailing circumstances which precluded such possession by China, it would not object to the occupation of the territory by any of the powers which respected China's independence.

After acquainting itself with the views of the Japanese Government, the British Government made representation to the Chinese Government on the lease of Weihaiwei. Sir Ernest Satow on April 1 communicated to Japan the British intention to decide by mutual agreement on the date of possession most convenient to Japan. On the following day, April 2, the Vice Minister of Foreign Affairs, Jutaro Komura, visited the British Minister and handed him the following memorandum in reply to the British notification:

"The Imperial Government express their concurrence in the contemplated lease by Her Britannic Majesty's Government from China of Weihaiwei after the evacuation of the place by the Japanese forces. In the event Japan should at any time in future find it necessary to take similar measures in order to strengthen her defences or to promote her interests, the Imperial Government trust that they may count upon the concurrence and support of the British Government."

The fact that the Japanese Government had asked for British concurrence and support, in case the Japanese Government should find it necessary to take the same measures against external pressures, marked the really first important step in the transformation of Japan's foreign policy as well as a move towards cooperation with Britain and away from her pro-Russian inclination.

Moreover, a leading member of the Cabinet privately intimated to Minister Satow that the Japanese Government, recognizing that China was not strong enough to maintain possession, greatly preferred that Weihaiwei should be occupied by Great Britain rather than by Russia or Germany.

It should be noted that in England, Prime Minister Salisbury, answering questions by Lord Kimberley in the House of Lords on May 18, publicly voiced for the first time Britain's cooperation with Japan, considered at the same time to be Britain's answer to the Japanese memorandum of April 2. In his speech, Lord Kimberley had stressed the importance for his country to establish friendly relations with Japan, a rising naval power, in the new Far Eastern situation. Asserting that it was highly desirable for Britain to count as its closest friend the most formidable naval power in that region of the world, Lord Kimberley supported the British policy of nonparticipation in the Triple Intervention directed at alienating Japanese friendship and depriving her of the fruits of victory.

To these utterances of Lord Kimberley, Lord Salisbury replied that he unreservedly agreed with the policy of the former Government. He affirmed that it was not the policy of the British Government to alienate the rising Japan, to whom Britain should rather express her sympathy and with whom she had many reasons to cooperate.

These words of Lord Salisbury were recognized as the first public avowal of Anglo-Japanese intimacy.

Between the years 1895 and 1898, antiforeign outbreaks were gaining momentum in China, the details of which have been related in preceding chapters, culminating in the Boxer Uprising of 1899 which had far-reaching political repercussions. Taking advantage of this confused situation, Russia poured her troops into Manchuria for an onslaught against Blagovshchensk, and in the name of protecting her railways was in full control of Manchuria by October 10, 1900. In addition, Russia seized control of the railways between Tientsin and Peking, and between Tientsin and north of Shanhaikwan, as well as Newchuang and other strategic points.

It was not difficult to understand the reasons for these bold Russian actions. She had correctly surmised that Great Britain—then deeply involved in the Boer War in which she had suffered initial reverses that seriously prejudiced her prestige all over the world—was in no position to offer any serious protest to these Russian incursions into Manchuria. Japan, then inclined towards a policy of compromise with Russia based on the so-called Manchuria-Korea Exchange Policy was also not expected to raise any efficacious objections.

In these grave circumstances, Great Britain, hoping to rely on Germany's influence to keep Russia in check, concluded an agreement with Germany on October 16, 1900, known as the Yangtze Agreement. But, as has been pointed out earlier, the two powers differed widely on the interpretation of the agreement, Germany insisting that the agreement did not apply to Manchuria as the region was not within the confines of her influence.

As the Far Eastern situation moved into a new phase, it was reported around October, 1900 that a secret agreement had been concluded between Russia and China concerning the occupation, administration, and supervision of Manchuria. Later, in December, 1900, the Peking correspondent of the London *Times,* Morrison, reported that the secret Sino-Russian agreement was signed by Korostvetz, acting Governor-General of Kwantung Province, and Tseng Chi, acting for the Governor-General of Mukden, at Port Arthur on November 22. The British Ambassador in Russia, Scott, informed his Government on January 5, 1901 that such an agreement had actually been concluded.

Under this agreement Manchuria was substantially stipulated as a Russian protectorate. However, dissatisfied with the provisional character of the agreement (modus vivendi), Russia exerted overwhelming pressure on the Chinese Government, climaxing in the conclusion at Levagiya of a formal treaty between the Russian Foreign Minister Count Lamsdorff and Chinese Minister Yang Ju. This Russo-Chinese accord relating to Manchuria became known as the Second Russo-Chinese Secret Treaty.

Under the terms of this treaty, China was to agree to several limitations on her sovereignty in Manchuria; Chinese troops were not to be stationed in Manchuria, pending the completion of the Chinese Eastern Railway, and China was to consult with Russia as to the number of troops she might subsequently wish to establish there; the importation of munitions of war into Manchuria was prohibited; and China should not, without the consent of Russia, grant to any other power, or the subjects thereof, privileges with regard to mines or other matters in Manchuria, Mongolia, Sinkiang, or Ili.

The Chinese Government appealed to the other powers to intervene in this case, without divulging the full text of the agreement because of her conviction that such publication of the text would be regarded as casus belli by Russia. But as soon as the terms were exposed, Japan, Great Britain, Germany, and the United States of America, feeling Russian monopoly of such special interests to be undesirable, urged the Chinese Government not to affix its signature to the agreement.

Meanwhile, Count Lamsdorff, in talks earlier with Sutemi Chinda, Japanese Minister to Russia, had stated that the question of Manchuria concerned Russia and China only, and that its occupation was the result of self-defense against Chinese attack. It was around this time that Russia, as a means of warding off Japanese opposition, proposed the neutralization of Korea under the joint guarantee of the powers.

In its reply of January 18, the Japanese Government, while conveying its feelings of deep uneasiness in the wake of the Russian occupation of Manchuria, stated that until the status quo ante was restored it considered that further negotiations should be postponed. On January 29, the Japanese Government through Minister Hayashi notified Lord Lansdowne, the British Minister for Foreign Affairs, of its stand, at the same time hinting at the possibility of an Anglo-Japanese common action to protest against the Russian advances in Manchuria.

The British Government, on its part, received the Japanese suggestion warmly. On behalf of his Government, Lord Lansdowne expressed Great Britain's boundless pleasure in being regarded with such intimacy and trust by the Japanese Government, and assured the Japanese Government that the British Government was determined in the future to act in a reciprocal manner. Not only did Great Britain accept the suggestion of a joint warning to China, but as had been intimated in the Japanese notification actively explored the possibility of German participation in this warning. In sympathy with this British approach, Germany despatched a similar warning, while Japan and Great Britain succeeded in arousing both Governor-General Liu Kun-i and Chang Chih-tung to submit the matter to the Throne and to implore the Emperor not to give sanction to the said secret treaty. They also vigorously protested directly to the Russian Government against the latter's action.

In these circumstances, the British Ambassador to Russia, Scott, on March 7, notified Lamsdorff that in view of the pros and cons concerning the alleged Russo-Chinese agreement relating to Manchuria, the Russian Government should submit the text of the agreement for deliberation by the interested powers. Under the pretext that the question of Manchuria was still under deliberation, Lamsdorff firmly refused to show the contents of the agreement, adding that in any case the affair concerned only Russia and China.

In view of Russia's act of insincerity, which came as no surprise, Foreign Minister Kato, concluding that the only course open to Japan was to launch an energetic diplomatic offensive, distributed a voluminous written opinion to members of the Cabinet attending a special session of the Cabinet on March 12, 1901 to determine Japan's policy of peace or war. In it, the Foreign Minister mentioned the following attitudes of the various powers concerning the China question:

"The British authorities have admitted that, in view of the cool public opinion, there is no determination to offer any strong resistance to Russia. The Boer War, moreover, has thoroughly depleted Britain's reserves. The German attitude on this question is sympathetic towards Japan and Britain, but her actions are restricted. The United States, on the other hand, while recognizing the need to call the special attention of the powers to the situation should it develop further, is maintaining a self-possessed attitude, unwilling at this stage to take any new steps."

The Japanese Government, therefore, could expect no assistance from a friendly third power. She had no other recourse but to formulate her policy independently. In the face of this situation, Foreign Minister Kato enumerated the following set of three policies, any one of which the Imperial Government could pursue:

1. Lodge an official protest, and if Japan's objectives could not be achieved peacefully to resort to the use of arms.

2. Proclaim to Russia that Japan would take appropriate steps to preserve equilibrium and for self-defense, and would take unilateral action in Korea in disregard of the Russo-Japanese Agreement on Korea.

3. Initially limit Japan's action to a formal protest against Russian violations or reserve Japan's right to act in behalf of her interests, and then take such steps in the future as the occasion demanded.

In his written opinion, Kato explained at great length the merits and demerits of each policy, but expressed his personal view that Japan would have no alternative but to select one of these policies. But the Foreign Minister concluded his exposition with an invitation to other members of the Cabinet to set forth their views on the question.

Cabinet meetings were held day after day from March 14. Hirobumi Ito, the Prime Minister, sought tirelessly to find an amicable way of negotiating with Russia, but the Japanese Government finally decided to send a protest to Russia. The members of the Cabinet agreed to entrust Kato with the task of negotiations, but emphasized their wish to avoid any provocations that might possibly lead to war.

The first protest to Russia was lodged by the Japanese Government on March 24, 1901, expressing Japan's view that Russia was acting beyond the scope of the secret Russo-Chinese agreement in the proper protection of her existing rights in Manchuria. Japan urged that as the current agreement upset the equilibrium in the Far East, it should be submitted to a conference of foreign representatives in Peking.

Lamsdorff firmly declined to entertain the Japanese proposal, declaring that the question concerned current negotiations between two independent states. But in a more conciliatory tone, he went on to intimate to Minister Chinda of Japan that the agreement in question was of a provisional character, a necessary preliminary for the purpose of evacuating Russian troops. In addition, it did not affect the sovereignty or integrity of China in Manchuria, nor the treaty rights of other powers. The question of Manchuria being a matter of exclusive Russian concern, it could not accept the Japanese proposal for a Peking conference to discuss the problem as this would be incompatible with the fundamental principles which Russia had hitherto upheld. A secret and lengthy conference attended by the Vice-Chief of the General Staff was held at the Ministry of War towards the end of March, 1901, which led the British press to speculate on Japan's war preparations. Upon receiving a military attaché's report on Russia's combat strength in Manchuria, General Oyama, Chief of the General Staff, convened on the morning of April 5 a Marshal's Conference at the Board of Marshals and Admirals of the Fleet in the Imperial Palace. A Cabinet meeting which followed in the afternoon continued late into the night.

The second note of protest to Russia was transmitted the

next day, regretting Japan's inability to concur with Count Lamsdorff's point of view but reserving the right of the Imperial Government to express its views in the present circumstances.

On receiving the Japanese protest, Lamsdorff evinced astonishment to Minister Chinda that Japan had now switched from her policy of Manchuria-Korea exchange to one of attaching grave significance to the problem of Manchuria. Nevertheless, Russia decided to bow to Japanese pressures, and on April 8 the Russian Minister to Japan, Iswalsky, handed to Foreign Minister Kato a formal note outlining the humiliating concession. In her note of reply, Russia stated her willingness to forego not only the hope of concluding the agreement on Manchuria being negotiated with China, but any intention of reaching any such agreement in the future as well.

Whether Japan at the time she was making these vigorous protests to Russia was prepared for a final showdown with Russia was a matter of conjecture. The British Minister in Japan, MacDonald, reported on March 22 that "in the words of Foreign Minister Kato, if the French fleet could be kept in check, matters might be different, but if unassisted Japan had no intention of going to war over the Manchurian question. On the other hand, he could not see how Japan could possibly avoid hostilities if her rights in Korea were violated."

There is ample evidence that Japan was making clandestine efforts to ascertain the attitudes of Great Britain, Germany, and France in the event of an armed clash with Russia. The German Vice Minister of Foreign Affairs informed Japanese Minister Inouye on March 6 that Germany viewed with disfavor any attempt to exploit the present situation, and emphatically denied that there was any secret understanding with Russia on the question of the Far East. He gave the German Government's assurance that it was well aware of the importance of Manchuria to Japan's national existence, and that in any crisis arising from developments in Manchuria, Germany would observe benevolent neutrality. He affirmed that this German stand would keep the French fleet in check and probably encourage England to actively support Japan.

Through Minister Hayashi in London, Foreign Minister Kato notified the British Government of Germany's attitude, but at the same time questioned Britain about the absolute reliability of such German assurance and the extent to which Japan could rely on Great Britain's support in case Japan found it necessary to "approach" Russia. To the use of the word "approach"—and, in particular, to the consequence of such an "approach"—the British Government attached two different interpretations. Bertie, Vice Minister of Foreign Affairs, after questioning Minister Hayashi, took it to mean "resist" and admitted that it also implied "war," while Lord Salisbury understood Britain's obligations to imply only "diplomatic support."

Bertie's memorandum, setting out the British Government's stand on the issue, showed Britain's desire to remain neutral, providing no third power entered the conflict, and to seek German cooperation. From the standpoint of checking Russo-Japanese rapprochement, Bertie's memorandum also emphasized the necessity of assisting Japan as part of Britain's future policy. He also contended that, if nothing was done to encourage Japan to look to Britain as a friend and possible ally against Russia and France, Japan might be driven to despair—an eventuality which might force her to come to some sort of settlement with Russia. This situation was described by Bertie as improbable, but not impossible, and a development which would inflict considerable damage to British interests.

The spring of 1901 marked an important epoch in the newly developing relations between Japan and Britain. The two nations were maintaining close liaison in respect to the Chinese affair. These contacts were also facilitated by the fortuitous presence in London of Baron von Eckardstein,

Chargé d'Affaires of the German Embassy in London, who visited Minister Hayashi on several occasions in March and April of 1901 and advocated an Anglo-German-Japanese alliance as a step to accelerate the negotiations on the Anglo-German alliance.

In order to maintain parity in the Far East, the German diplomat proposed a triple alliance between Japan, Great Britain, and Germany to deal with impending momentous changes in the area for a period of about five years. The provisions were:

1. Japan to be given a free hand in negotiations with Korea.

2. Should any one of the three allied powers become involved in hostilities against an enemy state, the other two powers should maintain neutrality. However, should a third power render assistance to the belligerent of an allied power, the two powers should intervene.

The principal aim was to form a triple alliance in the Far East similar to the one in Europe. The Eckardstein proposal was initially supported in England by Chamberlain, Balfour, and Lansdowne and shortly thereafter by Salisbury.

It being the understanding of the Japanese Government that the proposal had the blessings of the Kaiser and Bülow, Minister Hayashi, on instruction from Foreign Minister Kato, called on Lord Lansdowne on April 17, 1901. While on the question of China, the Japanese Minister pointed to the unstable conditions in China, adding that it had just occurred to him to inquire whether there was any possibility or likelihood of Japan and Britain reaching some permanent understanding. The seemingly surprised Lansdowne, in reply to the Minister's query, intimated that the conclusion of a permanent understanding need not necessarily be confined only to Japan and Great Britain, that a third power might possibly be invited—a hint suggesting German participation in the parleys.

On May 15, Minister Hayashi called on Lord Lansdowne

to outline Japan's foreign policy, based on the Open Door principle and the maintenance of her vital interests in Korea. Drawing attention to the fact that Japan and Great Britain had identical interests in China, he underlined that cooperation between them was imperative to prevent an alliance of other powers infringing upon their interests.

Two months later on July 15, Sir Claude MacDonald, the British Minister to Japan, who was in London for consultations with his Government, called on Minister Hayashi to state Great Britain's desire to consummate a permanent, not a provisional, alliance to cope with the Far Eastern situation, in which either party to the proposed alliance would remain neutral in case of war between an alliance member and a third power, but would assist the other party should a power or powers give aid to the opposing belligerent.

Continuing his talks on the following day with Hayashi, MacDonald mentioned that the idea of the alliance being contrary to Britain's traditional policy, a certain amount of time would lapse before the plan could be finalized. He hoped that the Japanese Government would not, in the meantime, conduct negotiations with Russia.

On the heels of these conversations, the Japanese Government began giving the matter of an Anglo-Japanese agreement its very careful consideration and study, making private inquiries through Minister Hayashi to confirm the intentions of the British Government as to (1) whether the alliance would be confined only to Japan and England, or whether the membership of Germany was contemplated; and (2) whether the scope of application of the alliance would be geographically restricted. On July 20, MacDonald relayed his Government's desire to have Germany participate in the alliance, but stated that on the matter of the scope of application, though it was intended to provide for geographical limitations, no final decision had yet been reached.

Then on July 30 in his conversation with Minister Hayashi, Lord Lansdowne, expressing his belief that the time had arrived for Japan and Great Britain to endeavor to reach some permanent understanding, asked the Japanese Minister whether Japan had real interests in Manchuria and what Japan expected to derive from the alliance.

In response to these inquiries, the Minister emphasized that although Japan's vital interests were in Korea, Japan desired primarily to keep Russia away from Manchuria as far as possible, and, secondly, in case of an unavoidable armed conflict with Russia she hoped to prevent any third party from giving assistance to Russia.

Consequently on August 14, Lord Lansdowne suggested to Minister Hayashi that, as Japan was the more interested of the parties to the agreement, it was rather for the Japanese Government to draw up the draft of the understanding. In order to pursue the matter in a more serious vein, Lord Lansdowne also advised that it would be well for the Minister to obtain formal instructions from his Government investing him with the necessary powers.

Following his assumption of the post of Foreign Minister, Jutaro Komura, former Minister to China, authorized the Japanese Minister in London to conduct the consultations. On October 16, the Minister informed Lord Lansdowne that the Japanese Government was primarily concerned about the maintenance of its peculiar interests in Korea, regarding it as a matter of life or death to crush at its inception any move by which Russia might gain paramountcy in that country.

On the question of China, the Japanese Minister added that the policy of Japan was in complete harmony with that of Great Britain: the maintenance of China's territorial integrity and the principle of the Open Door. Concerning the nature of the alliance, Hayashi emphasized that the Japanese Government did not propose that the alliance should take effect in case either England or Japan found herself at war with a single power. If Japan found herself at war with Russia alone, the British Empire's neutrality would suffice. The observance of strict neutrality, he continued, would be of tremendous assistance to Japan as it would keep the Russian fleet from using Britain's coaling stations.

Lord Lansdowne, asked by Hayashi whether in his opinion it would be desirable for Germany to be a party to the understanding, replied that at this stage of the negotiations it would be worth while for Great Britain and Japan to endeavor to arrive at a clear understanding of their requirements without reference to any other power. On coming to terms, Great Britain and Japan could then consider whether to solicit Germany's adherence.

In any case, Lord Lansdowne stressed, once an agreement has been reached, neither of the parties should, without prior consultations, enter into any separate arrangement or understanding with another power affecting the affairs of either China or Korea. He went on to hint that in time of peace, it would be of mutual benefit if the two navies could use each other's shipbuilding, port, and coaling-station facilities. This most friendly statement by Lord Lansdowne met with the Minister's expression of gratitude.

From these series of conversations, the framework of the alliance finally began to take shape. During an interview granted by Foreign Minister Komura to Sir Claude Mac-Donald, the British Minister, on November 1, the former apprised Sir Claude of the Japanese Government's desire to have the draft of the agreement submitted by the British Government. If the alliance was to be brought to a fruition, he said, every effort should be exerted to accelerate its conclusion. The British Government, for its part, regarded the materialization of such an agreement as "extremely hopeful."

On November 6, 1901, Lord Lansdowne handed to Minister Hayashi the following draft of an agreement between the Japanese and British Governments:

The undersigned, duly authorized by their respective Governments, actuated solely by a desire to maintain the status quo and general peace in the Far East, being moreover specially interested in preventing the absorption of Korea by any Foreign Power, and in maintaining the independence and territorial integrity of China, and in securing equal opportunities in that country for the commerce and industry of all nations, hereby agree as follows:—

ARTICLE I

If either Great Britain or Japan in the defence of the interests above described, should become involved in war with another Power, the other High Contracting Party will maintain strict neutrality, and use its efforts to prevent other Powers from joining in hostilities against its Ally.

ARTICLE II

Should another Power join in hostilities against the Ally, the other High Contracting Party will come to its assistance and will conduct the war in common, and make peace in mutual agreement with it.

ARTICLE III

The two High Contracting Parties agree that neither of them will, without consulting the other, enter into separate arrangements with another Power affecting the interests above described.

ARTICLE IV

Whenever, in the opinion of either Great Britain or Japan, the above-mentioned interests are in jeopardy, the two Governments will communicate with one another fully and frankly.

ADDITIONAL AGREEMENT ARTICLE I

It is further agreed between the High Contracting Parties that the naval forces of the two Powers shall, so far as is possible, act in concert at all times and that mutual facilities will be given for the docking of the vessels of war of one Power in the ports of the other, and also for the use of coaling stations and other advantages conducive to the welfare and efficiency of their respective navies.

While official negotiations for an Anglo-Japanese agreement were still in progress in both London and Tokyo, Marquis Ito accepted an invitation to attend the twentieth anniversary of Yale University to receive an honorary degree of LL.D. Immediately after the ceremonies, Marquis Ito set sail from New York for France, arriving in Paris on November 13, 1901.

In order to bring Marquis Ito up to date with the negotiations on the Anglo-Japanese agreement in London, and to obtain his assent, Foreign Minister Komura instructed Minister Tadasu Hayashi to brief the venerable statesman in Paris. On the day following his return from Paris, where he had stayed from November 14 to 19 to confer with Marquis Ito, Minister Hayashi called on Lord Lansdowne and Bertie. The British statesmen not only made no effort to hide their suspicions regarding Marquis Ito's visit to St. Petersburg, but also intimated that Britain would be extremely incensed if, at this advanced stage of the Anglo-Japanese negotiations, the Japanese Government would enter into a separate agreement with Russia.

Minister Hayashi assured them that the visit of Marquis Ito to Russia was of a purely personal nature. Moreover, the Marquis had received no authorization to discuss or negotiate on behalf of the Japanese Government. These explanations, however, did not appear to completely allay the fears of Lord Lansdowne and Bertie.

In the light of these circumstances, Minister Komura, while urging an acceleration in the Anglo-Japanese negotiations, also earnestly sought the approval of Marquis Ito to the general outline of the negotiations to date. He took extraordinary pains to impress upon the Marquis the importance of making no commitments in his conversations with the Russian

Government, commitments that might in any way adversely affect Anglo-Japanese relations.

In his cable of reply, Marquis Ito implied approval of the Anglo-Japanese discussions that were underway, and, at the same time, affirmed that during his trip to Russia he would do nothing that would in any way reflect upon the spirit of the Anglo-Japanese negotiations.

A Cabinet meeting held on November 28 sanctioned the Japanese amendments to the Lansdowne draft of November 6. These amendments, largely concerning the wording rather than the principle, proposed that:

1. The words "Far East" be amended to "Extreme East" and "any foreign power" to "another power," and the words "or powers" be included in the Preamble and Article II. Furthermore, the words "the independence and territorial integrity of China" be amended to read "the independence and territorial integrity of the Empire of China" in the Preamble.

2. The words "affecting the interests" in Article III be amended to read "to prejudice of the interests."

3. The following stipulation be inserted in the agreement as Article V since no provision was made as to the terms of validity: "This alliance shall remain in force for five years from the date of the signing of the present agreement, and it may be renewed at the pleasure of the High Contracting Parties."

4. The words "also for the use of coaling stations" be amended to simply "and coaling" in the Additional Agreement.

5. The following stipulations be inserted in the Additional Agreement:

SEPARATE ARTICLE II

Each of the High Contracting Parties shall endeavor to maintain in the Far East at all times naval forces superior in efficacy to the naval strength of any other Power which has the largest naval forces in the Far East.

SEPARATE ARTICLE III

Great Britain recognizes that Japan may take such suitable measures as she deems necessary to safeguard and promote the preponderating interests which she actually possesses in Korea.

When the Japanese amendments were reported to the Throne, the Emperor requested Prime Minister Katsura to ascertain the views of the *genro,* and those of Marquis Ito who was then in St. Petersburg. Instructed to obtain Marquis Ito's approval, Minister Hayashi despatched Keishiro Matsui, Secretary of the Japanese Legation in London, to St. Petersburg with the full text of the Japanese drafts.

Meanwhile, Prime Minister Katsura summoned the *genro* to Chounkaku in Hayama for an urgent meeting on December 7, 1901. Besides Prince Katsura, Navy Minister Admiral Yamamoto, and Foreign Minister Komura, representing the Cabinet, four leading *genro,* Marquis Yamagata, Marquis Oyama, Count Matsukata, and Count Inouye, attended the momentous meeting. Following a detailed report on the course of the negotiations by Foreign Minister Komura, those present unanimously approved and signed the amendments proposed by Japan. Only Count Inouye, who shared identical views with Marquis Ito, showed any hesitancy before finally affixing his signature to the document.

On the evening of December 8, the Government received a cable from Marquis Ito, requesting postponement of any definite reply to Great Britain until he had completed his talks in St. Petersburg. A Cabinet meeting, considering Marquis Ito's message, saw no necessity of changing its position on an issue which had been so thoroughly deliberated.

Accordingly, Premier Katsura and Foreign Minister Komura visited the Imperial Palace to report the Cabinet's decision. Having earlier received a cable from Marquis Ito to withhold Imperial sanction to the amendments, the Emperor ordered the *genro* to review the official decision. The *genro* who met again upheld the earlier Cabinet decision. Imperial sanction was obtained on December 10.

It is essential to grasp the significance of the relations between the proposed Anglo-Japanese agreement and the proposed Russo-Japanese agreement for a full understanding of the Japanese system of treaty alliances. As stated previously, Marquis Ito had always championed the Russo-Japanese agreement. He did not abandon his efforts in this direction until the Emperor had sanctioned the draft amendments to the Anglo-Japanese agreement.

Prince Katsura, on the contrary, was strongly convinced that the Anglo-Japanese agreement was more vital to the furtherance of Japan's interests, Never before in Japan's diplomatic history had such a bitter controversy developed over differences of foreign policy as between the two leading statesmen, Marquis Ito and Prince Katsura. It may not be altogether useless to take a closer look at the background of this dispute.

In his letter from St. Petersburg, to Count Inouye, a fellow champion of Russo-Japanese rapprochement, Marquis Ito wrote on November 28, 1901:

"It is my belief that Russia is leaning towards an agreement with Japan. The Tsar himself informed me that such an agreement would be welcomed, for it would not only benefit both Japan and Russia, but, at the same time, contribute to the maintenance of peace in the Far East. I am of the same opinion with you that Japan should sound out the extent of Russian concessions before finally making any decision concerning the pending negotiations in question."

In the opinion of Marquis Ito, the time was ripe to conclude a Russo-Japanese agreement. Should this opportunity be lost, the Anglo-Japanese agreement would rule out any chances of a future pact with Russia.

Furthermore, the primary objective of the Russo-Japanese accord remained the attainment of the so-called Exchange Policy affecting Manchuria and Korea. As soon as he arrived in St. Petersburg, Marquis Ito conferred on the Korean and other questions with Count Lamsdorff, Minister for Foreign Affairs, and Count Witte, Minister of Finance. Although Witte was quite receptive to Marquis Ito's proposals, Lamsdorff was noncommittal, fearing that the acceptance of the proposals would, in effect, mean the abandonment of Korea, a move which Russia could hardly countenance. Nevertheless, Lamsdorff said, Russia would send a reply to Japan after consulting with the responsible authorities.

Aware of Witte's favorable attitude and trusting in the Tsar's words, Marquis Ito was in an optimistic mood. In his two cables to Tokyo, he reaffirmed his conviction that a Russo-Japanese understanding should take precedence over an Anglo-Japanese agreement. However, his appeal for a postponement of the conclusion of an Anglo-Japanese agreement was overruled not only by members of the Cabinet, but also by the council of *genro,* who saw no necessity to veer from Japan's established path of diplomacy.

Shortly thereafter, Marquis Ito, then in Berlin, received a communication from Lamsdorff. In this reply, Lamsdorff amended many proposals made by the Japanese statesman on the subject of Korea, and demanded that Japan should recognize in Article VI Russia's "preponderant influence" over and "freedom of action" in Chinese territory adjoining Russia.

This unexpectedly sharp reply from Russia could hardly have been accepted by any responsible Japanese statesman. Even such an ardent Russophile as Marquis Ito was constrained to point out to Lamsdorff that—if no amendments were made—he was hesitant to recommend the draft to the Japanese Government, containing as it did a number of objectionable points. Assuring Lamsdorff that he would study the particulars of the Russian draft, Marquis Ito continued to adopt a compromising attitude.

Marquis Ito, in cabling the Russian reply to Tokyo, included his own views and earnestly requested the Japanese Government to take prompt action towards the finalization of a Russo-Japanese agreement.

Taking issue with Marquis Ito, Prime Minister Katsura declared as unacceptable to the Japanese Government any Russo-Japanese transaction embodying the exchange formula pertaining to Korea and Manchuria. These exchanges between Marquis Ito and Prime Minister Katsura are important in evaluating the true significance of the Anglo-Japanese alliance.

Emphasizing that the Japanese Government had obligations to the other powers, which she was honor-bound to respect, the Prime Minister in his reply insisted that such an agreement with Russia could not be negotiated.

He stated: "As it will be recalled, the Japanese Government gave unmistakable warning of grave consequences to the Chinese Empire during February, 1901, that it may compromise its territorial integrity by concluding with another power an agreement extending special territorial, financial or monopolistic privileges.

"Initiating a diplomatic offensive, the Japanese Government at the same time succeeded in getting Great Britain, Germany, the United States, Italy, and Austria to send similar warnings to the Chinese Imperial Government. This show of international unity is said to have forestalled the Russo-Chinese Agreement on Manchuria which allegedly had been under negotiation.

"In accordance with Japanese policy, I, as Prime Minister, advised China not to enter into any further agreement which would infringe on the treaty interests of a third power or the sovereignty of China. Acting in consonance with Japanese wishes, Great Britain and the United States offered the same advice to China.

"I am of the opinion that this joint advice to the Chinese Empire has not been in vain. In fact, its effect is becoming discernible. The Japanese Government has stated more than once that respect for Chinese territorial integrity and the principle of equal commercial opportunity are cardinal elements in Japan's policy towards China. It was this spirit which motivated Japan's participation in the Anglo-German Agreement. Whereas the German Government took a far-fetched interpretation of the agreement, by excluding Manchuria, the Japanese Government took the view that Manchuria should come within the purview of the said agreement."

Ruling out any possibility of Japan and Russia entering into an agreement, Premier Katsura asserted:

"Even if the question of an Anglo-Japanese Agreement were excluded, it would still be contrary to Japan's policy to conclude an agreement with Russia over the issue of Manchuria in exchange for concessions related to Korea. Japan would not only forfeit her national prestige, but lose the confidence of the powers and China in the pledges Japan had so solemnly given."

Referring to Article VI, the Premier stated that its acceptance would be contrary to the existing policy of the Japanese Government. He added: "Whereas Count Lamsdorff insists that the stipulation contained in Article VI of the proposed agreement is not contrary to the letter of Baron Nishi of 1898 and the proposition of Marquis Komura of 1900, the situation has now profoundly changed. The proposals of the individuals concerned were based on the cooperative principle. In other words, their proposals contained the proviso that Russia's position in Manchuria would be identical to Japan's position in Korea. The Russian agreement in question contained no such principle."

In a contentious reply from Brussels dated December 23 to Prime Minister Katsura, Marquis Ito restated his doctrine of favoring an Exchange Policy on Manchuria and Korea. Moreover, he asseverated that it would be more desirable to conclude an agreement that favored Japan rather than an agreement based merely on the principle of mutuality.

A week later on December 29, Prime Minister Katsura, replying to Marquis Ito, stated that the Russian counter-proposals, even if the objectionable points were amended, could hardly be acceptable as a basis for negotiating an early agreement. He went on to stress that Japan's policy was to exclude Russia from Korea, strategically and politically, and that it would be desirable to reach an agreement between Japan and Great Britain before opening negotiations with Russia. This reply was the last of the series of exchanges between Premier Katsura and Marquis Ito on Japan's fundamental policy.

On December 11, 1901, Foreign Minister Komura instructed Minister Hayashi to place the Japanese amendments before the British Government. These amendments were handed to Lord Lansdowne on December 12, exactly five weeks after the first British draft had been presented to the Japanese Government.

In presenting the Japanese amendments to Lord Lansdowne, Minister Hayashi explained the reasons for the revised text and added that Japan could not possibly accept the British plan to extend the scope of the alliance to include the protection of British interests in India should such a necessity arise. On December 6, Lord Lansdowne, in referring to this question, declared that British interests in the Yangtze Valley were not comparable in importance with those of Japan in Korea.

The position of the Japanese Government was that Japan and Great Britain had common and equal interests in China which were not opposed to the interests of other powers, but were more or less complementary. Reiterating Japan's stand, Minister Hayashi in his conversations with Lord Lansdowne on December 12 insisted that an extension of the scope of protection of their common interests in China to embrace India would be impractical. Furthermore, the Minister hoped that the provisions of the alliance would be fully published in order to dispel any suspicions on the part of other powers and that only the Additional Agreement should be kept secret.

After several Cabinet meetings in both the Japanese and British capitals to iron out the last remaining differences during a period of six weeks from the middle of December, 1901, to the end of January, 1902, the Anglo-Japanese Treaty of Alliance was signed on January 30, 1902.

During the course of the negotiations, the Japanese Government failed to receive the concurrence of the British Government to Separate Articles II and III of the Additional Agreement. In rejecting these two articles, Lord Lansdowne pointed out that their inclusion would confine British policy to regional interests, giving the alliance a unilateral appearance. However, the two Governments finally reached an understanding that Article II of the Additional Agreement would be incorporated into Article I of the secret official paper which would be exchanged between Japan and Great Britain simultaneously with the signing of the Anglo-Japanese Alliance.

In the case of Article III of the Additional Agreement, Great Britain expressed fears that, by acknowledging the wording of the Japanese proposition, she might be accused of encouraging Japan's aggressive policy, a position which the Cabinet could not possibly justify in Parliament. While acknowledging Japan's preponderant position in Korea, the British Government rejected Article III, for no other reason than that the article might draw Great Britain into a war with Russia in separated parts of the world as a direct outcome of a petty quarrel between Japan and Russia over regional interests.

Accordingly, Minister Hayashi, acting under instructions of Foreign Minister Komura, requested the British Government to insert the compromise plan in an official paper, but this proposal did not seem to please the British Government. In an effort to reach a settlement, the British Cabinet at its meeting on January 14 decided to insert Article II into Article I of the main agreement. The Japanese Government, which received the following amendment on January 24, expressed its satisfaction with the compromise formula.

ARTICLE I

The High Contracting Parties, having mutually recognized the independence of China and Korea, declare themselves to be entirely uninfluenced by any aggressive tendencies in either country. Having in view, however, their special interests, of which those of Great Britain relate principally to China, while Japan, in addition to the interests which she possesses in China, is interested in a peculiar degree politically as well as commercially and industrially in Korea, the High Contracting Parties recognize that it will be admissible for either of them to safeguard those interests if threatened either by the aggressive action of any other Power, or by disturbance arising in China or Korea, and necessitating the intervention of either of the High Contracting Parties for the protection of the lives or property of its subjects.

Following the Japanese Cabinet approval of the amended draft of the Anglo-Japanese Treaty of Alliance and subsequent Imperial sanction, the Government empowered Minister Hayashi to affix his signature to the document on January 29, 1902. This historic document was signed by Baron Hayashi on behalf of Japan and by Lord Lansdowne on behalf of Great Britain at the British Foreign Office at 5 P.M. on January 30, after which the official documents were exchanged.

The full text of this epochal treaty which terminated the traditional British policy of isolation and raised Japan to the status of a Great Power, consisting only of a preamble and six articles, was made public by Japan on February 11, and by Great Britain in the evening of February 11, 1902. The full text of the official document, which was rightly kept secret until the publication of the British diplomatic documents concerning the cause of wars, was as follows:

"In reference to the Agreement concluded by us today on behalf of our respective Governments, I have the honor to inform you that the British (Japanese) Government recognizes that the naval forces of Great Britain (Japan) should, so far as possible, act in concert with those of Japan (Great Britain) in time of peace, and that mutual facilities should be given for the docking and coaling of vessels of war of one country in the ports of the other, as well as other advantages conducting to the welfare and efficiency of the respective navies of the two Powers.

"At the present moment Japan and Great Britain are each of them maintaining in the Extreme East a naval force superior in strength to that of any third Power. Great Britain (Japan) has no intention of relaxing her efforts to maintain, so far as may be possible, available for concentration in the waters of the Extreme East a naval force superior to that of any third Power."

Before publishing the text of the Anglo-Japanese Treaty of Alliance, initialed by the two countries, the Japanese Government confidentially communicated the contents of the treaty to eight countries—Germany, Russia, the United States of America, France, Austria, Italy, China, and Korea. Particular consideration was given to Germany in view of her concern during the early stages of the negotiations on the treaty.

On February 3, 1902, shortly after the Treaty of Alliance was signed, its contents were privately communicated by Foreign Minister Komura to the German Minister in Tokyo and by Lord Lansdowne to the German Ambassador in London. The views of the German Government as relayed to the Japanese Government were as follows:

"The German Government regards the Anglo-Japanese Treaty as a most important instrument for guaranteeing and strengthening peace in the Far East. As her interests in both China and Korea are of a limited nature, Germany shall observe benevolent neutrality. Rather than adopt a positive attitude, the German Government feels her position of neutrality would better serve the interests of maintaining world peace."

The day after the publication of the Treaty, in the morning of February 12, Viscount Shinichiro Kurino, Japanese Minister at St. Petersburg, called on Count Lamsdorff to explain the nature of the Alliance. The Russian Foreign Minister appeared genuinely surprised to receive information of the conclusion of the Alliance.

After reading over the text of the Alliance, Count Lamsdorff observed that the Preamble and the Articles and terms outlining the object of the agreement were in such complete accord with the intimated views and repeated declarations of the Russian Government that he was disposed to ask the parties concerned to associate Russia with the agreement.

The Russian Minister went on to intimate that Russia had no intention of infringing or interfering with the territorial integrity of either China or Korea, and that she intended to evacuate from Manchuria at some opportune time in the future. However, he was at a loss to understand the underlying causes or necessity of the subsequent Articles relating to the event of either ally being involved in hostilities with other Powers. He emphasized that Russia's policy was to maintain harmonious ties with Japan, and that the possibility of war in the Far East had not occurred to him even in his dreams. If Japan and Russia were closely aligned, he declared, their influence would be so great that other powers would naturally attempt to sow discord between them.

The Treaty was favorably received in America. When Kogoro Takahira, Japanese Minister, visited the Secretary of State and handed him the text of the Alliance, he was told by the latter that the object of the Treaty was in complete accord with the wishes of the United States Government.

Other powers were informed on February 10 through Japan's representatives in the respective capitals.

Delcassé, French Minister for Foreign Affairs, appreciated the courtesy of the Japanese Government in informing him of the Alliance, but refused to make any comments. The Austrian Foreign Minister, on the other hand, opined that in view of the objectives of the Treaty, it could be a guarantee of the status quo or of peace. The Italian Vice Foreign Minister went even further in welcoming the pact. He had no doubt whatever of the peaceful intentions of the Japanese Government, and while expressing sympathy towards Japan earnestly wished the Japanese people peace and prosperity.

Prince Ching of the Chinese Empire, his face beaming with joy, told the Japanese diplomatic envoy that he was extremely pleased to learn that the conclusion of the Alliance was aimed at ensuring the integrity of the region in which China would be one of the leading beneficiaries. Turning to Sir Ernest Satow, the British Minister in China, Prince Ching intimated that the Treaty would no doubt considerably facilitate his negotiations for the evacuation of Manchuria.

Whereas Korean Foreign Minister Pak appeared to be relieved to learn of the Treaty, the Emperor of Korea evinced genuine surprise and appeared bewildered at the explanations on the Alliance given by Gonsuke Hayashi, Japanese Minister in Seoul.

Anglo-Japanese Agreement of Alliance of 1902

Signed at London, in English, January 30, 1902 (35th year of Meiji). Published February 11, 1902.

THE GOVERNMENTS of Japan and Great Britain actuated solely by a desire to maintain the status quo and general peace in the Extreme East, being moreover specially interested in maintaining the independence and territorial integrity of the Empire of China and the Empire of Corea, and in securing equal opportunities in those countries for the commerce and industry of all nations hereby agree as follows:—

ARTICLE I

The High Contracting Parties having mutually recognized the independence of China and of Corea declare themselves to be entirely uninfluenced by any aggressive tendencies in either country. Having in view, however, their special interests, of which those of Great Britain relate principally to China, while Japan in addition to the interests which she possesses in China is interested in a peculiar degree, politically as well as commercially and industrially, in Corea, the High Contracting Parties recognize that it will be admissible for either of them to take such measures as may be indispensable in order to safeguard those interests, if threatened either by the aggressive action of any other Power or by disturbances arising in China or Corea and necessitating the intervention of either of the High Contracting Parties for the protection of the lives and property of its Subjects.

ARTICLE II

If either Japan or Great Britain, in the defence of their respective interests as above described, should become involved in war with another Power, the other High Contracting Party will maintain a strict neutrality and use its efforts to prevent other Powers from joining in hostilities against its Ally.

ARTICLE III

If in the above event any other Power or Powers should join in hostilities against that Ally, the other High Contracting Party will conduct the war in common and make peace in mutual agreement with it.

ARTICLE IV

The High Contracting Parties agree that neither of them

will, without consulting the other, enter into separate arrangements with another Power to the prejudice of the interests above described.

ARTICLE V

Whenever, in the opinion of either Japan or Great Britain, the above mentioned interests are in jeopardy, the two Governments will communicate with one another fully and frankly.

ARTICLE VI

The present Agreement shall come into effect immediately after the date of its signature and remain in force for five years from that date. In case neither of the High Contracting Parties should have notified twelve months before the expiration of the said five years the intention of terminating it, it shall remain binding until the expiration of one year from the day on which either of the High Contracting Parties shall have denounced it, but if when the date fixed for its expiration arrives either Ally is actually engaged in war the Alliance shall, ipso facto, continue until peace is concluded.

In faith whereof the undersigned duly authorized by their respective Governments have signed this Agreement, and have affixed thereto their seals.

Done in duplicate in London, the 30th January, 1902.

(L.S.) (Signed) HAYASHI,
Envoy Extraordinary and Minister
Plenipotentiary of His Majesty the Emperor of
Japan at the Court of St. James.
(L.S.) (Signed) LANSDOWNE,
His Britannic Majesty's Principal Secretary
of State for Foreign Affairs.

CHAPTER 5

The Russo-Japanese War
1902-1905

~~~~~~

IT IS clear from the reactions of the powers to the Anglo-Japanese Treaty of Alliance that only Russia was notably displeased and disturbed. Although it would be presumptuous to describe the Alliance as a diplomatic defeat for Russia, there is little room for doubt that, while she maintained an outwardly calm attitude, the development did pose a diplomatic barrier.

In a move to counter the Alliance and maintain her prestige in the eyes of China, Russia invited both Germany and France to join her in issuing a warning to Japan. Meeting with German rejection, Russia finally issued a joint declaration with France on March 15. This declaration voiced satisfaction that Russo-French policy was in accord with the aims put forward in the Anglo-Japanese Alliance for the maintenance of the status quo and the general peace in the Far East as well as the preservation of the independence of China and Korea and the freedom of commercial and industrial access to these countries.

They affirmed that the "observance of these principles is at the same time a guarantee for their special interests in the Far East" and reserved "to themselves the right of consultation as to the means to be adopted for securing those interests" when faced with "the aggressive action of a third Power or the recurrence of disturbance in China" which might jeopardize the integrity and free development of the power concerned or become a menace to their own interests.

A few days later, Delcassé, French Minister for Foreign Affairs, referring in the National Assembly to the signing of the Declaration, stated that the French Government approved the extension of the Franco-Russian Declaration and Agreement to the Far East. Delcassé, however, took pains to inform London that the Declaration did not indicate a change of policy towards London, and that France did not wish to alienate British feelings towards France.

In the meantime, the Anglo-Japanese Alliance slowly began to have repercussions. The first significant effect was seen in the Russian evacuation of Manchuria. On April 8, 1902, only two months after the publication of the Alliance, the Russo-Chinese Convention relating to Manchuria was signed, providing, among other things, for the Government of Russia to gradually withdraw her forces from the three Eastern Provinces if no further disturbances occurred and no obstacles were caused by the other powers.

The Convention called for:

1. The evacuation of southwest Sheng-ching Province up to the Liao River before October 8, 1902;

2. The evacuation of the remainder of the Province of Sheng-ching and the Province of Kirin before April 8, 1903; and,

3. The evacuation of the Province of Heilungkiang before October 8, 1903.

Furthermore, the two Governments agreed that the Military Governors of the Manchurian provinces should be instructed to act in concert with the Russian military authorities in determining the number and movements of Chinese troops to garrison Manchuria until the Russian troops were withdrawn.

After the complete evacuation of the Russian forces from Manchuria, China could increase or reduce her armed forces merely by informing the Russian Government of her decision. There is no room to doubt that the Anglo-Japanese Alliance led Russia to make such an unexpected compromise.

The second effect of the Alliance was the sincere and unreserved support which Japan gave Britain during her diplomatic negotiations with China prior to her evacuation of Shanghai at the end of 1902.

The third undeniable effect was the strengthening of Japan's position in Korea. Britain's reaffirmation of Japan's special position in Korea enabled her ally to take a firm attitude towards Russia.

Russia carried out the first phase of her evacuation of Manchuria in accordance with the Russo-Chinese Convention before October 8, 1902. However, as the next expiry date approached, not only did the Russian troops show no disposition of fulfilling the terms of the second phase of the promised evacuation, but even sent troops into South Manchuria, an area which Russia had not hitherto occupied.

In a sudden and dramatic *volte-face,* Russia presented China with seven demands, seeking assurances that Manchuria would not be leased, transferred, or sold to any other power, and that the status quo would be preserved in Mongolia. Russia also sought the closure of Manchuria to foreign trade by demanding that no new ports or towns in Manchuria be opened up to foreign commerce.

These demands ignored not only the two cardinal principles of Open Door and respect for China's territorial integrity, but also violated the terms of evacuation stipulated in the Russo-Chinese Convention. Despite China's repeated refusal and the energetic protests of Japan, Britain, and the United States, Russia continued to pursue her uncompromising policy. Instead of honoring her pledge to evacuate Manchuria, Russia presented further demands, i.e.,

"That no portion of territory restored to China by Russia, particularly Newchuang and the Valley of Liao-ho, shall in any circumstances be leased or sold to another Power. Should such sale or lease to another Power be concluded, Russia will take decisive steps to safeguard her own interests as she considers such sale or lease to be of direct threat to her."

Taking a step further, Russia communicated to the Korean Government on April 13, 1903, that the timber interests acquired in 1896 would be used by the Russian Government. Early in May, Russia also occupied Yongampo and the entire region along the mouth of the Yalu River. This sudden change in Russian attitude indicated the ascendancy of the aggressive clique led by Bezobrazoff, Abaza, and Plehve.

This change in Russian policy shortly after the first stage of the evacuation of Manchuria in October 8, 1902, should be seriously considered as one of the main underlying causes of the Russo-Japanese War.

It is interesting to note here the role which the timber resources along the Yalu River played in changing Russian policy and consequently the Far Eastern situation. Brinell, a Russian merchant from Vladivostok, who secured a concession for timber along theYalu River in 1898, transferred his rights to Bezobrazoff and his group in 1902. Bezobrazoff, for his part, succeeded in persuading the Tsar that the timber interests formed the most valuable asset possessed by Russia in the Far East.

In April, 1903, there was a sharp clash of views between Alexieff, Commander-in-Chief of the Far Eastern Army, and General Kuropatkin who had changed his views in favor of Count Witte and Lamsdorff. Kuropatkin now felt that Russian security would best be served by withdrawing her troops from Manchuria in accordance with the Russo-Chinese Convention.

For reasons that were far from clear, Alexieff suddenly ordered the suspension of the evacuation of Manchuria in the name of the Commander-in-Chief of the Far Eastern Army, almost simultaneously with the first inspection tour in the Far East by Bezobrazoff. By November, 1902, the Tsar was completely won over to their project, and Bezobrazoff was despatched, with an enormous fund of two million rubles from the Russo-Chinese Bank at his disposal, to inspect the possibility of exploitation. Captain Bezobrazoff stayed in the Far East for about two months as a personal representative of the Tsar.

In Russia two distinct policies were being advocated, one represented by Witte, Kuropatkin, and Lamsdorff, holding moderate views. The other was represented by Bezobrazoff and his clique, which, backed by the Tsar, took an aggressive policy.

In May Bezobrazoff was appointed Minister without Portfolio, giving the lumbering enterprise a political character. The occupation of Yongampo, mentioned earlier, by forces under the command of Russian General Alexieff had as its purpose the protection of the timber interests.

Under these circumstances, the situation in the Far East in the months of June and July, 1903, took on a very complex character. The Chinese Eastern Railway, with its branch lines running to Port Arthur and Talien, was nearly completed at an enormous cost to the Russian Ministry of Finance. The importance of Vladivostok as the terminus of the Trans-Siberian Railway was reduced as frantic efforts were made to equip Talien as the trading port and to fortify Port Arthur as a naval port.

At the same time, the Russo-Chinese Bank, the monetary spearhead of Russian expansionism, broadened its sphere of interests. But it was becoming increasingly apparent that, despite its successes, Russian Far Eastern policy was marked by basic confusion, secrecy, deception, and universal suspicion.

Meanwhile, Bezobrazoff, Kuropatkin, and Witte inspected the Far Eastern situation, and the latter two, after returning to St. Petersburg, presented their recommendations on Russia's Far Eastern policy; but these were disregarded by the Tsar. The notorious Bezobrazoff already had the Tsar's ear. The gist of his Eastern policy was as follows:

"Russian policy lacks unity of purpose and trend. In co-operation with Germany, Russia can effectively block Great Britain in East Asia and prevent her from using Japan as a lever against Russia. Without the support of Great Britain, Japan is powerless and would be content with concessions in South Korea where she has a preponderant economic interest. Russia should, therefore, act with energy and determination. Russian evacuation from Manchuria is unthinkable, and the matter is one concerning Russia and China alone, not a question for international consultation. To silence the objections of the powers, Russia should reinforce her troops in the area.

"Moreover, Russia should protect her flank against any attack by Japan, or, in case of emergency, pose a threat to Japan by fortifying the Yalu River area. In short, Russia should abandon Witte's cowardly policy which can only lead to increasing difficulties. Russia should also further extend her economic interests in the Far East, attempting to cut off American support to Japan and inviting American capital to cooperate with Russia, thereby gaining American sympathy for Russia. Important industries in Manchuria should be controlled."

With the passage of time, the opinions of the Tsar began to take on added significance. In October, 1901, when the Tsar met Prince Heinrich, the Kaiser's brother, he revealed that originally he did not care about Manchuria, but only wished that it should not be seized by another power. He also intimated that he had little interest in Korea, but was against Japan gaining a powerful footing there. Japan's attempt to solidify its position would constitute casus belli for Russia, he asserted.

Late in the summer of 1902, the Tsar confidentially conveyed his views to the Kaiser, acknowledging that Russia was preparing for war, a war which would in all probability break out in 1904.

Even a cursory review of the overall situation reveals that

the Tsar was not only influenced by Bezobrazoff and his group, but also by the assessments given by his own military and naval authorities. The Russian naval expansion program to counter Japanese sea power, begun in 1897, was scheduled to be completed in 1904. The prediction made by the Tsar in his private conversation with the Kaiser that a Russo-Japanese conflict would erupt in 1904 seems to have been made in anticipation of the completion of the Russian naval expansion plan.

Insulting reports reaching the Tsar concerning Japanese armaments were confirmed by the Russian military attaché in Tokyo who informed his Government in 1900 that it would take almost a century for the Japanese army to have the basic morale necessary to confront even the weakest European army. He even described the Japanese army as an "infant" force.

Moreover, not only did General Kuropatkin guarantee a Russian victory in case of a war between Russia and Japan, but the Russia naval authorities were also confident of victory.

Misled by his informants, the question of war with Japan was not of serious importance to the Tsar. The policy of peaceful infiltration of Witte, Lamsdorff, Kuropatkin, and their associates held out no attraction to the Tsar, who preferred the high-handed policy of the Bezobrazoff group.

Whether the Tsar had any real intention of fighting Japan is open to question. There are evidences that the Tsar, who earlier predicted a Russo-Japanese war, was convinced that his policy of demonstrating Russia's massive strength would force Japan into submission without war. However, if the decision of war or peace involved major concessions or loss of prestige on the part of Russia, the Tsar was determined to uphold Russian rights by force of arms.

This then was the situation when Russia, completely dominated by Bezobrazoff and his group, ordered a major administrative reform in her Far Eastern policy on August 12,

1903, without informing Lamsdorff, Witte, Kuropatkin, and other leaders of the moderate wing. A special Vice-Regency known as the Far East Government-General was created to look after affairs in the Amur and Kwantung territories. General Alexieff, appointed the first Viceroy, was vested with supreme power over the civil and military administration of all Russian territories in the Far East.

Keeping pace with the grave transition in the Far East, a special committee on Far Eastern Questions was set up in St. Petersburg under the nominal jurisdiction of the Tsar. Constituted as the supreme organ for execution of Russia's Far Eastern policy, its members consisted of the four Ministers of Foreign Affairs, Finance, Army, and Navy, but the reins of power were firmly in the grip of Abaza and not the Ministers.

Having formed this machinery to suit their own ambitions, Bezobrazoff and his group succeeded in freeing themselves from governmental supervision, enabling them to materialize their designs without official intervention. The logical consequence of this development was the resignation of Count Witte as Minister of Finance.

Consequently, Russia's Far Eastern policy was now in the hands of three different organs, each acting independently. The weakest of the three organs was the Foreign Office, which did not enjoy the confidence of the Tsar. The other two were the special Vice-Regency and the Special Committee on Far Eastern Questions, a powerful organ having direct access to the Tsar. It was while Russia was in this confused state of affairs that Japan began negotiations with her giant Western neighbor.

Prior to these negotiations, a crucial conference had taken place at Murin-An, an estate of Prince Yamagata in Kyoto, on April 21, 1903, to decide Japan's policy towards Russia. The meeting was attended by two *genro,* Marquis Ito and Marquis Yamagata, and two leading members of the Cabinet, Katsura and Komura. The Cabinet as well as the *genro* went into every aspect of Japan's policy before the Imperial Conference was held in Tokyo on June 23, 1903, at which the following resolution was adopted:

1. In case there is no indication of Russian intention to evacuate from Manchuria, particularly from Liaotung Peninsula, Japan should seize this opportunity to bring the outstanding question of Korea to a satisfactory settlement.

2. Under no circumstances shall Korea transfer any part of her territory to Russia in the process of reaching a satisfactory settlement on Korea.

3. On the other hand, in view of her predominant position in Manchuria, there is room for a certain amount of concessions in the region named.

In effect, Japan came to the conclusion that she would endeavor to recognize Russian treaty interests in Manchuria in return for Russian recognition of Japanese interests in Korea. The Government was determined to achieve its objectives even at the cost of open hostilities.

Having come to this fateful decision, Japan was prepared to meet the new developments in Russo-Japanese relations in the Far East. Minister Kurino at St. Petersburg was instructed to begin direct negotiations with Lamsdorff, the Russian Minister for Foreign Affairs.

The Manchurian question naturally aroused great concern in Great Britain and the United States. Although Great Britain made recommendations to Japan that she should be in close contact with the United States, the Japanese Government replied that in view of the absolute need to maintain the strictest secrecy and the bilateral nature of the negotiations, it could see no advantage in communicating with the United States on the subject.

In explaining Japan's position, Foreign Minister Komura pointed out to Sir Claude MacDonald that the joint action of the powers might be construed as bringing pressure to bear on Russia, an act which was incompatible with the spirit of friendly negotiations with Russia as contemplated by the

Japanese Government. Moreover, the Japanese Government, anxiously desirous of peace, believed that the best and only means of attaining peaceful relations was direct negotiations with Russia. Japan felt that any delay in reaching a settlement might provoke hostilities.

The Japanese proposals, presented by Minister Kurino on August 12 to Lamsdorff, consisted of the following stipulations:

A mutual engagement to respect the independence and territorial integrity of the Chinese and Korean Empires, and to maintain the principle of equal opportunity for the commerce and industry of all nations in those countries (Article I);

A reciprocal recognition of Japan's preponderating interests in Korea and Russia's special interests in railway enterprises in Manchuria, and of the right of Japan to take in Korea, and of Russia to take in Manchuria, any necessary measures for the protection of these interests, subject to the provisions of Article I (Article II);

A reciprocal undertaking not to impede the development of those industrial and commercial activities, respectively, of Japan in Korea and of Russia in Manchuria, which were not inconsistent with the provisions of Article I (Article III);

An additional engagement on the part of Russia not to impede the eventual extension of the Korean Railway into Southern Manchuria so as to connect with the Eastern Chinese and Shanhaikwan-Newchuang lines (Article IV);

A reciprocal engagement that, in case troops should be sent by Japan to Korea, or by Russia to Manchuria, either to protect the interests mentioned in Article II or for suppressing insurrection or disorder liable to create international complications, troops so sent would in no case exceed the actual number required, and would be forthwith recalled as soon as their missions were accomplished (Article V);

The recognition on the part of Russia of the exclusive right of Japan to give advice and assistance in the interest of reform and good government in Korea, including necessary military assistance (Article VI);

This agreement to supercede all previous arrangements between Japan and Russia respecting Korea (Article VII).

The stipulations deserving the greatest attention in the Japanese proposals were, firstly, the Japanese demand of complete control over Korea and, secondly, the troop limitation proposed in Article V. These provisions had the expressed aim of preventing Russian administrative policy to extend over Manchuria and Korea.

When the Japanese Government's proposals were handed to the Russian Government, the conflicting policies, mentioned earlier, regarding the Far East had not yet been resolved. It was quite natural, therefore, that Russia should request the transfer of the venue of the preliminary negotiations from St. Petersburg to Tokyo inasmuch as the Office of the Viceroy of the Far East had been newly established and there was a need for substantial first-hand knowledge regarding local conditions.

This Russian move was received with strong indignation by the Japanese Government, which charged Russia with attempting to treat Japan as a vassal state. From the standpoint of not wishing to upset the peace of the Far East, the Japanese Government finally acquiesced to the Russian proposal. Hence, on September 7, 1903, the two parties agreed to invest Foreign Minister Baron Komura and Minister Baron Rosen with plenipotentiary powers to conduct formal negotiations as representatives of Japan and Russia respectively.

After a hurried trip to Port Arthur to meet General Alexieff, Baron Rosen presented a significant counterproposal of the Russian Government to Baron Komura on October 3. Russia suggested recognition of Korean independence and her territorial integrity as well as Japan's special interests (Articles I–IV), but at the same time sought to impose on Japan several impossible conditions regarding Korea, i.e., "not to use any part of the territory of Korea for strategical purposes" and "not to fortify the southern coast which would threaten the free navigation of the Korean Straits" (Article V), "to consider the territory lying north of the 39th Parallel as a neutral zone into which neither country should introduce troops" (Article VI), and "Manchuria and its littoral should be recognized by Japan as in all respects outside her sphere of interests" (Article VII).

In essence, the Russian counterproposal had no other aim but to exclude Manchuria from the field of discussion and to severely restrict Japan's actions in Korea. It also revealed Russia's uncompromising ambition to absorb and monopolize the whole of Manchuria and to carve out North Korea as part of her eventual sphere of influence, while at the same time refusing to recognize Japan's growing interests in those territories.

In an effort to bridge the wide gulf between Japan and Russia, Baron Komura, following a series of meetings with Baron Rosen initiated on October 6, presented Japan's second amended proposal to the Russian Minister on October 30.

In its revised proposal, Japan agreed not to fortify the Korean coast, but in return proposed a neutral zone extending fifty kilometers, not only on the Korean side, but on the Manchurian side as well. The proposal also declared that Manchuria was as far beyond the sphere of Japanese special interests as was Korea of the Russian, and that as a matter of course the treaty rights of Russia in Korea and those of Japan in Manchuria were to be respected. It also demanded that Russia refrain from impeding the economic activities of Japanese subjects in Korea. Other articles were mostly identical to the provisions stipulated in the first note.

These amendments represented an extensive concession on the part of Japan. However, by recognizing that Manchuria was far beyond the sphere of influence of Japan's special interests and by proposing a neutral zone, not only on the Korean side, but "on the Korean-Manchuria frontier extending 50 kilometers on either side," Japan was informing Russia that she had no intention of surrendering any part of Korean territory.

Despite these major concessions, Russia declined to reply promptly, using as a pretext the illness of the Empress and the need to consult the Viceroy of the Far East. When the reply was finally delivered on December 11, after repeated inquiries by Japan, it contained the second counterproposal.

Intent on restricting the agreement to Korea, Russia now was entirely silent on the subject of Manchuria, excepting the eventual extension of the Korean Railway into South Manchuria so as to connect it with the Chinese Eastern and Shanhaikwan-Newchuang Line. She not only persisted in the restrictions proposed earlier in October upon Japanese actions in Korea, but also insisted that the agreement concerning Korea contain the provisions "not to use any part of the territory of Korea for strategic purposes" and the establishment of the neutral zone.

Just before and after she communicated her second amended proposal, Russia began augmenting her forces, occupied Mukden and expelled Governor General Tseng I. General Alexieff made no secret of Russia's policy of intimidation, speedily constructing an elaborate fort at Port Arthur under the direction of General Stoessel, the Fortress Commandant.

Meanwhile, the Japanese Government, on the heels of fresh deliberations on the second Russian proposal, decided that it could not budge from its own amendments, but would, nevertheless, make one more attempt to appeal to the friendly sentiments of the Russian Government. A statement to this effect was delivered orally by Baron Komura to Baron Rosen on December 23. Baron Komura emphasized Japan's rights to offer advice and assistance to Korea for the reform of her administrative machinery, and proposed the removal of all fortifications which might hamper freedom of navigation along the Korean and Manchurian coasts.

The Russian Government, in replying to the Japanese proposal on January 6, 1904, asserted that, should Japan agree to the stipulations on the question of not using Korean territory for military purposes and on the question of a neutral zone, it would for its part respect the treaty rights and privileges enjoyed by Japan and other powers in Manchuria, excepting those concerned with settlement rights in the open ports. Russia, however, scrupulously avoided any mention of China's territorial integrity in Manchuria.

Disappointed with Russia's negative response, the Japanese Government verbally communicated another appeal to the Russian Government on January 16, urging it to reconsider its stand, with the following proposals:

1. To delete all reference to the military use of any part of Korean territory.

2. To delete the clause establishing a neutral zone.

3. To approve the amendment of the Russian proposal to read "Japan recognizes Manchuria and its coastline as lying beyond Japan's sphere of interest, providing Russia respect the territorial integrity of Manchuria and do not obstruct the enjoyment by Japan and other Powers of rights and privileges acquired by them under existing treaties with China."

4. To insert in the Russian counterproposal the words "Japan recognizes Russia's special interests in Manchuria and Russian rights to take measures necessary for the protection of those interests."

Despite these concessions and frequent reminders from Japan, Russia continued to remain unresponsive, declining even to give any indication of when a reply would be forthcoming. Instead she openly rushed military and naval preparations in Manchuria and along its coast, applying heavy pressure against Korea by massive troop concentrations along the borders.

Russian preparedness in the Far East exceeded all bounds of defensive requirements. In April, 1903, she added nineteen vessels with an aggregate tonnage of 82,415 tons to the Far Eastern Fleet, and despatched a further fifteen vessels of 37,000 tons to serve in Far Eastern waters. From June, 1903, Russia began transporting troops to Manchuria in alarming numbers. By February, 1904, their total exceeded 40,000, while another 200,000 were made available in case of emergency. Construction of forts at Port Arthur and Vladivostok went on day and night, while fortifications at Kungchuling, Liaoyang and other strategic points were reinforced. Huge quantities of arms and ammunition arrived by land and sea, followed in October, 1903 by fourteen trains from Russia carrying field hospital equipment.

Activities of Russian forces in Manchuria and Korea reached menacing proportions when two battalions of infantry and several artillery units were transferred from Port Arthur to the northern frontiers of Korea on January 21, 1904. On January 28, General Alexieff ordered the Russian troops near the Yalu River to be on a war footing. Tension heightened when the Governor of Vladivostok on February 1 requested the Japanese commercial agent at the port to prepare to withdraw Japanese residents to Habarovsk as he had received instructions from his Government to be ready to proclaim martial law at any time.

Fully aware of the grave implications of these Russian military moves, Japan began taking effective countermeasures to deal with this ominous threat. By January 13, 1904, Baron Komura, deeply disappointed by Russia's reactions to Japan's final proposal, became firmly convinced of Russian insincerity in conducting negotiations. Japan was left with no other alternative but to adopt appropriate measures designed to protect her interests.

A special council in the Imperial presence was summoned on February 4. Present on the occasion, besides Premier Viscount Katsura, Foreign Minister Komura, Finance Minister Sone, Navy Minister Admiral Yamamoto, and War Minister Terauchi, representing the Cabinet, were five leading *genro,*

Marquis Ito, Marshal Marquis Yamagata, Marquis Oyama, Count Matsukata, and Inouye. The Japanese Government, having reluctantly reached the decision to break off the hopeless diplomatic negotiations with Russia, notified the latter, who showed no signs of being deflected from her determination to invade Manchuria and Korea, that Japan would reserve the right to pursue an independent course of action in order to safeguard her acquired rights and legitimate interests and to resort to military action to protect her position.

Even Marquis Ito, known as a Russophile, recognized the inevitability of war with Russia. In his memoirs, *An Account of the Rupture of Russo-Japanese Negotiations,* he wrote as follows:

"It is unquestionable that Russia intended from the very outset to categorically reject Japanese demands, depending on the growing strength of its army and navy, to give free rein to its ambitions in Manchuria and Korea. If Japan should fail at this juncture to act forcefully to defend her own threatened interests, she will eventually be placed in a position of having to dance willynilly to the tune of an outlying Russian Government-General. In other words, she will only await her ultimate doom."

Finally on February 5, Minister Kurino in St. Petersburg received instructions to present a note to the Russian Government, setting forth the position of the Japanese Government, and giving notification of Japan's severance of her meaningless diplomatic relations with Russia.

The possibility that Japan was seriously contemplating armed action hardly seems to have entered the minds of the Russian leaders who had been pursuing a dilatory policy. It was Russia's belief that Japan would meekly surrender in the face of an overwhelming show of Russian military power, a power backed by a formidable navy and a massive land army capable of posing a grave threat to any potential adversary.

Even General Kuropatkin reported in August to the Tsar that he had no reasons to feel uneasy, particularly in view of

Russia's mounting strength in the past two years. In case of open conflict, he predicted that the war would end with Russian troops landing on the Japanese homeland. He held this confidence up to the beginning of hostilities. Public opinion in Russia shared this overbearing view.

Novoe Vremia, one of the leading Russian newspapers, commented in July that "Japan would be committing a suicidal act if she were to launch war against Russia. All her hopes would be dashed. Even the mighty armies of Napoleon had failed to subdue Russia. Having had this experience with the French army, no enemy is strong enough to be of any threat to Russia."

The Tsar could have had no more mistaken notion than to believe that the maintenance of peace depended simply on his divine will. When he granted an audience to Minister Kurino early in the new year of 1904, the Tsar defiantly declared: "Russia is a large country, but remember there is a limit to her patience."

While Japan's policy, based on justice, was concrete, clear, and mild, Russia's policy was from the very beginning ill defined, contradictory, and dominated by an ambitious lust for power and hegemony. Throughout the Russo-Japanese negotiations, Russia displayed no desire for compromise or conciliation.

Lately it has become customary for historians to try retrospectively to blame one or the other party for the outbreak of hostilities. As far as the Russo-Japanese War is concerned, evidence of responsibility weighs heavily against the Russians. There is hardly any divergence of opinion that Japanese policy was mainly dictated by circumstances, and her proclamation of war against Russia was an act of self-defence, a right which she justly exercised.

The situation in case of Russia was radically different. Whatever may be the arguments advanced by Russia, it is a fact that in 1904 she held no real interests in Manchuria and Korea except investments of an aggressive nature. She found it expedient to cut across Manchuria in order to acquire the shortest railway connection between the Russian capital of St. Petersburg and Vladivostok. Ostensibly to safeguard the railway, she sent armed guards, then demanded an ice-free port. In order to realize profits from the railway enterprise, Russia acquired mining and other concessions. To protect these vast concessions, she began fortifying Port Arthur. It is, of course, extremely difficult to judge and assess the extent of responsibility these situations had on the course of historical development.

In his memoirs, Count Witte disclaims any responsibility for the events leading to the outbreak of the war. While his denial of direct involvement is generally acknowledged, he cannot, in the last analysis, be absolved of all responsibility. After all, the ultimate aim of his seemingly pacific and conciliatory policy differed little in substance from the policies adopted by either General Kuropatkin and his militant group or Bezobrazoff and his clique of concession-hunters. The militaristic group and the concession-hunters were able to operate practically unhindered within the scope of Count Witte's policy—a policy which gave rise to grave uneasiness among the other powers, almost as if in conditions of military occupation.

As long as Russia persisted in pursuing this policy, an armed clash was unavoidable. Therefore, it would be superficial to lay the responsibility solely on the forces advocating war, led by Bezobrazoff and his clique. It was unfortunate that in the crisis of 1904 Russia lacked consistency in her policy.

Prior to the Russo-Japanese War, Russia's policy was a compound of vagueness and contradictory intrigues. With the passage of time, Japanese disappointment in Russian policy increased. She could no longer place faith in a government whose policy was contradictory, untrustful, and unjust. It was natural, therefore, that Japan began to feel that no reliance whatever could be placed on Russia's words.

During these crucial months, the Japanese Government kept the British Government fully informed about the progress of the negotiations. Japan hoped that Britain would recognize that the failure of the negotiations was not due to any lack of patience or forbearance on the part of Japan. The British Government was completely in accord with the basis of understanding which Japan had presented to the Russian Government.

Marquis Lansdowne, in his letter to Durand, the British Ambassador to the United States, stated that considering the nature of the demands upon which Japan was insisting, the British Government would not be justified in exerting even moral pressure on Japan to mitigate her demands. By depriving Japan of her present opportunity, Great Britain might incur her lasting resentment. If she missed her chance now, he wrote, she would suffer the consequences in the future.

The British Government fully recognized and supported the position of the Japanese Government. At the same time, Britain had no intention of inciting Japan to commence hostilities against Russia nor to make any recommendation to Japan to compromise with Russia. The British Government was careful to avoid giving Japan even the slightest impression of any moral pressure.

The attitude of the British Government was motivated by a desire to fulfil her treaty obligations, offering every possible assistance to Japan within the framework of the treaty of alliance. Britain also displayed understanding and sympathy for Japan's position in Korea. In a memorandum to Japanese Minister Hayashi on July 16, 1903, Marquis Lansdowne stated: "His Majesty's Government have never concealed the fact that the interests of Japan in Korea are of a special nature. . . . His Majesty's Government would welcome Russia's recognition of Japan's special interests in Korea. As a matter of fact, in the Anglo-Japanese Agreement, the British Government have already admitted that Japan has such interests and they would consider it to be to their advantage that the position of Japan in that country should be strengthened." Britain threw her full support behind Japan whose primary concern was the Russian evacuation from Manchuria.

Great Britain also promised that she would not permit a third power to mediate or intervene on behalf of the party opposing Japan. The Japanese Government made no secret of its distaste for mediation at this juncture of the negotiations. Reasons for taking this attitude were made abundantly clear in the instructions issued by Foreign Minister Komura to all Japanese Ministers abroad.

"Should Russia seek or accept mediation," emphasized Foreign Minister Komura, "her sole objective would be to gain time in order to strengthen and consolidate her position in the Far East and not with the aim of reaching a complete and permanent settlement on current issues. Any recourse to mediation rather than direct negotiations would compel the Imperial Government to modify its proposals, barring it from including any effective measures that would prevent complications to arise in the future. In view of these considerations, any attempt to bring about mediation, in whatever form, at this stage would, in the opinion of the Imperial Japanese Government, be ineffectual and of advantage only to Russia."

Paying due respect to these views, the British Government refused to entertain the mediation plan of Delcassé, the French Foreign Minister, and lent no support to Lamsdorff's demand for British assistance in reaching a peaceful settlement, based on the Tsar's strong aversion to war.

Immediately after the outbreak of the Russo-Japanese War, Great Britain formally proclaimed a policy of "strict neutrality." In due time, both Germany and France followed the British example. When France and Germany in contravention to the spirit of neutrality offered coaling facilities to the Russian Baltic Fleet on its voyage from Europe to the Far East, Great Britain remained unruffled and failed to change her neutral stand.

Fearful of the consequences if the Far Eastern conflict were to spread to Europe, Great Britain endeavored untiringly to restrict the combatants to Russia and Japan. She scrupulously avoided any act that would offend the Russians, whom she hoped to utilize in her policy towards Germany. How she intended to achieve this purpose is far from clear. The Japanese Government did not necessarily disapprove of this British attitude.

The Anglo-Japanese Alliance was an element of prime importance in determining the course of world history. If this Alliance had not been concluded prior to the Russo-Japanese War, it is highly improbable that Japan would have run the risk of resorting to war against Russia. Not only were the attitudes of Great Britain and Germany in a state of flux, but there was a real danger that Russia might call upon France to implement the provision of the Russo-French Alliance, in which case Japan would be faced by the combined armies and navies of Russia and France.

The Anglo-Japanese Alliance was a guarantee against a repetition of the Triple Intervention, and actually removed one of the greatest barriers to the outbreak of war. Although it failed to maintain peace in the Far East, the same Alliance was helpful in limiting the field of combat operations.

The British Government gave, without hesitation, the following pledge before the opening of hostilities to the Japanese Government:

"His Majesty's Government will on their side fulfil, both in letter and spirit, their obligations under the Agreement, which imposes upon them the duty of using their efforts in order to prevent other Powers from joining in hostilities against their Ally."

Moreover, the British Government intended to meet the grave situation in cooperation with the United States. In response to British entreaties, the United States took the stand of a spiritual ally. Marquis Lansdowne told the American Ambassador: "If there are any points in regard to which we are better informed than the United States Government, I would be glad to place any knowledge in my possession at your disposal." He expressed satisfaction on learning that the United States Government was taking a keen interest in the Far Eastern question.

In January, 1904, President Roosevelt of the United States, having already assured Japan of America's neutrality, solemnly warned both Germany and France that if either of these two powers should render active assistance to Russia, the United States would retaliate by assisting Japan and intervene.

However, France showed no desire to be drawn into the hostilities on the side of Russia. It was obvious that she had nothing to gain and everything to lose from such a war. But had not the Anglo-Japanese Alliance existed, it was likely that she would ultimately have been involved in the Russo-Japanese War. In such an eventuality, Great Britain would have extended a helping hand to Japan with the aim of maintaining the balance of power. Whether Germany joined one or the other side would then have been irrelevant; a World War would have ensued.

Japan, by the terms of the peace treaty, acquired complete and absolute administrative power over Korea and established her undisputed special interests in Manchuria. By virtue of Japan's victory in the Russo-Japanese War, crushing the Russian grandiose dream of a Far Eastern Empire, no longer did Great Britain have to fear a Russian advance into the Far East, endangering her special foothold in China, especially in the Yangtze Valley.

Furthermore, Great Britain took advantage of the Russo-Japanese War to recover her rights and interests in Persia, Afghanistan, and Tibet which Russia had violated during the Boer War. The Anglo-Japanese Alliance, as we mentioned earlier, had restricted directly or indirectly the sphere of war, contributed to the settlement of the Korean problem and set up Japan's special interests in Manchuria side by side with those of Russia. It had tightened Japanese and British foot-holds in China, and heightened the prestige of both nations in the imperial court at Peking. The First Anglo-Japanese Alliance having made such an outstanding achievement, there was no voice of opposition in Japan and Britain when the Second Alliance was concluded.

CHAPTER **6**

Second Anglo-Japanese Alliance
1903-1905

~~~~~~

THE Far Eastern situation underwent such a startling change
in the years following the Russo-Japanese War that it became increasingly difficult to maintain the original purpose
of the Anglo-Japanese Alliance. It was inevitable, therefore,
that a new treaty consonant with prevailing conditions would
have to replace the old arrangement existing between the two
countries.

Equally dramatic changes in the sphere of international
politics were also taking place in Europe. Recognizing the
futility of its four years of continuous efforts to reach an understanding with Germany, originating from 1898, Great
Britain finally took the path of rapprochement with Russia
and France.

In the spring of 1903, King Edward VII visited Paris in
an obvious attempt to signify Britain's desire to augment her
ties of friendship with France. Three months later, French
President Émile Loubet, accompanied by Foreign Minister
Delcassé and Colonial Minister Etienne, paid a return visit
to London.

Taking advantage of this visit, discussions were held between the representatives of the two countries on ways and
means of resolving their outstanding differences. As a result
of these exchanges, the two nations agreed that it would be
desirable to conclude an Anglo-French agreement. Respec-

tive signatures were affixed to a convention and the two attached declarations on April 5, 1904. On the basis of this agreement, known as the Anglo-French Entente Cordiale, Great Britain and France agreed to eliminate all major outstanding disputes existing between them in every part of the world.

Having won the amity of France, Great Britain made similar conciliatory moves towards Russia. The bone of contention between these two powers, however, lay in the Far East where Russia, with German assistance, continued her policy of aggrandisement. It was the view of certain leading British politicians that, notwithstanding the Anglo-Japanese Alliance, it would still be possible to attain some kind of understanding with Russia, providing that British policy was backed by unchallengeable power.

Against this complicated background, Great Britain made several attempts to reach an understanding with Russia, negotiating on issues which affected only the two countries, namely, questions concerning Persia, Afghanistan, and Tibet. The British Government, while generally supporting Japan's policy before and during the Russo-Japanese War, deliberately avoided incurring Russia's permanent hostility or displeasure and jeopardizing the chances of future reconciliation.

In formulating her policy towards Germany, the British Government took all pains to avoid any action that would throw Russia into the lap of Germany. A section of British opinion was apprehensive lest the Russians, in an effort to recover from the losses sustained in the Russo-Japanese War, should spearhead a drive into Central Asia and the Northwestern Frontier of India. Despite her defeat in the Far East, Russia remained a potential threat to British interests in India. In British eyes, the intimate relations between Russia and Germany also called for heightening vigilance.

Thus, the British politicians desired to reinforce the Anglo-Japanese Alliance by extending its scope to the frontiers of

India and by changing its character into a defensive and offensive alliance, hoping thereby to ensure Britain's national security and to have a trump card in negotiating with Russia.

In these circumstances, added significance was attached to the public statement of Foreign Minister Komura on the occasion of the celebration of the third anniversary of the First Anglo-Japanese Alliance on February 12, 1905, expressing his hope that the Alliance should continue to strengthen the existing close understanding between Japan and Great Britain.

Komura's declaration was favorably received in Britain as an indication of the probable policy and intention of the Japanese Government. Subsequently, on February 24, Lord Lansdowne, the British Minister for Foreign Affairs, in his meeting with Japanese Minister Tadasu Hayashi remarked —after reading the report from British Minister in Japan Sir Claude MacDonald—that he attached great importance to Komura's suggestion that the alliance might be given a more effective and wider scope.

Lord Lansdowne went on to outline the following three measures for the extension of the alliance which he felt would be acceptable to British public opinion:

1. Renunciation of the present alliance should become possible with a year's notification.

2. Period of validity should be defined.

3. The scope of the alliance should be enlarged, and the alliance itself placed on a broader foundation.

Describing the first measure as of minor importance, Lord Lansdowne privately informed Minister Hayashi that he would like to take up the other two measures as subjects of negotiation. The Japanese Minister was requested to transmit the proposals to Foreign Minister Komura with the suggestion that the Japanese Government intimate its views on the matter to the British Government and that the representatives of the two countries informally exchange opinions.

Concerning the question of revising the alliance, the fundamental policy of the Japanese Government was as follows:

1. The alliance should be continued.

2. The scope of the alliance should be limited to its present scope.

3. In view of its intention to eventually take charge of and direct the diplomatic affairs of Korea, the Japanese Government should obtain the prior approval and assistance of the British Government.

4. Every effort should be made to conclude the negotiations between Japan and Great Britain during the administration of the Balfour Cabinet. The term of validity of the alliance should be fixed as seven years in the attached protocol.

A somewhat different opinion was held by the British Government, which felt that:

1. The alliance should be continued.

2. The present defensive alliance should be transformed into a defensive and offensive alliance.

3. India should come within the geographical limits of the alliance.

4. Since the above conditions conformed to current British public opinion, their acceptance was essential in renewing the alliance before its expiration.

The Japanese Government at the time was faced with the urgent issue of settling the question of Korea. As early as May, 1904, at a formal Cabinet meeting the Katsura Cabinet had reached the following important decisions regarding the Korean question:

1. At an appropriate time, Korea should either be made a protectorate or be incorporated into the territory of Japan.

2. Until such time, Japan should acquire protective rights in the political, diplomatic, and military fields, and Japan's economic interests in Korea should be effectively developed.

In a positive move to achieve these objectives, an agreement was concluded between Japan and Korea on August 22, 1904, followed on October 15 by Korea's agreement to engage a Japanese subject as "Financial Adviser" to the Government of Korea.| Japan was gradually able to offer advice in all matters affecting Korea's diplomacy and finance. [On April 1, 1905, Japan was commissioned by Korea to operate communications within the country.

While it is true that Japan desired an early revision of the Anglo-Japanese Alliance to strengthen her position at the coming Portsmouth Peace Conference and to ensure her security against Russian revenge in the future, there is hardly any room for doubt that Japan's real and urgent object was the solution of the Korean question.

On March 27, 1905, Minister Hayashi received instructions from Foreign Minister Komura to sound out the views of Lord Lansdowne on the continuance of the alliance. A notable characteristic of these negotiations was the secrecy with which the talks were conducted from the very outset. It appears that the statement made by Lord Lansdowne to Minister Hayashi on May 17 decisively influenced a change in Japan's attitude towards the alliance. Lord Lansdowne intimated to the Japanese Minister that he could not help feeling that it would be advantageous to both parties to revise the conditions and strengthen the alliance in certain aspects.

In expressing his private observations on the treaty, Lord Lansdowne also stated that it was obvious that there were two courses to strengthen the alliance. One course would be to undertake to assist one another in the event either of the signatories was the victim of unprovoked attack, regardless of any prior interference by a third power. Great Britain would also undertake to assist Japan, in case of an attack by a single power, with the full might of her naval strength. In return, Japan would render land and naval assistance to Great Britain within certain geographical limits.

Giving a hypothetical example, Lord Lansdowne declared

that even if Japan were able to win a complete victory over Russia, the Russians would surely not rest until they had avenged their defeat. In any renewed hostilities, the Russians would bring to bear on Japan an irresistible force that would ultimately be ruinous for the island nation. By entering into a firm alliance with Great Britain, Japan would be able to remove this risk as Russia would hesitate to embark on any venture which would bring her into conflict with the combined naval strength of Great Britain and Japan. Faced with such a prospect, Russia would in all probability abandon any idea of reprisal in the Far East.

On the other hand, if Russia was unable to subdue her feelings of revenge, she would almost certainly turn her attention to other parts of Asia, seriously threatening the security of the Indian frontier or other strategic points. In exchange for shouldering a greater burden of responsibility, Lord Lansdowne pointed out that it was natural that Great Britain should receive some compensatory advantages.

In his biography, Prince Katsura clarifies the reasons for Japan having to accept the British position. He wrote: "From the Japanese standpoint, the nation needed a period of recuperation after the Russo-Japanese War, and, furthermore, the possibility of a Russian revenge could not be precluded. By concluding a firm alliance with Great Britain, Japan would be able to rebuild her strength and heal the scars of war."

Thus, at the Cabinet meeting and the *genro* conference on May 23 and 24, attended by all the elder statesmen and Cabinet Ministers, it was decided unanimously to accept the revised terms and enlarge the scope of the alliance as suggested by Great Britain. It is interesting to note that Marquis Ito was one of the strongest supporters of the British proposition. On May 25, Foreign Minister Komura wired Minister Hayashi in London that the Japanese Government would closely follow in principle the lines put forward by Lord Lansdowne, the geographic limits being East Asia including India.

Japan was also agreeable to changing the defensive First Alliance into a defensive and offensive alliance in the case of the Second Alliance, with both Great Britain and Japan to assist the other in the event either of·them was attacked by a third power without provocation.

At the same time, the Japanese Government transmitted the first draft, constituting six articles and three separate articles which were secret.

ARTICLE I

The objects of the Alliance are consolidation and maintenance of general peace in the Orient, conservation of common interests of all Powers in China, that is to say, territorial integrity of China and the Open Door policy therein, and the protection of respective territorial rights and special interests of the Contracting Parties in East Asia and India.

ARTICLE II

If either Contracting Party should be wantonly attacked by any other Power or Powers or should, owing to aggressive action of any other Power or Powers, become involved in war in defence of its menaced right or interests as above defined, the other Contracting Party will at once come to its assistance and will conduct war in common and make peace in mutual agreement with it.

ARTICLE III

The obligation of one Contracting Party to come to the assistance of the other as above described is territorially limited to the regions of Eastern Asia and India and no obligation in that respect shall arise unless and until hostilities or warlike operations have taken place in the said regions.

ARTICLE IV

The right of Japan to take such measures as she may deem right and necessary in order to safeguard her special political, military, and economic interests in Korea is fully recognized by Great Britain.

ARTICLE V

The Agreement shall remain in force for ten years from the date of signature.

ARTICLE VI

As regards the present war between Japan and Russia, England will maintain strict neutrality unless some other Power or Powers should join in hostilities against Japan in which case England will come to the assistance of Japan and conduct war in common and make peace in mutual agreement with Japan.

SEPARATE ARTICLES (SECRET)
ARTICLE I

Each of the Contracting Parties will endeavour to maintain at all times in the Far East a naval force superior in strength to that of any third Power having the largest naval force in the Far East.

ARTICLE II

The nature and degree of armed assistance and the means by which such assistance is to be made available will be arranged by the naval and military authorities of the Contracting Parties.

ARTICLE III

In case Japan finds it necessary to establish a protectorate over Korea in order to check aggressive action of any third Power and to prevent complications in connection with foreign relations of Korea, Great Britain engages to support the action of Japan.

When Minister Hayashi handed the above draft to Lord

Lansdowne, the latter inquired if the Japanese Government desired to alter the status quo in Korea by invoking the secret Article III. Minister Hayashi replied that the question of status quo could not be applied to Korea as the present condition in Korea resembled an area of conflict. The Japanese Government was of the opinion that Korea was the source of dangerous disturbances, and eternal peace in the Far East could not be hoped for until these alarming features were eliminated. It was for this reason that Japan was being compelled to tighten her control over Korea. The Minister denied any aggressive intent on the part of his country.

To the British Minister in Japan, Sir Claude MacDonald, Foreign Minister Komura made no secret of Japan's intention to establish a protectorate over Korea and take charge of that country's foreign relations. With regard to the geographical scope of the Alliance stipulated in Article III, Foreign Minister Komura informed MacDonald that it did not extend westward beyond India, thereby excluding Persia.

Concerning another important question, that of the nature and degree of armed assistance to be afforded by either power to the other, Minister Hayashi suggested that it would be better if the details were worked out later by the naval and military authorities of the Contracting Parties.

Referring to the secret articles of the treaty, Lord Lansdowne felt that it would be advisable, in the anticipation of questions in Parliament concerning the existence of such secret articles, that the matter be clarified during the exchange of documents between Great Britain and Japan. After consulting British army and naval authorities and several of his Cabinet Ministers, Lord Lansdowne handed the following revised version of the treaty to Minister Hayashi on June 10, 1905:

PREAMBLE

The Governments of Great Britain and Japan, being desirous of replacing the Agreement concluded between them on the 30th January, 1902, by fresh stipulations, have agreed upon the following Articles, which have for their object:

a. The consolidation and maintenance of the general peace in the East;

b. The preservation of the common interests of all Powers in China by insuring the independence and integrity of the Chinese Empire and the principle of equal opportunities for the commerce and industry of all nations in China;

c. The maintenance of the territorial integrity of the Possessions of the Contracting Parties in Eastern and South-Eastern Asia, and the defence of their special rights and interests in the countries in the proximity of such Possessions:

ARTICLE I

It is agreed that whenever, in the opinion of either Great Britain or Japan, any of the interests referred to in the Preamble of this Agreement are in jeopardy, the two Governments will communicate with one another fully and frankly, and will consider in common the measures which should be taken to safeguard those interests.

ARTICLE II

If in consequence of hostilities due to unprovoked attack, or aggressive action on the part of any other Power or Powers, the rights and special interests of either Party mentioned in section (c) of the preamble should be endangered, the other Contracting Party will at once come to its assistance, and will conduct the war in common, and make peace in mutual agreement with it.

ARTICLE III

The right of Japan to take such measures as she may deem right and necessary in order to safeguard her special political, military, and economic interests in Korea is fully recognized by Great Britain, provided always that such measures do not infringe the principle of equal opportunities for the commerce and industries of all nations.

ARTICLE IV

Japan, on the other hand, equally recognizes the special interests of Great Britain in the regions adjacent to the Indian frontier and her right to take such measures as she may deem proper and necessary in order to safeguard those interests.

ARTICLE V

The High Contracting Parties agree that neither of them will, without consulting the other, enter into separate arrangements with another Power to the prejudice of the interests above described.

ARTICLE VI

The present Agreement shall, subject to the provisions of Article VII, come into effect immediately after the date of its signature, and remain in force for ten years from that date.

In case neither of the High Contracting Parties should have notified twelve months before the expiration of the said ten years the intention of terminating it, it shall remain binding until the expiration of one year from the day on which either of the High Contracting Parties shall have denounced it. But if, when the date fixed for its expiration arrives, either ally is actually engaged in war, the alliance shall, ipso facto, continue until peace is concluded.

ARTICLE VII

As regards the present war between Japan and Russia, Great Britain will continue to maintain strict neutrality unless some other Power or Powers should join in hostilities against Japan, in which case Great Britain will come to the assistance of Japan, and will conduct the war in common, and make peace in mutual agreement with Japan.

NOTES
(A)

After the conclusion of the present war, each of the Contracting Parties will endeavour to maintain at all times available for concentration in the waters of the Far East a naval force superior in strength to that of any European Power in those seas.

(B)

It is agreed that Japan will, in the event of war, provide and maintain a force which shall be equal to the force of British troops from time to time in India up to a limit of ,000.

(C)

Subject to the above obligation, the conditions under which armed assistance shall be afforded by either Power to the other in the circumstances mentioned in the Agreement signed this day, and the means by which such assistance is to be made available, will be arranged by the Naval and Military authorities of the Contracting Parties, who will from time to time consult one another fully and freely upon all questions of mutual interest.

In presenting the revised draft, Lord Lansdowne amplified some of the major points in the following vein:

1. Insofar as Article II was concerned, Great Britain would come to the assistance of Japan with her naval force. The zone of hostilities would extend throughout the world. On the other hand, in case Japanese land forces were made available to Great Britain, the zone of hostilities would be limited to a certain area.

2. With reference to Article IV, the proximity of the Indian

frontier involved no economic interests whatsoever, only strategic considerations.

3. Concerning the paragraph marked "A" in the note, Great Britain deliberately stipulated "European Power" in deference to the unlikelihood that Great Britain and Japan would ever become involved in a war with the United States. The strong naval force maintained by the United States in Philippine waters was outside the purview of the note in question.

The counterproposal of the Japanese Government was presented on June 23, 1905, to the British Foreign Minister Lord Lansdowne, who, in turn, handed the British revised draft of the proposed Anglo-Japanese Agreement to Minister Hayashi on July 1. A few days later, on July 6, the Japanese Government submitted its counterdraft.

It is not surprising that the counterproposals and amendments exchanged between Great Britain and Japan were primarily concerned with Article III, dealing with Korea, and Article IV, dealing with India.

The British Government proposed that the words, "the treaty rights of other nations" be inserted before "the principle of equal opportunity" in Article III. The Japanese Government responded by declaring that it desired to be given as free a hand as possible in Korea without such restriction, fearing that another nation might seek to claim the same position as Japan enjoyed in Korea. Britain's ally had misgivings that the recognition of the most-favored-nation clause in Korea might be exaggeratedly interpreted.

The Japanese Government persistently rejected the British proposal, pointing out that it would infringe Japan's special interests in Korea, neither did she conceal the fact that the settlement of the Korean question was the primary object of the whole alliance.

As to the second half of Article IV of the British draft relating to India, laying down that "Japan equally recognizes the special interests of Great Britain in the regions adjacent to the Indian frontier . . . ," the Japanese Government concurred that Great Britain had every right to take whatever steps were necessary to guard her interests along the Indian frontier. However, as Japan had absolutely no interests in those regions, she considered that the second half of Article IV of the English draft might be struck out as irrelevant. Actually, Japan entertained fears that the English wording meant that Japan might be called upon to take part in punitive expeditions into Tibet, Afghanistan, and Persia. Furthermore, concerning the secret notes, Japan proposed their total elimination, excepting for "C" in the British draft.

Subsequently, on July 19, 1905, Lord Lansdowne handed to Minister Hayashi the second counterdraft of the British Government. Pertinent points in this revised draft were as follows:

1. Since the British proposal to insert in Article III the words having reference to "the treaty rights of other nations" before "the principle of equal opportunity" was rejected by the Japanese Government, a Note should be exchanged on the interpretation of Article III.

2. On grounds of its interdependency with the Korean Article, the British Government believed that it was imperative to include the clause concerning India.

In its final counterdraft, the Japanese Government concluded on August 1, 1905, that it did not see any necessity for the exchange of the proposed notes concerning the Korean Article, and that although it felt that the point at issue was covered sufficiently by the Preamble and Article II Japan would agree to the retention of Article IV in a modified form. On the question of assistance, stipulated in the second paragraph of Article VII, the Japanese Government felt that the stipulation could be excluded on the ground that the nature and scope of the assistance to be given should be the subject of arrangement between the military and naval authorities of the two Powers.

On August 3, 1905, Lord Lansdowne notified Minister

Hayashi that the British Government had decided to dispense with the exchange of the proposed notes, trusting the Japanese assurance that a war resulting from Japan's infringement of the treaty rights of other powers in Korea would not be regarded as hostilities due to unprovoked attack, as defined in Article II. The rewording of Article IV relating to India by the British Government stated that "Great Britain having a special interest in all that concerns the security of the Indian frontier, Japan recognizes her rights to take such measures in the proximity of that frontier as she may find necessary for safeguarding her Indian possessions."

The Japanese Government's concurrence with the interpretations of the British Government regarding Articles III and IV, covering the knotty problems of Korea and India, removed all major obstacles in the way of revising the Anglo-Japanese Alliance. Thus, after six months of intensive negotiations the new agreement between Japan and Great Britain was finally concluded.

That the British Minister to Japan, Sir Claude MacDonald, had persistently supported Japan's position and had urged his Government to accept the Japanese draft is clear from the publication of the British *Documents on the Origins of the War,* Vol. IV. Pointing out that the scope of the new alliance weighed in Britain's favor, the British Minister stressed the importance of accepting the Japanese demands, warning that any undue delay might rupture the entire agreement.

In contrast to the First Alliance, the Second Anglo-Japanese Alliance expanded its scope of application as follows:

1. The consolidation and maintenance of the general peace in the regions of Eastern Asia and India.

2. The preservation of the common interests of all powers in China by insuring the independence and integrity of the Chinese Empire and the principle of equal opportunities for the commerce and industry of all nations in China.

3. The maintenance of the territorial rights of the High Contracting Parties in the regions of Eastern Asia and of

India, and the defence of their special interests in the said regions.

It is worth noting that specific references to Korea were eliminated from the Preamble. The Second Alliance also substituted the principle of a defensive alliance, committing each of the Contracting Parties, in case of war, to come to the assistance of its ally, to conduct the war in common, and to make peace only in mutual agreement.

Unlike the First Alliance wherein China and Korea were treated alike, Great Britain now specifically recognized, "Japan possessing paramount political, military, and economic interests in Korea, the right of Japan to take such measures of guidance, control, and protection in Korea as she may deem proper and necessary to safeguard and advance those interests, provided always such measures are not contrary to the principle of equal opportunities for the commerce and industry of all nations."

Having agreed to extend the scope of the First Alliance, Japan recognized, "Great Britain having a special interest in all that concerns the security of the Indian frontier," the British rights "to take such measures in the proximity of that frontier as she may find necessary for safeguarding her Indian possessions." While the validity of the First Alliance was for five years, the two powers agreed to a term of ten years for the Second Alliance.

The Treaty renewing the Anglo-Japanese Alliance was signed at the private residence of Lord Lansdowne on August 12, 1905, only three days after the opening of the Portsmouth Peace Conference. Deeply concerned about its adverse effects on the peace negotiations, the Governments of Japan and Great Britain agreed to postpone the announcement. The new Treaty was not announced in Tokyo and London until September 27, 1905, after the successful conclusion of the Portsmouth Peace Treaty.

Prior to the formal announcement of the new Treaty, the British Government transmitted the text of the Treaty to Sir

Francis Bertie, Ambassador to France, and Sir Charles Hardinge, Ambassador to Russia, suggesting that it should be communicated to the respective Governments together with explanations before the publication of the Treaty.

In communicating the text of the new Alliance to Count Lamsdorff, Russian Minister of Foreign Affairs, Sir Charles Hardinge explained that in light of their special interests, the Contracting Parties were only insisting on their legitimate rights. Britain felt that the Russian Government would undoubtedly recognize that any of the powers interested in the affairs of the Far East would take no exception to the new Agreement.

The British Ambassador drew Count Lamsdorff's attention to the wording of Article II, that the Treaty was applicable only in case of an unprovoked attack made on one of the Contracting Parties by another Power or Powers. Article III, dealing with the question of Korea, the British envoy added, also deserved special notice, recognizing as it did in clearest terms the paramount position which Japan at that moment occupied and must henceforth occupy in Korea, and her right to take any measures which she might find necessary for the protection of her interests in that country. Hence, the British Government observed "with satisfaction that this point was readily conceded by Russia in the Treaty of Peace recently concluded with Japan."

Responding to the remarks of the British Ambassador, Count Lamsdorff stated that, after consulting the view of the Tsar and others on the agreement, the Russian Government could reach no other conclusion than that the Treaty was directed with hostile intent against Russia, judging from certain wordings in the Treaty. The Russian Government could not, therefore, be expected to welcome the conclusion of such a Treaty.

Expressing Russia's friendly sentiments towards Great Britain, Count Lamsdorff regretted that he had received many conflicting reports about the existence of such an agreement, including an allusion that the agreement was inimical to Russian interests.

The Russian Foreign Minister was evidently referring to Germany, which had been actively engaged in seeking information about the agreement, as the source of his information.

On the other hand, the French Foreign Minister informed Sir Francis Bertie, British Ambassador to France, that he could find nothing objectionable in the treaty. Referring to Article II, the French Minister declared that "unprovoked attack" might in some cases be difficult to interpret.

The Japanese Government had, in the meantime, instructed Minister Inouye to communicate the full text of the new Anglo-Japanese Alliance to Prince von Bülow and attempt to dispel reported misapprehensions among some German officials and individuals that the Alliance contained provisions detrimental to Germany's vested interests. After studying the document, Bülow informed Minister Inouye on September 2, 1905, that Germany had no reasons to take exception to the new Alliance, since German Far Eastern policy was aimed at the maintenance of sovereignty, Open Door principle and commercial freedom in China.

Through its Minister in Paris, Motono, the Japanese Government also informed the French Government about the real nature of the Alliance. The French Minister of Foreign Affairs appreciated the fact that Japan did not publicly disclose the Treaty while peace negotiations with Russia were proceeding. Other nations receiving notification of the finalization of the revised Anglo-Japanese Alliance, either unofficially or on its publication, included the United States, Austria, Italy, China, Siam, Korea, and Holland. Acknowledgments were received from all nations except Korea. British sentiments definitely welcomed the conclusion of the revised Treaty of Alliance.

CHAPTER 7

Franco-Japanese and Russo-Japanese Agreements 1904-1907

~~~~~~

JAPAN'S PUBLICLY declared policy since the Sino-Japanese War and the Triple Intervention was directed towards the establishment of good relations between Japan and Russia, based on the Exchange Policy of Korea and Manchuria. The Anglo-Japanese Alliance notwithstanding, this policy was not forsaken until the rupture of Russo-Japanese diplomatic relations. In Russia, there existed an influential group which advocated the enhancement of friendly relations with Japan, notably Rosen and Iswalsky, who served as Russian Ministers to Japan, and Witte, the Minister of Finance.

Before assuming his diplomatic post in Japan, Minister Rosen in a memorandum to Foreign Minister Muraviev expressed his deep desire to avoid jeopardizing Russo-Japanese relations along the path to war. This memorandum, meant also for the Tsar's perusal, strongly denounced the Russian War Department's scheme to organize a Korean Army to be trained by 120 Russian officers as a dangerous step likely to provoke armed conflict with Japan. Rosen advocated a policy of friendly understanding with Japan as well as China as the best guarantee of a solid and lasting peace.

Minister Iswalsky who succeeded Rosen in 1900 also supported the policy of friendship. In his memoirs, Iswalsky refers to some of his efforts in this direction.

"In my capacity as representative of the Russian Govern-

171

ment in Tokyo," writes Iswalsky, "I sincerely recommended the conclusion of an agreement with Japan regarding the urgent problems of Manchuria and Korea. The European trip of Japan's famous statesman Marquis Ito, aimed at improving relations between Japan and Russia, is one of the fruits of my efforts. If his mission had been a success, it would not only have changed the course of events but war might well have been avoided."

Although it is superfluous to point to Witte's policy of collaboration with Japan, the fact remains that these efforts towards conciliation proved of no avail. Up until the frontal clash of the two powers, they continued to urge upon their Government the necessity of Russo-Japanese collaboration, stressing that this could be attained through a treaty clearly demarcating the spheres of rights and interests of both nations.

Russia's defeat in the Russo-Japanese War offered new opportunities to the advocates of the cooperative policy. Rosen and Witte, well-known members of the conciliatory group, were appointed plenipotentiaries to the peace negotiations with Japan. Lamsdorff was replaced by Iswalsky as Minister for Foreign Affairs. Iswalsky describes his views in his memoirs as follows:

"The Portsmouth Treaty may be considered as favorable to Russia herself. Aside from its value in restoring peace with Japan, it paves the way to a rapprochement and possibly even an alliance between Russian and Japan."

The Russo-Japanese War liquidated the question of the Exchange Policy involving Manchuria and Korea, leaving only the issues of what Russia could salvage from Manchuria and the extent of Japan's advance into the region. These were the major issues which the Portsmouth Peace Conference had to settle. Lasting peace could only be founded on the basis of a satisfactory formula.

A detailed study of each stipulation of the historic Portsmouth Peace Treaty, signed on September 5, 1905, reveals that the foundation of future cooperation between Japan and Russia rested on the clarification of the rights and interests of both nations in Eastern Asia.

Under Article II, Russia acknowledged that "Japan possesses in Korea paramount political, military, and economical interests" and engaged not to "obstruct or interfere with any measures of guidance, protection, and control which Japan finds it necessary to take in Korea." It is further stated in the same Article that in order to remove all causes of misunderstanding Japan and Russia would mutually abstain' from taking any military measures on the Russo-Korean frontier which might menace the security of Russian and Korean territory.

Moreover, Japan and Russia mutually engaged in Article III, (1) to evacuate completely and simultaneously Manchuria except the territory affected by the lease of the Liaotung Peninsula, and (2) to restore entirely and completely to the exclusive administration of China all portions of Manchuria occupied by Japanese or Russian troops or under their control, with the exception of the above-mentioned territory. By this stipulation, Japan and Russia hoped to prevent the occurrence of any collision.

Under Articles V and VI, Russia pledged to transfer the Russian leases of the Leased Territory of Kwantung, including Port Arthur and Dairen, and transfer to Japan, subject to the consent of the Chinese Government, the portion of railway south of Changchun and all its branches together with all rights, privileges, and properties appertaining thereto.

From the standpoint of Russo-Japanese rapprochement and cooperation, the Portsmouth Treaty was entirely negative in nature. Any positive significance of the said Treaty had to await the progressive development of Russo-Japanese relations.

In order to understand the real meaning of the rapprochement and conciliation between Japan and Russia after the conclusion of the Peace Treaty, it is necessary to take a look at the postwar international situation. Like her late adversary, the costly war left Russia exhausted militarily as well as financially. Plagued by internal crisis, Russia no longer possessed the power to cope singly with the combined power of Japan and Britain in the Far East.

As a result, it became increasingly imperative for Russia to find a powerful ally willing to support her Far Eastern policy. It was natural for her to move in the direction of closer relations with France, but the latter had, in the meantime, arrived at an understanding with Great Britain in 1904.

In view of these circumstances, Russia could rely only on Germany to support her Asian policy. Taking advantage of this opportunity, the Kaiser naturally attempted to reach an agreement with Russia. A Russo-German Preliminary Treaty of Alliance, concluded on December 11, 1904, was succeeded by the Björkö Agreement of July 24, 1905. This Agreement, however, proved abortive, owing to Russian anxiety about the attitude of France and the opposition of the German Chancellor Bülow.

After scrapping the Björkö Agreement and failing to counter the Anglo-Japanese Alliance, Russia finally embarked on a policy of compromise with Great Britain. Considering the interests of the two countries, it was not surprising that the Anglo-Russian Agreement had an anti-German tinge. Russia not only felt the need to compromise with Great Britain from a political as well as a military point of view, but also to obtain Japan's assurance before undertaking a bold policy against Germany and Austria in the Balkans and the Middle East.

In the midst of recovering from the grievous wounds of war, Japan regarded peace as indispensable to her rapid recovery. Furthermore, in order to carry out her plans in China—the real object of her policy—Japan keenly realized that Russian cooperation was a prerequisite. This policy was inspired by the provisions of the Treaty of Portsmouth.

Faced with this situation, the *genro* Yamagata and Ito saw eye to eye on the necessity of cooperating with Russia. By appointing a Russophile, Motono, as Ambassador to Russia under Foreign Minister Hayashi, the Saionji Cabinet was fully prepared to enter into discussions on the Russo-Japanese Agreement.

In Russia, on the other hand, the proponents of a conciliatory policy towards Japan gained ascendancy in the aftermath of the disastrous defeat, but an uncompromising faction led by elements in the Army and Navy Departments as well as a section of the press defiantly regarded the Portsmouth Treaty as only an armistice. They openly manifested their intention to renounce the treaty as soon as Russia had recuperated from the exhausting conflict.

Having mutually agreed at the time of the conclusion of the Peace Treaty of Portsmouth to iron out the details at a later date, Japan and Russia initiated talks in December, 1905. During the prolonged negotiations, which lasted until December of the following year, Japan was greatly annoyed at the lack of any progress. The favorable turn in the diplomatic talks on an Anglo-Russian Agreement, however, provided a stimulus to the Russo-Japanese talks in which Great Britain and France played the mediatory role. France was particularly in favor of Russia's rapprochement towards Japan because of the Franco-Russian Alliance and the Anglo-French Entente Cordiale. Not only did she offer friendly advice, but France also took the initiative in promoting closer ties with Japan.

Shortly after commencing negotiations in Paris on the conclusion of a political agreement, the French Minister for Foreign Affairs, Pichon, and the Japanese Ambassador to France, Kurino, signed the Franco-Japanese Agreement on June 10, 1907. By this Agreement, reached without any major difficulty, Japan and France agreed to respect the independence and integrity of China as well as the principle of equal treatment in that country for the commerce and subjects (i.e. *ressortissants*) of all nations. They also voiced their special interest in guaranteeing order, especially in the regions of the Chinese Empire adjacent to the territories where they had the rights of sovereignty, protection, or occupation, and agreed to support each other for assuring the peace and security in those regions, with a view to maintaining their respective situations and territorial rights in the continent of Asia.

This Agreement not only confirmed the principles of the Anglo-Japanese Alliance with regard to China, but in it France also recognized the results of the Russo-Japanese War. France also succeeded in having Japan agree to respect her territorial rights in French Indo-China. It is worth taking note of the fact that Japan and France confirmed their respective spheres of influence in China. In the exchange of official documents, France designated the three provinces of Kwantung, Kwangsi, and Yunnan as her regions of special interests, and in return, Japan stipulated Fukien Province, Manchuria, and Mongolia as her regions of special interests. Moreover, in a separate note, the two Governments also agreed upon a mutual most-favored-nation arrangement concerning the protection of Japanese subjects and their properties in French Indo-China.

The publication of the Franco-Japanese Agreement was given a warm reception in France, Great Britain, and Russia. The Agreement, promising good relations between Japan and France, was also a happy augury for the conclusion of future important agreements between other powers and the friendly nations of Japan and France which would vastly affect the political situation in the Orient and Occident. Only Germany appeared visibly disappointed at the conclusion of such an agreement.

The Franco-Japanese Agreement was undoubtedly one of the primary factors influencing Russia to adopt a more conciliatory attitude. It also expedited the talks between Japan and Russia over the details of the Portsmouth Treaty, culminating in the successive agreements on the Chinese Eastern Railway and the South Manchurian Railway on June 13 in Moscow as well as the fisheries agreement concerning fishing in the Japan Sea, the Sea of Okhotsk, and the Bering Straits on July 28. On July 30, 1907, the two countries at long last inked the documents of the first Russo-Japanese Agreement: the Motono-Iswalsky Agreement.

In this Agreement, Japan and Russia, "desiring to consolidate the relations of peace and good neighborliness which have happily been established between Japan and Russia, and wishing to remove for the future every cause of misunderstanding in the relations of the two Empires," agreed in Article I "to respect the actual territorial integrity of the other and all the rights accruing to one and the other Party from the treaties, conventions and contracts in force between them and China," insofar as these rights were not incompatible with the principle of equal opportunity. In Article II they recognized "the independence and the territorial integrity of the Empire of China and the principle of equal opportunity in whatever concerns the commerce and industry of all nations in that Empire," and engaged "to sustain and defend the maintenance of the status quo and respect for this principle by all the pacific means within their reach."

Further, in the Secret Convention consisting of four articles, both parties agreed on the line of demarcation in Manchuria by which they were to sustain their mutual interests in each sphere of influence, and they mutually acknowledged Japan's free action in Korea and Russia's special interests in Outer Mongolia.

The full text of the Secret Convention is as follows:

The Government of His Majesty the Emperor of Japan and the Government of His Majesty the Tsar of all the Russias desiring to remove for the future all cause of friction or misunderstanding concerning certain questions relating to Manchuria, Korea and Mongolia have agreed upon the following provisions:

ARTICLE I

Having in view the natural gravitation of political and economic interests and activities in Manchuria, and desiring to avert the complications likely to arise from competition, Japan engages not to seek, for her own account or on behalf of Japanese subjects or others, any railway or telegraph concessions in Manchuria to the north, and not to obstruct, directly or indirectly, applications for such concessions in that region supported by the Russian Government.

Russia, on her part, inspired by the same pacific motives, engages not to seek, for her own account or on behalf of Russian subjects or others, any railway or telegraph concessions in Manchuria to the south, and not to obstruct, directly or indirectly, applications for such concessions in that region supported by the Japanese Government.

ARTICLE II

Russia, recognizing the relations of political solidarity existing between Japan and Korea in consequence of the Japanese-Korean Conventions and Agreements (copies of which have been communicated to the Russian Government by the Japanese Government), engages not to obstruct or interfere with the further development of those relations, and Japan, on her part, engages to extend to the Government, Consular Officers, subjects, commerce, industry and navigation of Russia in Korea, pending the conclusion of a definitive treaty, the treatment in all respects of the most-favored nation.

ARTICLE III

The Imperial Government of Japan, recognizing the special interests of Russia in Outer Mongolia, engage to abstain from all interference which may bring prejudice to those interests.

ARTICLE IV

The present Convention shall be strictly confidential between the two High Contracting Parties.

ADDITIONAL ARTICLE

The line of demarcation between northern Manchuria and southern Manchuria mentioned in Article I of the present Convention is established as follows:

Starting at the northwest point of the Russo-Korean frontier and describing a succession of straight lines, the line runs, after passing by Hunchun and the northernmost point of the Lake of Pirteng, to Hsiushuichan, thence it follows the Sungari River to the mouth of the Nunkiang to ascend thereafter the course of this river to the mouth of the Tola-ho. From this point the line follows the course of this river to its intersection with 122 degrees of longitude east of the meridian of Greenwich.

It is understood that an official document was exchanged between Japan and Russia, explaining that the provisions of Article III of the secret convention relating to Mongolia in no way constituted an impairment of the principles of status quo and equal opportunity laid down in Articles I and II of the ostensible convention.

This principle had to be treated with the greatest discretion in the light of the misunderstanding in Great Britain and the United States that Japan appeared to be taking advantage of her political supremacy to violate the principle of equal opportunity in the regions of Manchuria and Mongolia.

In conclusion, it is necessary to stress the significance of the Franco-Japanese Agreement and the Russo-Japanese Agreement, especially in view of the fact that the two Agreements with their secret conventions made an important contribution in removing the causes of disputes among the three nations by demarcating their spheres of influence and their special interests in East Asia, particularly in China.

Historically, these two agreements served to cement the bonds of amity between the Franco-Russian and the Anglo-Japanese Alliances, formerly the source of conflicts in the East Asian sphere. Thus, Japan became not only a strong nation, but an important element in world history.

CHAPTER **8**

Japanese-American Agreement
1907-1908

~~~~~~

DURING the Russo-Japanese War, the sympathy of the United
States Government and public opinion were unreservedly on
the side of Japan. Besides extending diplomatic and financial
assistance, President Roosevelt took the initiative in assuming
the role of peacemaker and mediator. The conclusion of the
Portsmouth Treaty owes much to the great prestige enjoyed
by the American President.

The subsequent emergence of Japan as a major power,
however, aroused growing anxiety among the American public. With sharpening rivalry between Japan and the United
States in various spheres, relations between the two countries
quickly began to deteriorate. Among the major events which
stirred national sentiments on both sides of the Pacific were
the discriminatory ban imposed on Japanese immigration
and the exclusion of students of Japanese parentage from
attending public schools in San Francisco. These controversial
questions for a time seriously strained the ties between the
two nations.

Parallel with this brewing crisis in the Pacific were two
international maneuvers which could not be overlooked. One
was the failure of the Kaiser's attempt to conclude a tripartite
alliance between Germany, the United States, and China.
The other was the miscarriage in the design of President
Roosevelt to reach an accord with Great Britain and Canada

180

on the questions of immigration and the Far East, owing to British rejection of the American scheme. The underlying causes leading up to the Japanese-American Agreement are little known to the general public, but they have been clarified beyond any possible doubt by the publications of the German and British diplomatic documents concerning these abortive moves.

The consummation of the Franco-Japanese Agreement of June, 1907, was a severe shock to Germany, if for no other reason than that Germany feared the agreement would isolate her still further from the European political arena and spark a scramble among the Western Powers to carve up the Celestial Empire. Germany could see only two alternatives: either she should obstruct any partitioning of China, or if partitioning was inevitable she should be prepared to stake out her proportionate claim.

Faced with this situation, German newspapers variously commented on the possibility of the formation of a quadruple alliance composed of Japan, Great Britain, France, and Russia. Fears of encirclement or *einkreisung,* of which the German Chargé d'Affaires in London, Eckardstein, had earlier warned, began to haunt the German Government.

Convinced that Russia could be alienated from the Western Powers and Japan, the German Government on June 2, 1907, formally protested to the Russian Government through Herr Schoen, German Ambassador in Russia, on the subject of the imminent quadruple alliance reported in the *Berliner Lokalanzeiger.* The German protest pointed out that, while the German Government had no objection to Russian attempts to resolve their disputes with Japan and Great Britain, it would take exception to any moves directed towards Russia's participation in an alliance with Japan, Great Britain, and France aimed at Germany. Regardless of whether that alliance was ostensibly for defensive purposes, Germany would oppose it from the standpoint of her own national security.

This German protest deeply disturbed the Russian Minister for Foreign Affairs, Iswalsky. In a desperate attempt to assure Germany that his country harbored no malicious intent, the bewildered Iswalsky disclaimed any aim other than reaching an understanding with Japan and Great Britain on limited issues within a restricted area. The sole purpose was the removal of the causes of disputes, and the move in no way envisaged a third power, not to mention any counteraction against Germany.

Realizing that Germany would have to embark on a positive counteroffensive against Russian diplomatic maneuvers, the German Government instructed its Ambassador to Japan, Mumm von Schwarzenstein, to study the possibility of concluding an agreement with Japan similar to the Franco-Japanese Agreement. After careful consideration, the German envoy concluded that such an alliance was superfluous in view of Japan's recognition of the principles of the Anglo-German Agreement of October 29, 1900, affirming the independence and territorial integrity of China and the policy of the Open Door. The German Ministry of Foreign Affairs concurred with this view.

Regarding the Franco-Japanese Agreement as a prelude to a scramble for concessions in China, the German Ambassador in China, Count Rex, proposed that Germany should act in concert with the United States to meet such a situation. Accepting this idea, the Kaiser began nursing a fantastic notion of concluding a triple alliance of Germany, the United States, and China to oppose the alleged quadruple alliance of Japan, Great Britain, Russia, and France.

Meanwhile, Japanese-American relations had become highly strained as a result of the stern measures adopted by the United States against the rising tide of Japanese immigration and the exclusion of Japanese students from schools in California. In an effort to turn this situation to the advantage of Germany, the German Ambassador in the United States, on the advice of Count Rex, was instructed to sound out America's attitude towards the proposed triple alliance.

After preliminary inquiries, Ambassador Speck von Sternberg reported to the German Government that in view of the conciliatory attitude of President Roosevelt towards Japan it was unlikely that such an alliance would pass the United States Senate. China, on the other hand, was pursuing an obscure foreign policy, making progress on the negotiations for the triple alliance impossible beyond the exploratory stage. The Kaiser, however, still hopeful that the alliance could be materialized, persisted in his efforts until the conclusion of the Japanese-American Agreement.

From the very outset President Roosevelt paid scant attention to the formation of the triple alliance, describing it as the Kaiser's pipe dream caused by opium smoking. Moreover, he felt that the restriction against Japanese immigration was as much in the interests of Great Britain, Canada, and Australia as of the United States. Concerning China, he could see no reason why his country could not cooperate with Great Britain on the basis of the principles of the Open Door and equal opportunity.

Diplomatically the immigration question was regarded with great seriousness by President Roosevelt, who regarded the immigration companies responsible for the outflow of Japanese laborers as being exceedingly influential in Japan. Although he did not consider that Japan could possibly be provoked into open hostilities, he did not rule out the possibility of a diplomatic break precipitated accidentally.

In any emergency arising from the passage of the Immigration Law in June, 1906, the American President hoped to enlist the complete understanding of Great Britain. In line with his policy, he informed the British Ambassador to the United States, James Bryce, that the American Government deemed it desirable and useful, should the necessity arise, to tell the Japanese Government in a direct and forcible way that the inflow of their laborers could not be allowed to continue. He hoped that the British Government would echo the American view and speak with the same decisive voice.

Simultaneously, the American Ambassador in Japan, O'Brien, questioned the British Ambassador in Japan, Mac-Donald, as to the possibility of the two Embassies working together on the immigration question. The United States Government, while dismissing any possibility of a war between Japan and Anglo-America, nonetheless felt that, if any risk of war did arise, it could only be averted through simultaneous joint warnings by the two Governments.

Despite these diplomatic maneuvers, the British Government remained unperturbed. On the question of Anglo-American cooperation, the British Ambassador MacDonald met the Canadian representative in Tokyo and informed the latter that his Government did not necessarily hold the same views as the American Government on the problem of immigration. Canada, for her part, could not legislate against immigration unless she first abrogated her treaty with Japan.

Ambassador MacDonald was of the opinion that anything like joint action between Great Britain and the United States in this matter would only antagonize Japan. Agreeing with the view of the British envoy, the British Minister for Foreign Affairs, Sir Edward Grey, informed President Roosevelt through Ambassador Bryce that it was unwise at this stage to say anything to Japan since only harm would result. In the light of these circumstances, President Roosevelt could not but accept the views of the British Government.

There is no doubt that this British rebuff had its effect on America's policy. The British position was dictated by the fact that she had not only to consider her relations with Japan under the Anglo-Japanese Alliance, but also the existence of the Franco-Japanese, the Russo-Japanese, and the Anglo-Russian Agreements as well as the shifts in the delicate international situation in the Far East. Having branded the German proposition for a triple alliance as Utopian and unrealistic, and having realized that common action with Great Britain was unattainable as a result of British commitments to Japan and Russia, the United States singly had no other alternative but to adopt a conciliatory policy towards Japan.

Despite the exclusion act and discrimination against Japanese students, the Japanese Government continued to maintain a conciliatory attitude towards the United States. Entering into a so-called "Gentlemen's Agreement" in December, 1907, the Japanese Government voluntarily instituted controls on immigration of Japanese laborers from June, 1908.

To demonstrate America's determination, President Roosevelt despatched the American Atlantic Fleet on a world cruise in 1907–08. Although its main purpose was to impress Japan without paying any call at Japanese ports, the Japanese Government was unaware of the seriousness of the international situation. Sincerely disappointed that the fleet would cross the Pacific without visiting Japan, the Government negotiated with the United States Government for the visit of the American warships.

Immediately responding to this request, President Roosevelt ordered the fleet to anchor at Yokohama Harbor on October 18, 1908. The Japanese Government and people accorded the fleet an enthusiastic welcome. Referring to this visit, President Roosevelt later wrote:

"The most noteworthy incident of the cruise was the reception given to our fleet in Japan. . . . The event even surpassed my expectations. I cannot too strongly express my appreciation of the generous courtesy the Japanese showed the officers and crews of our fleet; and I may add that every man of them came back a friend and admirer of the Japanese."

The Japanese Government, of course, had no intention of resorting to arms over the controversial immigration question. On questions pertaining to the Pacific Ocean, Japan desired to reach an amicable settlement, leading to friendly ties between the two countries.

To give effect to this policy, the Japanese Foreign Minister Komura authorized Ambassador Takahira in Washington to initiate negotiations with the American Government. Japan hoped that the cordial welcome extended to the American fleet in Japan would be regarded by the United States Government and people as proof of the sincere desire of Japan for better understanding.

On October 25, 1908, Japan transmitted her wish to negotiate with the United States on an agreement which would:

1. Encourage the free and peaceful development of commerce of the two nations on the Pacific Ocean;

2. Maintain the existing territorial status quo of the important outlying insular possessions of the two nations in the regions of the Pacific Ocean;

3. Support and defend, by all means at their disposal, the principle of equal opportunity for the commerce and industry of all nations in China.

Ambassador Takahira presented an outline of the Japanese-American Agreement to President Roosevelt for his approval, and explained to Secretary of State Root the Japanese Government's intention to strengthen the relations of friendship existing between Japan and the United States and to preserve the general peace.

While expressing his wholehearted approval, Secretary Root presented some modifications during the successive exchanges of views with Ambassador Takahira. In Paragraph 3, the United States Government desired to add the clause "the independence and integrity of China," in keeping with the purport of the Anglo-Japanese Alliance, and to insert the words "administrative entity."

The Japanese Government had no objection to the inclusion of the former clause, but rejected the second insertion, fearing that this might cause misunderstanding in the future over Japan's management of Manchurian affairs and prove incompatible with the administrative power in Japan's leased territory and the land attached to the South Manchuria Railway. The United States Government finally accepted the contention of the Japanese Government.

Thus, the exchange of notes commonly known as the Root-

Takahira Agreement was effected between Secretary of State Root and Ambassador Takahira on November 30, 1908, and later published on December 2, 1908.

The Note addressed to Root from Takahira ran as follows:

"The exchange of views between us, which has taken place at the several interviews which I have recently had the honor of holding with you, has shown that Japan and the United States holding important outlying insular possessions in the region of the Pacific Ocean, the Governments of the two countries are animated by a common aim, policy, and intention in that region.

"Believing that a frank avowal of that aim, policy, and intention would not only tend to strengthen the relations of friendship and good neighborhood, which have immemorially existed between Japan and the United States, but would materially contribute to the preservation of the general peace, the Imperial Government have authorized me to present to you an outline of their understanding of that common aim, policy, and intention:

1. It is the wish of the two Governments to encourage the free and peaceful development of their commerce on the Pacific Ocean;

2. The policy of both Governments, uninfluenced by any aggressive tendencies, is directed to the maintenance of the existing status quo in the region above-mentioned and to the defense of the principle of equal opportunity for commerce and industry in China;

3. They are accordingly firmly resolved reciprocally to respect the territorial possessions belonging to each other in the said region;

4. They are also determined to preserve the common interests of all Powers in China, by supporting, by all pacific means at their disposal, the independence and integrity of China and the principle of equal opportunity for commerce and industry of all nations in that Empire;

5. Should any event occur threatening the status quo as

above described or the principle of equal opportunity as above defined, it remains for the two Governments to communicate with each other, in order to arrive at an understanding as to what measures they may consider it useful to take."

In reply to the Note of Ambassador Takahira, the Note of the same date from Secretary of State Root to Ambassador Takahira affirmed the American-Japanese declaration of policy and stated as follows:

"It is a pleasure to inform you that this expression of mutual understanding is welcome to the Government of the United States as appropriate to the happy relations of the two countries and as the occasion for a concise mutual affirmation of that accordant policy respecting the Far East, which the two Governments have so frequently declared in the past."

It is not too much to say that the unofficial advice of Great Britain had played an important part in inducing the Japanese Government to make the proposal to conclude the American-Japanese Agreement. Ambassador Takahira asked the advice of James Bryce, the British Ambassador in the United States, in a rather guarded way as to whether it would be desirable that Japan should conclude such an agreement, to which Ambassador Bryce replied that the conclusion of such an agreement would have a good effect on the relations between Japan and the United States.

On the other hand, the United States confidentially communicated the text of the proposed agreement before its consummation to Sir Edward Grey, the British Foreign Minister, who stated that the Government of Great Britain had learned with sincere satisfaction of the impending conclusion of such an agreement, and that they were confident that the agreement could not fail to have beneficial results not only to the respective interests of the United States and of Japan but to the general peace in the Pacific and Far East. The Japanese Chargé d'Affaires in London also informed Foreign Minister Grey that Japan had made an agreement with the United States, to which Grey stated that "it was very good news.

I welcomed it sincerely and all my colleagues would do so too. As the ally of Japan we were very pleased with it, because we ourselves were especially desirous of remaining on good terms with the United States."

At the time of the conclusion of the Japanese-American Agreement, critics charged Japan with having fallen into a trap set by herself. However, it is undeniable that the Agreement helped to dispel all major doubts that had contributed to the strained relations between Japan and the United States ever since the end of the Russo-Japanese War. Together with the Anglo-Japanese, the Franco-Japanese, and the Russo-Japanese Agreements, it may be safely assumed that the Japanese-American Agreement constituted one of the props to guarantee the general peace in the Far East.

CHAPTER 9

Second Russo-Japanese Agreement
1905-1910

~~~~~~

IT was a startled world that greeted the proposal made in
1909 by Philander Knox, the Secretary of State in the Taft
Administration, known as the "Knox Neutralization Plan for
the Manchurian Railways." So serious were the implications
of the Knox proposition that Japan and Russia entered into
immediate negotiations to realize the second Russo-Japanese
Agreement, the so-called "Motono-Iswalsky Agreement"
aimed at protecting their respective interests. As a prominent
British diplomat remarked at the time, however plausible
may have been the explanations offered by the United States
to clarify the situation, there was little room to doubt that it
was the absurd proposal of Secretary Knox which accelerated
the conclusion of the Agreement signed in July, 1910.

In order to understand the background of events leading
to the "Knox Neutralization Plan for the Manchurian Railways," it is important to be acquainted with the circumstances in which Edward H. Harriman offered his plan for
the joint control of the South Manchurian Railways by Japan
and the United States. Having had a long-abiding interest
in the Far East, it was not difficult for this great American
railway tycoon to see the potentialities offered by the South
Manchurian Railway.

Harriman envisaged a round-the-world transportation
system, entailing the acquisition of the right to manage the

South Manchurian Railway, the purchase of the Chinese Eastern Railway and the procurement of the right of passage over the Western Siberian Railway up to the Baltic Sea, whence the system would extend westwards across the Atlantic Ocean to link up with the American transcontinental railway over which he had controlling interests.

With this grandiose scheme in mind, Harriman visited Japan in August, 1905, at the invitation of the American Minister in Japan, Lloyd C. Griscom. He was heartily welcomed by the Japanese Government and people. In his interviews with Premier Count Katsura and the *genro,* Harriman outlined his proposal for the joint Japanese-American control of the South Manchurian Railway as a vital link for the establishment of a global transportation network.

So impressed was Marquis Inouye, the Finance Minister, by this fabulous proposal that he readily expressed his unbounded enthusiasm for the plan, declaring that it would be the height of folly for Japan to throw away this golden opportunity. By jointly operating the railway, Marquis Inouye foresaw the possibility of utilizing the railway as a buffer zone against any Russian attempt to seek a war of vengeance. Consequently on October 12, 1905, Count Katsura and Mr. Harriman affixed their signatures to the provisional memorandum concerning the Joint Japanese-American Control of the South Manchurian Railway. Extremely elated over the successful outcome of the first stage of his plan to set up a global transportation system, Harriman left Japan for the United States, little suspecting that his ambitious dreams would soon be dashed.

The deliverer of this coup de grace, Foreign Minister Komura, was at the time on the high seas en route home from the Portsmouth Peace Conference. When details of the Harriman proposal reached him, Baron Komura could hardly restrain his profound wrath. Uncompromisingly opposed to the very idea of a joint management, he charged the Government with gross indiscretion for having attempted to sign away the only tangible asset that Japan had gained from the Russo-Japanese War.

Foreign Minister Komura returned home to a nation seething with dissatisfaction and disappointment over what it considered unfavorable peace terms without indemnity. Firmly convinced that he was acting in Japan's national interest, Komura tried to persuade the Premier, the Cabinet Ministers, and the *genro* to nullify the provisional agreement. Baron Komura's forceful protestations finally swayed Premier Katsura and his Cabinet to decide in favor of renouncing the Katsura-Harriman provisional memorandum, thereby permitting Japan to retain and develop her acquired rights in Manchuria completely free of American interests.

Harriman, who had arrived in San Francisco on October 23, was subsequently informed by the Japanese Consul in San Francisco, Uyeno, of Premier Katsura's urgent message, informing him that the "Imperial Japanese Government, recognizing the need for further closer examination and study of the provisional memorandum, desires that the memorandum be considered in a state of temporary suspension pending notification of detailed information."

In view of these circumstances, it became imperative for Japan to reach a new Sino-Japanese understanding on Far Eastern issues, not only because of the changed situation brought about by the Portsmouth Peace Treaty, but also in the wake of the Harriman affair. To achieve this objective, Baron Komura proceeded to Peking early in November, 1905, and signed in the Chinese capital on December 22, 1905, a Treaty as well as an Additional Agreement with the Government of China. Under this Treaty, Japan secured China's agreement that only nationals of Japan and China should be able to participate in the management of the railways in Manchuria. The two Governments also agreed to restrict capital investments in the railways to the signatories of the Treaty, namely Japan and China. On the basis of this agreement, Harriman was formally notified that Japan had no alternative but to renounce the Katsura-Harriman provisional memorandum, as third power interests could no longer participate in the operation of the railways in Manchuria. So ended the bold and imaginative plan espoused by Harriman.

However, there still remained the serious international question concerning the Chinchow-Aigun Railway, closely related to the Harriman project, forming another scheme through which American financiers hoped to revive the original Harriman plan.

Ostensibly to check Japanese and Russian railway enterprises in Manchuria, the Chinese Government in November, 1907, secretly granted a concession to Pauling and Company, a British construction firm, to construct a short line between Hsinmintun and Fakumen. Japan reacted immediately, warning Peking that the Hsinmintun-Fakumen scheme was totally unacceptable on the basis of the protocol annexed to the Peking Treaty of December 22, 1905, in which China agreed, "for the purpose of protecting the interests of the South Manchuria Railway, not to construct . . . any branch line in the neighborhood of and parallel to that railway, or any branch line which would be prejudicial to the business of the above-mentioned railway." This warning and two subsequent energetic protests made during November had no perceptible results on the Chinese Government.

Considering that it was a British firm to which China had granted the concession for the Hsinmintun-Fakumen extension, Great Britain as an ally of Japan was deeply interested in the controversy. Foreign Minister Sir Edward Grey, supporting the Japanese contention, informed the Japanese Ambassador in London on February 3, 1908, that he had already instructed the British Minister in China that Great Britain regarded the construction of the new line as unjustifiable and improper. When questioned in the House of Commons as to the attitude of the Government, Foreign Minister Grey defended Japan's position, replying that "it was open to the contractors (Pauling and Company) to prove to the satisfaction of Japan that the proposed line would not prejudice the South Manchurian Railway, and so would not violate the agreement." Thus, the project for the new line was temporarily stalled.

In this delicate situation, Mr. French, a representative of Pauling and Company, called on Japanese Minister to China Mr. Ishuin in an effort to ascertain the views of the Japanese Government regarding the construction of a line from Chinchow to Tsitsihar should there be uncompromising opposition to the Hsinmintun-Fakumen line.

It was during these series of negotiations between Japan, Britain, and Pauling and Company that French became intimately associated with Willard Straight, the United States Consul-General in Mukden, who was closely in touch with Harriman and a group of New York financiers. With Straight's cooperation, French was able to secure from Hsi Liang, Viceroy of Mukden, on October 2, 1909, a provisional concession for the construction of a railway from Chinchow on the Gulf of Pechihli to Aigun on the Amur River. Straight, viewing this turn of events as a golden opportunity to realize the Harriman project, sought to obtain the approval of the Chinese Government with Hsi Liang's backing.

China, however, fearing Japan's reaction and wary about the Harriman scheme, showed no inclination to support the latest project. It soon became evident that only heavy diplomatic pressure and British and United States financial commitments could change the policy of the Peking Government.

On December 18, 1909, Mr. O'Brien, the American Ambassador in Tokyo, communicated a memorandum to Foreign Minister Komura, stating that a provisional agreement concerning the financing and building of the Chinchow-Aigun railway had been signed at Mukden between China and Anglo-American financiers and inviting Japan as an interested power to participate in the financing and construction of the said railway. It will be recalled that the American Government had also advanced a suggestion to Japan known as the Knox Neutralization Proposal for Manchurian Railways.

It was largely with a view to protecting American interest in the Chinchow-Aigun railway concession then under negotiation that Knox had suggested in his plan that the powers, namely, Japan, Russia, Great Britain, the United States, Germany, and France should advance credits to China to enable the latter to buy back the Japanese and Russian railways in Manchuria. The railways would then be operated on a commercial basis, and not for military or political purposes, by an international syndicate of participating powers during the term of the loan. Knox relayed his proposal to Great Britain, France, Germany, Russia, and other nations, but the contents were not necessarily the same.

Although the Knox proposal for the neutralization of the Manchurian railways is frequently referred to as a typical example of dollar diplomacy and as representative of America's aggressive activities in the Far East, Japanese politicians cannot be entirely absolved from blame for this situation.

Notwithstanding Harriman's failure to realize his ambitious scheme, principally through Foreign Minister Komura's opposition, it was nevertheless a fact that the American financier had succeeded in acquiring Japan's provisional agreement to jointly manage the Manchurian railway. There is every reason to assume, of course, that Harriman had informed President Taft and Secretary Knox of the views of Premier Katsura and the *genro* and the chain of events leading to the breakdown of the understanding. Washington was aware that the plan to jointly manage the railway had once been authorized and then canceled as a result of strong pressures exerted by certain influential politicians in Japan who had also conducted the negotiations with China. It is important to bear this fact in mind in trying to understand America's policy towards the Manchurian railway question in later years.

It is difficult to confirm to what extent the project of neutralizing the Manchurian railways was a national policy of the United States and the role which the American financiers personally played in influencing the materialization of this project. Being an officer of the State Department, Willard Straight could not possibly have negotiated in behalf of the American financiers without the tacit approval of the Secretary of State.

There were indications, on the other hand, that Secretary of State Root was hesitant to officially assist the neutralization project. Choosing rather to advance American interests in Manchuria by means of the Open Door policy, Root favored negotiations with Japan and was against any antagonistic policy.

Knox's proposition that the Manchurian railways be placed under an impartial administration of interested powers was said to have been initiated at the request of the Chinese Government. It is doubtless true that the prime mover of American investments in Manchuria and the neutralization plan of the Manchurian railroads was Harriman himself. The original ideas behind American capital investments in Manchuria had come from Edward Harriman and Willard Straight, and not directly from the United States Government.

Japan and Russia naturally could not remain indifferent to these American moves. Immediately after Knox despatched his notes to the interested powers on December 18, 1909, Ochiai, the Japanese Chargé d'Affaires in St. Petersburg, met the Russian Foreign Minister Iswalsky at the latter's request. At this meeting, Iswalsky explained Russia's view regarding the American notification and expressed his desire to exchange concrete opinions with Japan, if Japan so desired, before replying to the United States.

Shortly thereafter the Japanese Government communicated to the Russian Government through Ochiai that it was interested in a frank exchange of views on ways of protecting their common interests before their formal replies were made to the United States.

Acting concertedly, the Japanese and Russian Governments held several confidential discussions. Having confirmed their identity of views, Japan expressed her objection to the American plan on January 21, 1910, followed a day later by a similar Russian objection. Both countries gave explicit reasons for their action.

It was obvious that Japan and Russia, feeling that their special position in Manchuria had been threatened, had taken action, though independently, to defend their common interests to the utmost of their ability. The British Government, while noncommittal, desired only to know the views of Japan and Russia on the proposal. The French Government also declined to make its views known as long as Japan and Russia could not approve of the proposal. Notwithstanding Germany's warm response in favor of the proposal, the Knox Neutralization Plan failed to win any more adherents.

America's action in Manchuria brought Japan and Russia, which had already expressed a common purpose in the first Motono-Iswalsky Agreement of 1907, even closer together, foreshadowing the imminence of the Second Russo-Japanese Agreement. Negotiations for the new agreement were due to be held upon Ambassador Motono's return to St. Petersburg in accordance with Government instructions. Before entering into formal talks, Ambassador Motono was asked by Foreign Minister Iswalsky in April if there was any definite plan Japan wished to incorporate into the agreement. Ambassador Motono replied that he wished to be acquainted with the Foreign Minister's views on the matter during the exchange of views before seeking final instructions from his Government.

Thereupon, Iswalsky suggested that the new agreement, like the earlier Russo-Japanese Agreement of 1907, should be composed of two conventions, one ostensible and the other secret. The ostensible treaty should contain a clause proclaiming to the entire world that Japan and Russia held completely identical views on the issue of the Manchurian railways. While remaining reticent regarding what should be contained in the secret convention, Iswalsky solicited the opinions of Ambassador Motono.

The Ambassador in expressing his opinion declared that, considering the situation in China and anticipated future circumstances which would necessitate more precise stipulations than those contained in the Agreement of 1907, the secret convention should include a clause that would adequately safeguard and defend the respective nations' privileges and interests within the spheres of influence indicated in the previous agreement.

Without making any objection to the Ambassador's statement, Foreign Minister Iswalsky expressed a desire to confirm whether it would be necessary to add a clause with reference to the policy of both nations towards the whole of China. The Japanese Ambassador did not feel that this was necessary as once they had come to an understanding on the subject of Manchuria, it would not be difficult to act in concert on questions relating to China. Generally satisfied with the purport of these talks, Iswalsky was prepared to conclude a new Russo-Japanese agreement on the basis of these opinions.

Further negotiations on the agreement were held in abeyance during Iswalsky's tour abroad, but were resumed in May, 1910, when Ambassador Motono called on the Russian Foreign Minister. Following a number of exchanges on their respective drafts, Japan and Russia signed the Second Motono-Iswalsky Agreement on July 4, 1910.

In a preamble of the ostensible convention of this Agreement, the Russian and Japanese Governments were declared to be sincerely attached to the principles established by the convention concluded between them in 1907, and desirous to develop the effects of that convention. Article I stated that "the two High Contracting Parties mutually engage to lend each other friendly cooperation, with a view to the amelioration of their respective railway lines in Manchuria, and the improvement of the connecting service of the said railways, and to abstain from all competition prejudicial to the realization of this object." Under that instrument, the two nations further agreed in Article II "to maintain and respect the status quo in Manchuria resulting from the treaties, conventions or other arrangements concluded up to this day, between Russia and Japan, or between either of these two Powers and China," and pledged in Article III that "in case any event arises of a nature to menace the status quo above mentioned, the two High Contracting Parties shall, in each case, enter into communication with each other, in order to arrive at understanding as to the measures they may judge it necessary to take for the maintenance of the said status quo."

The stipulations contained in the Secret Convention were as follows:

The Imperial Government of Japan and the Imperial Government of Russia, desirous to consolidate and develop the provisions of the Secret Convention signed at St. Petersburg on the 30/17 July, 1907, have agreed as follows:

ARTICLE I

Japan and Russia recognize as delimiting the respective spheres of their special interests in Manchuria, the line of demarcation fixed by the Additional Article of the Secret Convention of 1907.

ARTICLE II

The High Contracting Parties engage reciprocally to respect the special interests in the spheres above indicated. They consequently recognize the right of each in its sphere freely to take all measures necessary to safeguard and defend such interests.

ARTICLE III

Each of the two High Contracting Parties engages not to

obstruct in any manner the further consolidation and development of the special interests of the other Party in the limits of the sphere above mentioned.

ARTICLE IV

Each of the two High Contracting Parties engages to abstain from all political activities in the sphere of special interests of the other in Manchuria. It is moreover understood that Japan shall not seek in the Russian sphere, and Russia shall not seek in the Japanese sphere, any privilege or concession of a nature to bring prejudice to the special interests of each other, and that the two Governments of Japan and Russia shall each respect all rights acquired by the other in its sphere, by virtue of the Treaties, Conventions or other Arrangements mentioned in Article II of the Ostensible Convention of this day.

ARTICLE V

In order to ensure the satisfactory working of their reciprocal engagements, the two High Contracting Parties shall from time to time enter frankly and loyally into communication in all that concerns the affairs touching in common their special interests in Manchuria. In case those special interests are menaced, the two High Contracting Parties shall concert with each other upon the measures to be taken, in view of common action or support to be lent to each other in order to safeguard and defend those interests.

What is still not clear is which nation, Russia or Japan, actually suggested rephrasing the Russo-Japanese Agreement. Although Russia maintains that the new Agreement originated with Foreign Minister Komura, Japan credits Iswalsky for making overtures for the renewal of the Agreement. Sir Claude MacDonald, the British Ambassador in Japan, was informed by Komura that, while Japan was satisfied with the existing convention between Japan and Russia, the Russian Government was anxious to consolidate it.

What is undeniable is the fact that America's new policy towards the Far East had driven Japan and Russia closer together and prompted the conclusion of the Second Motono-Iswalsky Agreement. Foreign Minister Komura assured Ambassador MacDonald more than once that the Japanese Government had no intention whatever of departing from the policy of the Open Door, adding that the ostensible convention had laid down in the preamble that the signatory Governments were "sincerely attached to the principles established by the Agreement of 1907," and that the 1907 convention, in Article II, clearly stated that Russia and Japan "agreed to recognize the principle of equal opportunity for the commerce and industry of all nations in the Chinese Empire." Furthermore, he drew Ambassador MacDonald's attention to the fact that the new Agreement contained a provision for the maintenance of the status quo in Manchuria.

The British Government expressed satisfaction over the new Agreement, feeling that so long as it did not impair the Open Door in Manchuria it would increase good relations between Japan and Russia and ensure peace in the Far East.

It should be noted here that Kaiser Wilhelm II of Germany described the new Russo-Japanese Agreement as a signal for a scramble by the two powers for concessions in the Celestial Empire, emphasizing at the same time that the Slavs had no intention of supporting Europe against the so-called Yellow Peril. He strongly maintained that the only effective countermeasure against this new agreement would be an American-German agreement with Chinese participation.

CHAPTER 10

Third Anglo-Japanese Alliance 1909-1911

~~~~~~

ENTHUSIASM in Britain for the treaty of alliance with Japan reached its highest point during the Second Anglo-Japanese Alliance in 1905, but steadily declined in public favor as a result of the Russo-Japanese and Anglo-Russian Agreements and the consequent loss of a potential enemy which had instigated the original accord. Added to this were such factors as the strained relations between Japan and America, the anti-Japanese and pro-American tendencies in the British Dominions and the growing conflict of interests in China in the fields of investments and trade.

Japan's prosperous commerce and industry had begun to cut deeply into the trade of the Far East, especially in China, gradually driving out the more expensive British goods. There were also grave misgivings in Britain that the exclusion of British capital from the Fakumen railway and the Chinchow-Aigun railway schemes in Manchuria was part of Japan's policy directed against the principles of the Open Door and equal opportunity in Manchuria and Mongolia.

A culmination of these events began to deepen the impression in Britain, both within Parliament and without, that Japanese policy in China was seriously menacing British interests.

In an editorial on the question of concluding the Third Anglo-Japanese Alliance, one of Britain's leading newspapers, the *Daily News,* even went so far as to comment that anyone predicting a year ago that the alliance would be renewed would have become a laughing stock. Another paper, the *Manchester Guardian,* repeatedly called for the discontinuance of the Anglo-Japanese Alliance.

Amidst this storm of criticisms, some voices in Britain were also vehemently urging the augmentation of the British Far Eastern Fleet in preparation for the expiry of the Alliance in 1915. In British Dominions overseas, public opinion was apprehensive lest the Anglo-Japanese Alliance might one day drag Great Britain into a dispute with the United States, a country with whom she desired to maintain cordial relations.

The British Government, on the other hand, could not lend its ears entirely to public opinions at home and in the Dominions, but had to pursue a policy within the framework of the Anglo-Japanese Alliance and with regard to the nation's far-flung interests throughout the world, of which China was only a part.

Looming ominously on the horizon was the growing strength of Germany, engaged not only in a gigantic naval construction program but vying with Great Britain in commerce and in the acquisition of colonies. To meet this new situation and the possible eventuality of war with Germany, the British Government laid great stress on her alliance with Japan, relying on it to enable Britain to concentrate the bulk of her naval might in the North Sea and its neighborhood in case of an emergency.

Acting with circumspection, the British Government made no move to support the British company of Pauling when China granted it a concession for extending the Hsinmintun-Fakumen Line, nor did it outwardly approve or disapprove of Secretary Knox's formal proposal for the neutralization of the Manchurian railways.

Furthermore, Great Britain took a similar stand in connection with the Chinchow-Aigun Railway, not only offering no positive support but even recommending Japan's participation in the said railway to the United States. The annexation of Korea by Japan was also accepted calmly by Britain. Judging from these repeated official manifestations of British goodwill, there was clearly a split between the official and popular attitudes on the question of renewing the alliance with Japan.

The desire to continue the Anglo-Japanese Alliance on the part of the British Government was not a separate entity in itself. In order to encircle Germany, Great Britain required such an alliance in the Far East and a triple alliance in Europe, both working to place an effective damper on German imperialism which, if unrestrained, could threaten the very existence of the British Empire. Despite possible Japanese and Russian maneuvers in the Far East, likely to be injurious to British economic and commercial interests, as well as the rising popular tide of national sentiment against Japan, the British Government made strenuous efforts to renew the alliance as part of Britain's strategic policy towards Germany.

There were several compelling reasons why Japan also positively favored a renewal of the alliance. Japan regarded the alliance as an indispensable stabilizing factor for the maintenance of peace in the Far East, and beneficial for the promotion of economic expansion on the Asiatic Continent. Japanese politicians were also gratified that the British Government remained aloof from the activities of British and American capitalists in Manchuria and Mongolia.

There were, however, some *genro* and leading politicians in Japan who felt that, in view of the unpopularity of the alliance, the country should rely on the Russo-Japanese Agreement to circumvent any chances of a Russian war of retaliation. At the same time, lurking fears could not be dispelled that Russia, while presently friendly, would attempt with German assistance to recapture the ice-free ports in Manchuria, once she had sufficiently recovered from the crippling blows of the Russo-Japanese War. In such a likelihood, only Great Britain could be relied upon to side with Japan to curb Russia's ambitions. Premier Katsura and Foreign Minister Komura, who favored a policy of continuing the alliance, were ultimately supported by the *genro*.

On the subject of prolonging the alliance with Britain, even Prince Ito, who had been known for his disinclination to support the pact, told British Ambassador MacDonald, before his departure for Harbin on May 13, 1909, that he felt the maintenance of Great Britain's predominance in China was a decisive element for the preservation of peace in the Far East, and that as long as the Anglo-Japanese Alliance continued, there was little or no danger of stability being upset in the area.

Continuing, Prince Ito declared that he had never lost an opportunity to drive home this point on members of the Japanese Government, urging them to consistently uphold the Alliance and to act loyally and honestly in all dealings with Great Britain. "The mere fact that we are geographically so far apart so that our local interests do not clash is, in my opinion," he said, "an important feature in the stability of the Alliance."

Premier Katsura not only echoed Prince Ito's statement, but proclaimed unreservedly that the active existence of the alliance ensured that all would be well in the Far East, although affairs in China would require constant vigilance.

Rather unexpectedly, it was the contemplated Anglo-American arbitration treaty which provided the opportunity for the early revision of the Anglo-Japanese Alliance. When the Japanese Ambassador to Great Britain, Takaaki Kato, called on British Foreign Minister Sir Edward Grey on September 26, 1910, he was informed that the United States and Great Britain, through the initiative of a person who was not officially connected with the United States Government, were contemplating the advisability of conducting a general and unlimited arbitration treaty, but that Great Britain would not proceed further with such a treaty in view of its incompatibility with the present Anglo-Japanese Alliance.

The British Foreign Minister added, however, that his Government was ready to reply to the United States with two alternative propositions, namely:

1. "to reserve the Anglo-Japanese Alliance from the effective sphere of the proposed arbitration treaty and to revise the Treaty of Alliance at the time of its expiration so as to conform to the general principle of the arbitration treaty," or

2. "to suggest to the United States the participation of Japan in the proposed arbitration treaty, if the United States did make formal overtures."

Concerning these propositions, Foreign Minister Grey privately expressed a desire to be apprised of the Japanese Government's reaction after they had been duly studied.

Upon receiving the British Government's suggestions on a general arbitration treaty between the United States and Great Britain from Ambassador Kato, the Japanese Government, after carefully considering its implications, rejected the second of the two alternative propositions of the British Government on the ground that it could not possibly accept an arbitration award on matters which might possibly affect the very existence of a nation and place Japan in an unfavorable position since most of the arbitrators would be Europeans and Americans who had different cultural, racial, and religious backgrounds.

The Japanese Government finally decided in favor of the first proposition, it being clear that Great Britain would endeavor under all circumstances to avert war with the United States, if only out of economic necessity and her relations with Canada, and to avoid becoming entangled in any explosive issues between Japan and the United States. Realizing that the Anglo-Japanese Alliance would not be applicable in matters involving the United States, the Government instructed

Ambassador Kato to communicate Japan's decision to Foreign Minister Grey on January 17, 1911.

The Japanese Government had cause to fear that, in case the proposed arbitration treaty proved unsuccessful, the Anglo-Japanese Alliance would be regarded as a chief obstacle, thus jeopardizing the future renewal of the Alliance and spelling disaster for international relations in the Far East.

Hence, Foreign Minister Komura decided to take this opportunity of completing the revision for the renewal of the Alliance. His decision was communicated to Lord Grey by Ambassador Kato with the proposal (1) to clarify the inapplicability of the Treaty of Alliance on matters involving the United States, thus removing fears of British involvement in any American-Japanese dispute, (2) to revise the Treaty of Alliance in accordance with the changed situation in the Far East, including the annexation of Korea, and (3) to extend the Alliance for another ten years.

On March 29, 1911, Foreign Minister Grey transmitted to Ambassador Kato the British Cabinet's concurrence on the general principles for the revision and extension of the Anglo-Japanese Alliance which would not affect the unlimited arbitration treaty between the United States and Great Britain. Negotiations were immediately started through Ambassador Kato on the terms for the renewal of the alliance.

The draft of the treaty which Ambassador Kato presented to Minister Grey as the basis for discussion was similar to the Second Treaty of Alliance in its Preamble, Article I, and Article II, but with some notable exceptions. In the first place, all references to Korea were eliminated and replaced by a stipulation concerning Japan's special interests in all that concerns the security of her frontiers, stating that "Great Britain recognizes her right to take such measures in the proximity of those frontiers as she may find necessary for safeguarding her possessions."

In the second place, while Article IV and Article VI were identical to Articles V and VII of the prior Agreement, Article V proposed that "it is understood that this Agreement is not to apply in case either of the High Contracting Parties becomes involved in hostilities with any third Power with which the other Contracting Party has in operation a Treaty of General Arbitration."

An important proviso added, however, "unless such third Power is joined in such hostilities by one or more other Powers or joins in hostilities against either of the Allies." Eliminated were Articles III and VI of the Second Anglo-Japanese Treaty of Alliance. Article VII stipulated that the new Alliance should remain in force for ten years. In short, the two major differences were the revision of Article III and the insertion of the proviso to Article V.

Foreign Minister Grey and Ambassador Kato conferred on a number of occasions on the basis of the Japanese draft proposals. In his introductory remarks during his meeting with Ambassador Kato on June 26, 1911, the British Foreign Minister stated that the British Government, having already submitted a draft amendment of the arbitration treaty to the United States, was desirous of the earliest revision of the Treaty of Alliance that would conform to the general principles of the arbitration treaty.

Britain also proposed the elimination of Article III, relating to British special interests in India, in view of the improved Anglo-Russian relations, and the proviso to Article V. It was even suggested that the treaty include a clear statement that the Alliance did not impose any obligation on either Great Britain or Japan to enter into hostilities with the United States. After careful consideration and repeated discussions, the Japanese Government finally agreed to strike out the whole of Article III and the proviso to Article V.

Four years before the Second Anglo-Japanese Alliance was to expire, the Third Anglo-Japanese Treaty of Alliance was signed between Ambassador Kato and Foreign Minister Grey on July 13, 1911.

The new treaty of 1911 retained the preamble and the main

provisions of the 1905 Agreement, but deleted Articles III and IV relating to the special interests respectively of Japan in Korea and of Great Britain in India as well as Article VI relating to the Russo-Japanese War. The most significant addition to the 1911 treaty was Article IV, which read: "Should either of the High Contracting Parties conclude a treaty of general arbitration with a third Power, it is agreed that nothing in this Agreement shall entail upon such Contracting Party an obligation to go to war with the Power with whom such treaty of arbitration is in force."

Shortly after the revised Anglo-Japanese Treaty was signed, the Anglo-American Arbitration Treaty was initialed in Washington on August 3, 1911, but since it failed to get United States Senate ratification, Article IV lost its original significance and became an idle provision.

The following is the full text of the Third Anglo-Japanese Treaty of Alliance:

PREAMBLE

The Government of Japan and the Government of Great Britain, having in view the important changes which have taken place in the situation since the conclusion of the Anglo-Japanese Agreement of the 12th August, 1905, and believing that a revision of that Agreement responding to such changes would contribute to general stability and repose, have agreed upon the following stipulations to replace the Agreement above mentioned, such stipulations having the same object as the said Agreement, namely:

(**a**) The consolidation and maintenance of the general peace in the regions of Eastern Asia and of India;

(**b**) The preservation of the common interests of all Powers in China by insuring the independence and integrity of the Chinese Empire and the principle of equal opportunities for the commerce and industry of all nations in China;

(**c**) The maintenance of the territorial rights of the High Contracting Parties in the regions of Eastern Asia and of

India, and the defence of their special interests in the said regions:

ARTICLE I

It is agreed that whenever, in the opinion of either Japan or Great Britain, any of the rights and interests referred to in the preamble of this Agreement are in jeopardy, the two Governments will communicate with one another fully and frankly, and will consider in common the measures which should be taken to safeguard those menaced rights or interests.

ARTICLE II

If by reason of unprovoked attack or aggressive action, wherever arising, on the part of any Power or Powers, either High Contracting Party should be involved in war in defence of its territorial rights or special interests mentioned in the preamble of this Agreement, the other High Contracting Party will at once come to the assistance of its ally, and will conduct the war in common, and make peace in mutual agreement with it.

ARTICLE III

The High Contracting Parties agree that neither of them will, without consulting the other, enter into separate arrangements with another Power to the prejudice of the objects described in the preamble of this Agreement.

ARTICLE IV

Should either High Contracting Party conclude a treaty of general arbitration with a third Power, it is agreed that nothing in this Agreement shall entail upon such Contracting Party an obligation to go to war with the Power with whom such treaty of arbitration is in force.

ARTICLE V

The conditions under which armed assistance shall be afforded by either Power to the other in the circumstances mentioned in the present Agreement, and the means by which such assistance is to be made available, will be arranged by the Naval and Military authorities of the High Contracting Parties, who will from time to time consult one another fully and freely upon all questions of mutual interest.

ARTICLE VI

The present Agreement shall come into effect immediately after the date of its signature, and remain in force for ten years from that date.

In case neither of the High Contracting Parties should have notified twelve months before the expiration of the said ten years the intention of terminating it, it shall remain binding until the expiration of one year from the day on which either of the High Contracting Parties shall have denounced it. But if, when the date fixed for its expiration arrives, either ally is actually engaged in war, the alliance shall, *ipso facto,* continue until peace is concluded.

In faith whereof the Undersigned, duly authorised by their respective Governments, have signed this Agreement, and have affixed thereto their Seals.

Done in duplicate at London, the 13th day of July, 1911.

There were varying repercussions from the new Treaty of Alliance. Public opinion appeared split. For instance, the *Hochi Shimbun,* labeling the Treaty as disadvantageous to Japan, went so far as to claim that the Treaty undermined the fundamental basis of Japan's foreign policy. Count Shigenobu Okuma charged that the Treaty placed an unequal burden on Japan, requiring the country to render assistance to Great Britain while under certain circumstances being unable to call on her support in Japan's hour of need.

However, by and large, the nation regarded the new Treaty as advantageous in view of its role in easing tensions between Japan and the United States and encouraging cooperation between them. Japanese Government circles also held similar views.

The new Treaty also received a mixed reception overseas. While Great Britain and the United States were generally satisfied, particularly the President and the Secretary of State of the United States over Article IV which would facilitate passage of the Anglo-American Arbitration Treaty, the European powers were critical of the Treaty, declaring that it was so decidedly unfavorable to Japan that its days were numbered.

It is thus questionable whether the early revision of the Anglo-Japanese Alliance was advantageous to Japan. Moreover, to have given the impression unnecessarily that the Treaty had been revised to the disadvantage of Japan was, to say the least, ill considered. The revision should have been carefully weighed against the progress of the negotiations on the Anglo-American Arbitration Treaty. In this connection, Foreign Minister Lord Grey preferred to renew the Alliance only after the Treaty of Arbitration was concluded.

Misjudging that Great Britain had no intention of renewing the Alliance and fearful of the instability in China and the anti-Japanese movement in the British Dominions, the Japanese politicians unintentionally exposed the weakness of the Japanese Government and failed to contribute towards the stability of the Far Eastern situation.

The unsoundness of Japan's diplomacy was glaringly revealed during the first Chinese Revolution which took place shortly thereafter. As Chancellor von Bülow once said, diplomats should never forget the golden saying *"Pas trop de zèle,"* or "Don't be too zealous."

CHAPTER 11

Third Russo-Japanese Agreement 1910-1912

~~~~~~

THE first organized attempt at international loan operation in China was made in 1907 by Harriman for a Manchurian loan of $20,000,000. Neither this effort nor the Chinese scheme to float a loan of $30,000,000 in the United States in 1908 was successful.

During 1908–09, British, French, and German banking groups also began to show interest in possible Manchurian loans, while President Taft in 1909 encouraged the formation of an American banking syndicate to undertake Chinese loans.

The combined interest of these European and American bankers culminated in the formation of the so-called "Four Power Banking Group" or the Quadruple Agreement of November 10, 1910. The first definite loan agreement between the Peking Government and the Four Power Banking Group, signed on April 15, 1911, covered both the loan agreement for the Chinese currency reform and the Manchurian Industrial Development Loan. The Four Power Banking Group comprised the Banque de L'Indo-Chine (French), the Deutsch-Asiatische Bank (German), the Hongkong and Shanghai Banking Corporation, Ltd. (British), and an American group of banks, namely, J.P. Morgan and Company, the National City Bank of New York, the First National Bank, and Kuhn, Loeb, and Company.

The Imperial Chinese Government Five Percent Currency

Reform and Industrial Development Sinking Fund Gold Loan of 1911 specified a loan which was not to exceed £10,-000,000 at 5 percent interest, with the bond to be sold at 95.

A vigorous protest was immediately lodged by Japan and Russia against the four powers. This joint action also hastened the conclusion of the Third Russo-Japanese Agreement.

The energetic Japanese protests to the various foreign ministries were accompanied by demands that her nation's financial groups be admitted into the Four Power Consortium. The Government felt that it was grossly unjust that Japanese and Russian banking interests should be excluded. The Japanese Government interpreted Article XVI of the Four Power Agreement of April 15, 1911 to mean that a preference in loan operations, especially in Manchuria, would be given to the participating banking groups. This article meant, asserted the Japanese protest, that "in the whole of the three Manchurian provinces the four powers' financial group is accorded priority over all other foreigners and foreign institutions, not only as regards enterprises contemplated by the agreement, but in the matter of any other activities which may hereafter be associated with such enterprises."

It would have been strange indeed if Japan and Russia had neglected to protest against the arrangement which was harmful to their national prestige and interests. The two countries conferred on the matter of obtaining precise statements from the Consortium Governments as to the use of the loan and the collateral involved.

As a result, on June 26, Japan requested that Article XVI either be amended or expunged. Naturally objecting to the same Article, Russia also demanded its deletion, charging that "it seems that the syndicate, utilizing the Article, pretends to a monopoly of financial and industrial enterprises in the regions in which Russia possesses important special interests."

While the Consortium was seriously considering the steps to be taken to ameliorate the protests filed by Japan and Russia, an unexpected and dramatic incident developed to lead the two countries into closer relationship.

This was the overthrow in 1911 of the Manchu dynasty which had ruled China for 300 years, by the Chinese revolutionary forces led by Dr. Sun Yat-sen. Later, on March 10, 1920, a provisional constitution was proclaimed and the Republic of China was established with Yuan Shih-kai as President.

It is of relevance to refer briefly to conditions in Japan, where the nation was going through a turbulent period at the time of the Chinese Revolution. The uprising in China came as a great shock to the nation. Japan's first concern was to undertake unilateral intervention in case China should request assistance in defending the Imperial Throne.

At the same time, there was deep concern in Japan that such an action might cast an unfavorable shadow on her intentions, precipitating an international dispute and fanning anti-Japanese movements among the revolutionary forces. Japan proposed to Great Britain that they should cooperate in helping China through joint intervention. In accordance with this policy, Japanese Minister Ishuin in Peking was instructed to confer with the British Minister, and Consul-General Ariyoshi was informed of the Japanese Government's intention to offer, in concert with the British Government, its good offices to conciliate between the Manchus and the revolutionary forces.

In Peking the Ministers of Japan, Great Britain, the United States, France, Germany, and Russia cooperated in the task of restoring peace between the opposing Chinese forces, and on December 20, 1911, the Consuls-General of the six nations in Shanghai presented their joint recommendation to Tang Shao-i, representative of the North, and Wu Ting-fang, representative of the South.

Shortly thereafter on January 24, 1912, Germany made a representation to the United States Secretary of State Knox, appealing for American assistance to check Japanese intervention in China's internal affairs. Having failed in his scheme to neutralize the Manchurian railways, Secretary Knox was very wary about Far Eastern questions. While agreeing with the principle of preventing Japanese intervention, Knox declined to take any positive stand without first consulting Great Britain and Russia, particularly the former.

Furthermore, the United States desired to ascertain the real motive behind Japan's unilateral intervention. The German objective was later incorporated in the official note exchanged between Germany and the United States and despatched to the powers concerned. Japan's unconditional approval of the note was regarded by Germany and the United States as a great success which they had not anticipated.

It was largely Great Britain's hesitancy to cooperate with her ally in the Far East that forestalled active Japanese intervention. Under these circumstances, a compromise was effected between Yuan Shih-kai and the revolutionaries at a peace conference held in Shanghai under the auspices of British Minister Jordan, at which both the British and Japanese Consuls-General were present.

This meeting eventually led to the abdication of Emperor Hsuan Tung, more commonly known as Henry Pu Yi, on February 12, 1912, and the subsequent election three days later of Yuan Shih-kai as the provisional President of the new Republic. Yuan took the oath of office on March 10 and promulgated the Provisional Constitution, while the National Advisory Council met on April 29, 1912, and the first Parliament was convened on April 8, 1913.

Taking advantage of Japan's preoccupation with measures to deal with the Chinese Revolution, Russia made strenuous efforts to expand her vested interests in northern Manchuria, Mongolia, and Turkistan. Russia had already, in December, 1910, applied pressure on China to promise to respect the status quo in Mongolia and to promise not to engage in any military operation in the region.

While Japan and the other powers were fully prepared to

respect the independence and territorial integrity of China, Russia was openly pursuing a policy of instigating secessionist actions on the part of China's adjacent dependencies and later of amalgamating them into the Russian Empire. When the Four Power Consortium, inimical to Russia's special interests, came into existence, the Manchurian situation became more complicated than that of Mongolia. However, having identified her interests as similar to those of Japan, Russia was obliged to discuss the implications of the Consortium with the Japanese Government.

Meanwhile, a series of negotiations had taken place to consider the requests by Japan and Russia to be allowed to participate in the Consortium and in the granting of future loans to China, including Manchuria. Considering the straitened financial condition of the Chinese Government, the four powers finally approved the entry of Japan and Russia into the Consortium.

In response to the approval, Japan notified the Four Power Consortium that she would join the Consortium on the understanding that her special rights and interests in southern Manchuria and Inner Mongolia should not be menaced, and Russia also requested similar respects for her rights and special interests in northern Manchuria, Mongolia, and Western China.

Thus, in a general multipower agreement signed at Paris on June 18, 1912, the Reorganization Loan to the Chinese Government was extended under an arrangement which deleted the clause concerning the enterprises in Manchuria and inserted the Japanese-Russian reservations in the minutes of the proceedings of the Paris meetings. In these negotiations, the Japanese and Russian banking groups reserved the right to withdraw from the Consortium in case it undertook to offer a loan or loans "contrary to the interests of Russia and Japan."

At the time of the conclusion of the Reorganization Loan, Japan reserved for herself special rights in the region of

South Manchuria and contiguous Inner Mongolia, while Russia did the same with respect to the regions of North Manchuria, Mongolia, and Turkistan. Through the secret instrument of the Third Russo-Japanese Agreement, the two powers pledged to respect the regions of special interests of both nations by confirming the division of Inner Mongolia into East and West in which they would—as they did in Manchuria in 1907—maintain separate spheres of influence.

The gist of the Secret Agreement signed between Ambassador Motono and Foreign Minister Sazonoff on July 8, 1912, was as follows:

The Imperial Government of Russia and the Imperial Government of Japan, desirous of precisely clarifying the arrangements of the political conventions entered into by them on July 30, 1907, and July 4, 1910, aimed at removing all causes of misunderstanding regarding their special interests in Manchuria and in Mongolia, have decided to extend the line of demarcation fixed in the Additional Article of the Convention of July 30, 1907.

In Article I, the two powers demarcated the lines of their respective spheres of interests on the basis of various rivers flowing in the region.

In Article II, the signatories divided Inner Mongolia into two parts, one to the east and the other to the west of the meridian of Peking (116° 27′ East of Greenwich). The Imperial Government of Russia agreed to respect the special interests of Japan in the part of Inner Mongolia to the east of the above mentioned meridian and the Imperial Government of Japan agreed to respect the special interests of Russia in the part of Inner Mongolia to the west of the said meridian.

In Article III, the two powers agreed to keep the Convention strictly secret.

CHAPTER 12

Franco-Russian Schemes for Alliances and the Quadruple Alliance 1914-1915

THE outbreak of World War I afforded both France and Russia a compelling opportunity to conclude an alliance with Japan. Although these efforts proved abortive, owing chiefly to Foreign Minister Kato's evasive tactics, they do throw an interesting sidelight on the frantic international diplomatic maneuvers which accompanied the global conflict, maneuvers which had Japan as the object of the Allied Powers. In this connection, it is important to know the circumstances which led to the Russian and French propositions for alliances.

Shortly after the outbreak of World War I, the Japanese Government decided in August, 1914, to become a belligerent in compliance with the British Government's request for assistance under the terms of the Anglo-Japanese Alliance. No sooner had this decision been made, than the British Government not only retracted its earlier statement, but even voiced its opposition to any hasty involvement in the war by Japan, ostensibly in order to defend her trading interests in China.

However, when prospects for an early victory became uncertain, Britain urged Japan to enter the war, pointing out that the German Ambassador in Tokyo had threatened Japan's interests by employing intimidating words to Vice Foreign Minister Matsui.

This vacillating British policy appears to have been strongly influenced by pressures which were exerted by the United States, Russia, and France. When Britain first changed her attitude towards Japan's participation, the decision was most likely swayed by American and Chinese propositions for the neutralization of the Far East. In order to block German and Austrian intrigues which might jeopardize her position in the Far East, Britain decided to support Japan's involvement in the world conflict. Throughout this period, also, Britain could not ignore Russian and French maneuvers to benefit from the unsettled conditions in Asia.

All indications are that the British Government endeavored to confine Japan's military actions to the Far East and the Pacific Ocean, while on the other hand paying due attention to the demands of the United States and China as well as Russia and France.

Having no direct cause for going to war against Germany, advocates of a neutral stand found wide support among the Japanese public. An example of this view, shared by many politicians of the Seiyukai Party, was the following statement made by Korekiyo Takahashi, former Minister of Finance, to Prime Minister Shigenobu Okuma:

"Although there is a rumor that we are to join the conflict, isn't this an extremely rash action? How would it be if Japan negotiated with Germany for a peaceful settlement of the Far Eastern situation?"

Some Japanese military leaders also presupposed a German victory, and this respect for Germany's fighting capability was even expressed at one of the memorable sessions of the council of *genro* on August 8, 1914, as a valid reason for hesitating to actively side with the Allied Powers. Members of the Japanese Cabinet also could not conceal their apprehensions over the country's participation.

On the other hand, the Allied Powers also watched Japan's attitude with profound anxiety. They feared that if Japan joined the Central Powers, the entire strategic picture of the war would radically alter in favor of their enemies. Japan would gain control of the Western Pacific Ocean, the China Sea, and the Indian Ocean, and by threatening Russia's rear, paralyze her offensive strength in Europe.

These grave forebodings prompted both Russia and France to send out repeated feelers and proposals for alliances with Japan. Motivated also by the existence of the Anglo-Japanese Alliance, they hoped to acquire material support and, at the same time, check any eventual Japanese ambitions.

1

FRANCE was the first to send out a feeler. When the French Ambassador in Tokyo called on Foreign Minister Kato on August 4, 1914, he abruptly suggested, though in personal capacity, the formation of a Franco-Japanese alliance. Taken by surprise, Baron Kato discreetly declined to express any opinion on such an informal suggestion. Upon Great Britain's declaration of war against Germany on August 7, the French Ambassador again called on Baron Kato and officially inquired about Japan's reaction to the proposal to include France in the Anglo-Japanese Alliance.

In order to avoid any misunderstanding, Baron Kato requested that the proposal be made in the form of an official communication. Curious to know the real intention of France in making such an unexpected proposal, Baron Kato invited the French Ambassador to express his views candidly. Without the slightest hesitation, the French envoy disclosed that the purpose of the proposal was to protect French Indo-China. Thereupon, Baron Kato quickly reassured the Ambassador that Japan had no intention of taking advantage of the present situation in order to invade the territories of other powers in the Far East.

The French memorandum containing the draft of the Franco-Japanese Alliance reached Foreign Minister Kato the following day. The broad objectives of the alliance, substantially the same as those of the Anglo-Japanese Alliance, were to strengthen the friendly relations between Japan and France. The draft also included a stipulation that neither of the contracting parties would engage in acts of hostility against Great Britain or Russia.

Article I stated that each of the Contracting Parties would endeavor to observe all agreements and treaties previously concluded between them. The treaty would also incorporate Articles I to VI of the Anglo-Japanese Alliance. The French Ambassador, who followed up the memorandum with another visit to Foreign Minister Kato on August 12, was informed that in view of the extreme importance of the proposition the Japanese Government would require more time for consideration and study.

The French Ambassador then asserted that in the event of Japan's participation in the war, it would be expedient to conclude the Franco-Japanese alliance, the existence of which would favorably affect the course of the war. Baron Kato's attention was also drawn to the fact that Russia was contemplating a similar move.

The Ambassador was promised an early reply after the subject had been discussed with Great Britain, and was informed that the Japanese Government intended to consider the Russian proposal together with the French overture. However, the question of a Franco-Japanese alliance was never followed through, and no further allusion was ever made to the alliance.

Strangely enough, there is not a single page in the *Documents Diplomatiques Français* which concerns the negotiations for a Franco-Japanese alliance, and even the French Ambassador, M. Gerard, who had originally brought up the proposition at the time had tactfully deleted any reference to the alliance in his memoirs, *Ma Mission au Japon*.

Accordingly, it is not clear what the circumstances were which led France to send out such feelers to Japan and then suddenly drop the negotiations at a halfway stage. Was the

French action the result of her conclusion that Japan had no territorial designs? Then, too, was she satisfied that a closer collaboration between Japan and Russia would be sufficient to meet her requirements?

Moreover, despite the French Ambassador's statement to Baron Kato on August 7 that France had no intention of obliging Japan to enter the war, did not the proposition itself assume that under the alliance Japan would become a belligerent and despatch troops to the European front? Another valid reason for abandoning the talks could be the fact that Japan had categorically rejected any scheme for sending her troops to fight in the European zone of operations. The absence of any official French documents on this episode make it impossible to ascertain the true state of affairs.

2

RUSSIA was just as eager as France to join the Anglo-Japanese Alliance. On August 10, 1914, the Russian Foreign Minister Sazonoff informed Ambassador Motono that only two weeks before the outbreak of the war the Russian Government, through its Ambassador in London, had suggested to the British Government that Russia be included in the Anglo-Japanese Alliance. The British Foreign Minister had welcomed the Russian suggestion, but had taken no positive action in view of the constantly changing situation.

Foreign Minister Sazonoff then expressed Russia's eagerness to give effect to the proposal for the sake of peace in the Far East and the preservation of Russian and Japanese interests on a permanent basis. He also specifically requested that Japan make common cause with Great Britain, Russia, and France in their war against the Central Powers.

To understand the significance of the statement by the Russian Foreign Minister, it is imperative to closely examine Anglo-Russian relations immediately before World War I.

The relations between the two countries were especially tense in Asia where the conduct of the Russian Consul in Persia was disconcerting to the British. The situation in Afghanistan was a source of deep anxiety to the Government of India.

In addition, Russia made no secret of her disappointment over the results of the treaty with Great Britain in 1907, and her displeasure at the acquisition of mining interests by a British company in the Persian neutral zone. At home, influential quarters in the Imperial Court of Russia and the armed forces stressed the need to seek German assistance to maintain the monarchy against the danger of revolutionary elements.

Britain could ill afford to overlook these dangerous situations and made energetic efforts to reach a better understanding with Russia. An outstanding example was the Anglo-Russian naval conference which had been taking place in London since the spring of 1914. Convinced of Britain's friendliness, Russian Foreign Minister Sazonoff suggested to Sir George Buchanan, the British Ambassador at St. Petersburg, in early July, the signing of a triple guarantee of territorial nonaggression by Japan, Great Britain, and Russia. There is ample evidence to suppose that the Sazonoff proposal for a triple guarantee was only an extension of the scheme proposed earlier to Ambassador Motono to include Russia in the Anglo-Japanese Alliance.

In the light of these circumstances, Foreign Minister Kato felt that it would be appropriate to consider the Russian proposition in relation to the French overture for a Franco-Japanese alliance. However, he saw no compelling reason to take immediate action because the French approach was prompted by a desire to protect French Indo-China and the Russian objective was Japan's participation in the war on the side of the Allied Powers.

Since Japan had declared war on Germany on the basis of the Anglo-Japanese Alliance, Baron Kato doubted the wisdom of actively pushing the negotiations with Russia. Recognizing that the alliance with Britain would be weakened by additional signatories, Baron Kato instructed Ambassador Motono on September 15 to find out whether Russia still entertained the idea of participating in the Anglo-Japanese Alliance.

Simultaneously, Ambassador Inouye in London was instructed to solicit the views of Britain on this question. Motono informed Baron Kato that to the best of his belief, the Russian Government still desired to take part in the Anglo-Japanese Alliance. Ambassador Inouye in his communication reported the results of his meeting with Foreign Minister Grey, who had informed him that since the Russian representation to Ambassador Buchanan in July, 1914, had been obscure no serious consideration had been given to the conversation.

Furthermore, since Japan, Great Britain, and Russia were already leagued together, the matter itself had lost its urgency. Grey took the stand that if the Russian motive was political, then the negotiations should be suspended until after the war. On the other hand, if Japan preferred to negotiate with Russia at this juncture, the British Government would not be averse to conducting joint negotiations.

Fearing that the inclusion of Russia in the Anglo-Japanese Alliance would change the original character of the Alliance and weaken its effect, Baron Kato refused to entertain the idea. Lord Grey, for his part, agreed wholeheartedly with Baron Kato that the question of Russian inclusion should be postponed until peace was restored, that the question would be under constant study, and that if any change should occur in the policies of the two powers they would consult each other reciprocally.

Later, on January 2, 1915, Foreign Minister Sazonoff intimated to Ambassador Motono Russia's desire to reopen negotiations immediately in view of the change in Lord Grey's attitude in favor of the conclusion of the Anglo-Japanese-Russian alliance even during the hostilities. Baron Kato's rejection of the idea, on the ground that he had received no information of the change of British policy from Lord Grey and that no new situation had arisen to renew consideration of the question, greatly disappointed the Russian Foreign Minister.

Prior to this approach, from around September 20, 1914, the question of forming an Anglo-French-Russian-Japanese alliance on a permanent basis in the event of the failure of the Russo-Japanese and Franco-Japanese alliances to materialize had been raised by France and Russia with both Britain and Japan. The ultimate aim of these moves was to combine the Anglo-Japanese and Franco-Russian Alliances into a single grand alliance for the control of Eurasia.

3

As previously stated, the failure of the French and Russian Governments to form a Franco-Japanese alliance and the proposed inclusion of Russia in the Anglo-Japanese Alliance developed into the four-power alliance proposal and an invitation to Japan to join the London Declaration of September 5, 1914.

On visiting Foreign Minister Kato on September 26, 1914, the French Ambassador in Tokyo strongly urged the formation of the Anglo-Franco-Russian-Japanese alliance, and expressed the wish to convey the Minister's views to Delcassé, newly appointed French Minister for Foreign Affairs. Replying that it would not be too late to decide on the question after the end of the war, Baron Kato on September 28 instructed his Ambassador in London, Inouye, to ascertain the attitude of the British Foreign Minister on the question.

Lord Grey, in his reply, reiterated his view that the question should be negotiated after peace was restored, and that the British Government would notify the Japanese Government in advance of any change of opinion. For their part,

France and Russia insisted upon continuing the discussion, instructing their Ambassadors in London to call on Lord Grey on January 9, 1915, to propose the formation of the Anglo-French-Russian-Japanese alliance on a permanent basis, failing which Japan should be invited to become a party to the London Declaration of September 5, 1914.

Thus, the question of the grand alliance of the four powers shifted to the issue of Japan's participation in the London Declaration. Lord Grey told the French and Russian envoys that the British Government, while welcoming the principles of the Russian and French propositions for a quadruple alliance, took the view that the question should await the conclusion of hostilities, a view which Japan also shared.

Pointing to Article II of the Anglo-Japanese Alliance, Lord Grey explained that since Japan was waging war in common and was pledged to make peace in mutual accord with Great Britain, France, and Russia, it was hardly necessary to invite Japan at this belated stage to join the London Declaration. Lord Grey, whose efforts were appreciated by Baron Kato, also promised, in response to the Japanese Foreign Minister's request, to clarify Japan's position regarding the London Declaration to the Russian and French Governments, thereby removing any chances of a misunderstanding.

Following these diplomatic maneuvers, the Russian Foreign Minister Sazonoff accepted Japan's stand, declaring in the Duma that under the Anglo-Japanese Alliance, each of the High Contracting Parties pledged to conduct war in common and make peace in mutual agreement; thus Germany could not make peace separately with Japan before making peace with Great Britain.

The French Foreign Minister not only approved of Japan's stand, but informed Ambassador Ishii in Paris that the views of the two Governments were in complete accord.

Although Foreign Minister Kato consistently opposed the four power alliance in order to maintain the Anglo-Japanese Alliance—the only alliance which Japan had signed—intact, and hesitated to join the London Declaration, he exerted every effort to assure Japan a voice at the peace table. This he was able to do by convincing Britain, Russia, and France that Japan was entitled to an equal voice under the terms of Article II of the Anglo-Japanese Alliance, an obligation that was as binding as the London Declaration.

CHAPTER **13**

Japan's Adherence to the London Declaration 1915

~~~~~~

TAKING into account the failure of all efforts before and after Japan's entry into World War I to conclude an alliance between Japan, on the one hand, and France and Russia, on the other, as well as the quadruple alliance of Japan, Great Britain, France, and Russia, Lord Grey became increasingly alarmed at the deteriorating condition of the Russian troops on the Eastern Front. He feared that unless some political assistance was quickly given, Russia might seek a separate peace with Germany in an attempt to stave off a serious internal crisis.

Contrary to Lord Grey's view, Russia was apprehensive that Japan might conclude an independent peace with Germany. This fear that Germany might succeed in wooing Japan away from the Entente Powers had moved Foreign Minister Sazonoff to insist on the conclusion of an alliance with Japan.

In a memorandum dated August 2, 1915, the British Ambassador informed the Japanese Foreign Minister Kato of Lord Grey's view regarding the rapprochement between Japan and Russia. It stated: "The most attentive question at present should be the policy of supplying Russia with material and political assistance. The former should be the supply of necessary arms and ammunitions of war and the latter must be the establishment of greater intimacy between Japan and

229

Russia, maintaining the principle of the Anglo-Japanese Alliance. Therefore, Japan's formal participation in the London Declaration would be effective in bringing closer relations between Japan and Russia. It might well be left unsaid, however, that Japan has already been linked up with the said Declaration under the provisions of the Anglo-Japanese Alliance."

Baron Kato lost no time in replying that such an important question affecting the future policy of the nation could not be lightly considered. Even while Kato was studying the subject, Lord Grey on the following day invited Japan, through Ambassador Inouye, to join the London Declaration as a means of appeasing Russia.

Opposed to any initiative on the part of Japan to join the London Declaration, yet realizing that the request of Japan's ally could not be ignored, Foreign Minister Kato requested Japanese envoys in Europe to submit their respective views on the country's terms for such a participation.

In his reply from St. Petersburg Ambassador Motono stated that, while it would be advisable to share the benefits of the Anglo-French-Russian Secret Treaty of 1915, it would be impossible to stick to this proviso since the British Foreign Minister had publicly denied its existence. Ambassador Motono also felt that insofar as the interests of Great Britain, France, and Russia in the Far East and Pacific Ocean area were not affected, the three powers should agree not to oppose the transfer to Japan of German-Austrian interests at present under the control of Japan.

From London, Ambassador Inouye replied that Japan would not be justified in attaching any condition as long as Japan had no intention of assuming any new obligation in the conduct of the war. Ambassador Ishii in Paris also believed that Japan should not set conditions if she felt that participation in the London Declaration was beneficial to her interests. Ambassador Hayashi in Rome aroused Baron Kato's uneasiness by reporting the possibility that Britain,

France, and Russia might solicit some military assistance from Japan when she became a member to the London Declaration.

When the formal invitation to Japan to adhere to the Declaration was issued in the name of the British Government on August 19, 1915, Marquis Okuma was holding the portfolio of Foreign Minister concurrently with the premiership. As a result of a bribery affair, known as the "Oura Incident," Baron Kato had earlier resigned from his post. Although the Baron's involvement in the Oura incident was said to have been the primary cause of his resignation, there are other facts which lend support to the theory that he was dismissed by the *genro* and military chiefs who were dissatisfied with his negative foreign policy.

With Prime Minister Okuma also holding the foreign ministership, the way was now clear for Japan to participate in the London Declaration. He informed the British Ambassador in Tokyo that the Japanese Government was prepared to adhere to the Declaration, but desired to know whether any terms were connected with Japan's participation, such as the despatch of Japanese troops to Europe.

The British Ambassador assured Marquis Okuma that, in view of the fact that there was now no obligation attached to Japan's adherence to the Declaration, the Japanese Prime Minister should bend every effort to expedite a Cabinet decision on this matter.

Summoning the British, Russian, and French Ambassadors, Foreign Minister Okuma informed them that Japan's adherence to the London Declaration had been unanimously approved by the Cabinet and had received the Imperial sanction. He added that procedural arrangements would be made by the Japanese Ambassador in London with the British Foreign Minister.

After Viscount Ishii assumed the post of Foreign Minister, Japan's formal adherence to the Declaration was effectuated in London by the exchange of notes between Ambassador

Inouye, Lord Grey, and the French and Russian Ambassadors on October 19, 1915, and these exchanges were made public by the nations concerned on October 30.

After joining the Allied Powers as a belligerent, Italy also became a party to the London Declaration on November 30, 1915, thus making it a five-power war pact between Japan, Great Britain, France, Russia, and Italy. Although the Russian Revolution in 1917 eliminated Russia from the *entente,* her place was taken over by the United States. These five powers eventually constituted the "Big Five" as the Allied and Associated Powers of the Peace Conferences at Paris and Versailles.

Japan's participation in the London Declaration was widely criticized domestically, especially in the Diet and the Privy Council, but these criticisms were largely motivated by party politics. Viscount Ishii, who attached great significance to Japan's participation, wrote in his diplomatic memoirs as follows: "That Japan was able to take part in the important deliberations of the Versailles Peace Conference as one of the leading members of the Allied and Associated Powers and furthermore assure her position and honor as a major power of the world was principally due to her adherence to the London Declaration."

From the very outset, it was the British Foreign Minister Lord Grey who showed no inclination to have Japan adhere to the London Declaration, despite repeated Russian and French moves to extend the invitation to Japan. The ostensible reason for Lord Grey's rejection of the proposal was that Japanese interests were well protected by Article II of the Anglo-Japanese Alliance.

However, the underlying reasons appear to have been Lord Grey's anxiety that Japan's participation in the Declaration would carry with it an obligation to acquaint Japan with the existence and contents of the Anglo-French-Russian Secret Treaty of 1915, relating to Constantinople and the Straits, Asia Minor, Alsace-Lorraine, and the Western frontiers of

Russia, consummated at the time of the Declaration itself. He might also have feared that he would no longer have any excuse to reject Japan's claim regarding the German South Sea Island possessions.

On the question of Shantung, however, Lord Grey had already categorically stated to Ambassador Inouye on August 9, 1914, that Great Britain would have no objection whatever to Japan's acquisition of Kiaochow Bay in the event of war between Japan and Germany. The British Minister, however, took a different view towards the disposition of the German South Sea Island Territories.

On the Japanese demand for the conclusion of an agreement on the German possessions in the South Seas following their occupation by Japan, Lord Grey replied that Great Britain could not turn a deaf ear to the demands of other nations by agreeing to Japan's permanent occupation.

Urging the settlement of all matters concerning these islands by postwar agreements, he firmly rejected Japan's demand. Though Great Britain fully recognized that Japan should be adequately compensated for her war efforts, the British Government took the view that Japan should not use her territorial occupation as an obstacle to a postwar agreement.

It was Lord Grey's anxiety about the question of the final disposition of the German islands in the Pacific Ocean which lay behind Britain's reluctance to invite Japan's participation in the London Declaration. On the other hand, although Foreign Minister Kato concurred fully with the views of Lord Grey, he held grave fears that adherence might involve a request for the despatch of Japanese troops to the European front.

Baron Kato had consistently opposed the sending of any Japanese naval or army units to the European war theater. In September, 1914, Great Britain requested Japan to despatch units of the Japanese navy to the Mediterranean area, and, in November, to the Dardanelles, in order respectively to support British operations in the Baltic Sea and to blockade the German-Turkish navies. Foreign Minister Kato failed to respond favorably to the British appeal, pointing out that the Japanese navy was not adequately equipped to operate offensively in foreign waters, being based primarily for defensive action in home waters against potential aggressors. Moreover, he said "the existence of the main strength of the Japanese navy in the Far East is proving to be an indispensable guarantee for peace in the Far East."

Prior to the British request, informal talks concerning a Japanese expeditionary corps to Europe were held between the Russian Foreign Minister and the Ambassadors of Britain and France in St. Petersburg. As a result of these talks, Russia requested Japan through the British Government to despatch three army corps of Japanese troops to the European front. Russia reiterated her demand for Japanese troops to join the Allied armies in Europe, on the ground that Turkey had joined the Central Powers, and by so doing assure herself of a more powerful voice at the peace conference. On April 11, 1915, Russia made a more specific demand, requesting the Japanese expeditionary corps to assume the responsibility for a sector of the Western Front along with the British forces.

To these repeated and insistent demands, Foreign Minister Kato replied that the Japanese army and navy existed only for defensive purposes, and the despatch of these forces to distant foreign lands would be incompatible with the principle and constitution of the Japanese armed forces. In addition, the competent Japanese military authorities also could not agree to a Japanese expedition to the European theater. Once Japan became a signatory to the London Declaration, Baron Kato felt that Japan could no longer reject the Allied demands.

As stated earlier, it was only after Kikujiro Ishii, former Ambassador to France, succeeded Baron Kato as Foreign Minister that Japan affixed her signature to the document of the London Declaration. Viscount Ishii had basically regarded the Declaration as beneficial to Japan's interests. Unless the country adhered to the Declaration, in the event Russia and France concluded a separate peace or negotiated secretly with Germany, Japan would have no means of knowing the details of such developments. It was with the aim of assuring Japan an effective voice at the peace conference that Viscount Ishii made Japan a party to the Declaration. The text of the London Declaration runs as follows:

DECLARATION between Great Britain, France, and Russia, engaging not to conclude Peace separately during the present European War.

Signed at London, September 5, 1914.

The undersigned, duly authorized thereto by their respective Governments, hereby declare as follows:—

The British, French, and Russian Governments mutually engage not to conclude peace separately during the present war.

The three Governments agree that when terms of peace come to be discussed, no one of the Allies will demand conditions of peace without the previous agreement of each of the other Allies.

In faith whereof the undersigned have signed this Declaration and have affixed thereto their seals.

Done at London, in triplicate, this 5th day of September, 1914.

CHAPTER **14**

Fourth Russo-Japanese Agreement and the Secret Treaty of Alliance 1914-1917

THE conclusion of the Second Russo-Japanese Agreement gave birth to a number of influential advocates of an alliance between Japan and Russia, the most prominent supporter being Marshal Aritomo Yamagata who stood at the top of the list of *genro*. Another ardent advocate was the Japanese Ambassador to St. Petersburg, Ichiro Motono, who frequently suggested such an alliance to the Russian authorities and, at the same time, made similar recommendations to his home Government.

At the behest of Marquis Inouye, who had been urging the conclusion of an alliance with Russia as the best means of overcoming the critical situation facing the nation since the winter of 1914, the three *genro* Yamagata, Matsukata, and Oyama, following a thorough deliberation of the question, joined Inouye in a written opinion forwarded to Prime Minister Okuma and Foreign Minister Kato.

This memorandum pointed out that Russia was too preoccupied with operations on the battlefield in the West to have any time to appraise calmly the situation in the East. Thus, the time was most appropriate to broach with Russia the question of an alliance which could only be of benefit to Japan. The *genro,* on the other hand, believed that it would not necessarily be difficult to enter into such an alliance upon the termination of the war and the consequent restoration of peace.

Judging from the present circumstances, all indications were that Great Britain would welcome the conclusion of an alliance between Japan and Russia. Should there be any objection to the use of the term "alliance," the *genro* felt that this could be circumvented by merely expanding the scope of the present Russo-Japanese Agreement by including the following stipulations:

a. If by reason of unprovoked attack on the part of any third power, either High Contracting Party should be involved in war, the other High Contracting Party will at once come to the assistance of its ally, and will conduct the war in common.

b. The High Contracting Parties will respect the territorial integrity of China.

c. The High Contracting Parties should communicate with one another in advance fully and frankly, and will consider in common the diplomatic and economic policies (especially concerning railways) and other important matters concerning China.

d. The High Contracting Parties should communicate with one another in advance fully and frankly, and will consider in common the important matters concerning Mongolia and Manchuria, and especially the important matters which should be negotiated with China, and the High Contracting Parties should reciprocally respect and safeguard their special interests in those regions.

While Marquis Okuma was for the most part not averse to accepting the purport of the written opinion, Foreign Minister Kato appeared reluctant to accept the proposition of the *genro* who, for their part, showed no willingness to lightly withdraw their draft proposal for a Russo-Japanese alliance.

It is plausible that the Russian Government might have made an overture through the British Government for the conclusion of a Russo-Japanese alliance in view of the aggravating domestic and foreign situation at the time, but an even more compelling reason may have been Russia's astute judgment.

When the British Ambassador in Tokyo, in his memorandum delivered on July 24, 1915, mentioned that the Russian proposition for the conclusion of an alliance was based on "Foreign Minister Sazonoff's impression from his talks with the Japanese Ambassador in St. Petersburg and the report of the Russian Ambassador in Tokyo that the Japanese Government had been actively entertaining the idea of better relations between Japan and Russia, including even its serious consideration," he was being neither presumptuous nor wide of the mark.

Giving scant attention to the aspirations of the *genro* and the repeated solicitations of Russia, Foreign Minister Kato stood by his policy of offering no comfort to the Russians. Thus, in his memorandum dated July 28 to Foreign Minister Sazonoff, the Japanese Foreign Minister stated that the Japanese Government had not received any report from its Ambassador in St. Petersburg on the nature of the conversations he had had with the Russian Foreign Minister, nor was it acquainted with the information despatched by the Russian Ambassador to his Government. Moreover, there was no evidence that the Japanese Government was considering the question of strengthening relations between Japan and Russia.

But one month later, Baron Kato left the Foreign Ministry post in the aftermath of the "Oura Incident." As stated earlier, his resignation undoubtedly came about as a result of the dissatisfaction of the *genro* over his negative attitude on the question of the Russo-Japanese alliance.

Viscount Ishii, who succeeded Kato, did not hesitate to give effect to his cherished opinion. Not only did he participate in the London Declaration, but went on to establish a more intimate relationship among Russia, France, and Japan.

The already crucial domestic and foreign situation facing the Tsarist regime was seriously aggravated by the desperate position of the Russian troops on the Western Russian front. They were retreating along the entire Galician front, and German troops were in occupation of the greater part of Poland. Rumors that Russia was clandestinely negotiating for a separate peace with Germany and Austria began to cause deep consternation in British and French circles.

To stabilize the situation on the East European front, preparations were made in the early summer of 1916 to recapture the lost territory in Galicia. Russia, though possessing an abundance of youths of conscription age, was short of guns and war materials of all kinds. Moreover, the supplies could be delivered only by cracking through the icy waters to the northern Russian ports of Archangel and Murmansk.

But Russia's European allies were not in a position to ship such supplies. Their production of arms and munitions could hardly meet their own requirements. To be able to carry on protracted war in these conditions, Russia could not but rely on Japan's assistance and the positive support of the latter's ally, Britain. She had to make concessions to Japan if she were to get the necessary sinews of war.

With the resignation of Foreign Minister Kato who had been a major obstacle to a Russo-Japanese alliance, the *genro* renewed their demands for the early realization of the alliance, persuading both Prime Minister Okuma and Foreign Minister Ishii to resume negotiations with Russia. To conclude such an agreement with Russia, Foreign Minister Ishii took the initial step of adhering Japan to the London Declaration.

In referring to the Russo-Japanese Agreement in his diplomatic memoirs, however, Foreign Minister Ishii did not allude to Russia's repeated propositions for the alliance or to the *genro's* recommendation to the Japanese Government, but simply stated that "the conclusion of the new Russo-Japanese Agreement was initiated by Japan." Although he asserts that Japan's purpose in reaching a new agreement was designed to prevent Russia from concluding a separate peace, the importance of the secret treaty attached to the new agreement makes it highly unlikely that Japan was motivated by this reason alone.

The Fourth Russo-Japanese Agreement was signed between Ambassador Motono and Russian Foreign Minister Sazonoff at St. Petersburg on July 3, 1916. The ostensible convention of this Agreement was composed of two articles. In Article I it was agreed that neither Russia nor Japan would enter into any agreement or alliance which would be antagonistic to the political interests of either of the High Contracting Parties. In Article II the two nations further agreed that if the territorial rights or special interests of either party in the Far East were menaced, the two High Contracting Parties should concert with each other upon the measures to be taken, in view of common action or support to be lent to each other in order to safeguard and defend those interests.

The First Article meant that both Japan and Russia pledged not to conclude a separate peace. It should be recalled that Russia feared that Japan would seek a unilateral peace, just as Foreign Minister Ishii suspected Russia's intentions. The violator of the special interests preconceived in Article II was not necessarily Germany; the article should be construed as being applicable also to the westward advance of the United States. More significant than the ostensible convention was the following Secret Convention:

The Imperial Government of Japan and the Imperial Government of Russia, desirous to consolidate the good relationship between the two countries stipulated by the Secret Conventions signed at St. Petersburg on July 30 (17), 1907, July 4 (June 21), 1910, and July 8 (June 25), 1917, have agreed as follows:

ARTICLE I

Considering that the two countries have vital interests in

China and recognizing that it is essential that China will not come under the political influence of the third power who entertains a hostile feeling against Japan or Russia, the two governments shall from time to time enter frankly and loyally into communication and shall concert with each other upon the measures to be taken to prevent the occurrence of such situation.

ARTICLE II

Should either of the High Contracting Parties involve in war with the third power referred to in Article I as a result of the measures taken in common referred to in the stipulation of Article I, it is agreed that the other Contracting Party will come to the assistance of its ally complying with a request, and, in this case, neither of them will, without consent of the other, enter into separate peace.

ARTICLE III

The conditions under which armed assistance shall be afforded by either Power to the other in the circumstances mentioned in Article II, and the means by which such assistance is to be made available, will be arranged by the authorities concerned of the Contracting Parties.

ARTICLE IV

It is fully understood, however, that neither of the High Contracting Parties, without being assured by its allies of the assistance respondent to the serious proportions of an imminent war, will have any obligation to afford the armed assistance referred to in Article II to the other.

ARTICLE V

The present Convention shall come into effect immediately after the date of its signature, and remain in force until July 14, 1921 from that date.

In case neither of the High Contracting Parties should have

notified twelve months before the date fixed for its expiration the intention of terminating it, it shall remain binding until the expiration of one year from the day on which either of the High Contracting Parties shall have denounced it.

ARTICLE VI

The present Convention shall be strictly confidential between the two Contracting Parties.

Unlike the earlier Russo-Japanese Agreements, whether secret or open, which confined themselves to the regions of Manchuria and Mongolia, the fourth accord extended the spheres of influence to the whole of China.

It should be noted here that for the phrase "special interests," hitherto used in the Russo-Japanese Secret Conventions, was substituted the phrase "vital interests." It is not clear what particular country was designated as "the third power who entertains a hostile feeling against Japan or Russia" mentioned in Article I, but it was meant to describe a country which intended to have political control over China.

Both Foreign Minister Ishii in his diplomatic memoirs and Foreign Minister Sazonoff in his conversations with the United States Ambassador in St. Petersburg, Francis, alluded to Germany. Germany not being specifically mentioned as the third power in the convention, the stipulation in Article I was applicable to the United States in case she attempted to control China politically.

It was rumored at the time of the consummation of this Secret Convention that an additional agreement, containing the following clauses, was signed between Japan and Russia:

1. The transfer to Japan of approximately seventy-one miles of railway between Kuanchengtsu and the south bank of the Sungari River as well as the land attached to the railway and all the rights related thereto.

2. The right of navigation along the Sungari River.

3. The establishment of a Japanese post office in Harbin and the right to convey mail between Changchun and Harbin.

4. The commencement of Japanese telegraphic messages between Changchun and Harbin.

5. The settlement of fishery questions in the Prinmorskaya region.

6. The continuing supply of war materials to Russia by Japan.

The preliminary arrangement concerning the above was duly signed in July, 1916, but the said additional agreement did not come into effect. The reasons for the miscarriage were the inability to obtain China's necessary consent, the knotty commercial problems related to the Sungari River and Japan's right of navigation, not to mention other obstacles.

The Fourth Russo-Japanese Agreement was of short duration, being operative for only eight months before it was nullified by the Russian Revolution of 1917 which overthrew the Romanoffs and established the Soviet regime following the signing of a separate peace at Brest-Litovsk with Germany and Austria on March 13, 1918. The circumstances and the precise provisions of these agreements were not universally known until the Russian revolutionary Government in December, 1917, divulged the hitherto unrevealed contents of these agreements.

CHAPTER 15

Lansing-Ishii Agreement
1917-1923

~~~~~~

THE Anglo-Japanese Treaty of Alliance was the first international document to recognize that the Japanese Government possessed special interests in China. The subsequent Franco-Japanese and Russo-Japanese Agreements both recognized, whether openly or secretly, the special interests of Japan in China. With the United States and Germany, no similar agreement existed. Before any negotiations could take place with the latter, the two countries had become antagonists in World War I.

During this period, Japan was not afforded favorable opportunity to negotiate with the United States on the question of China. Choosing to disregard the Sino-Japanese Agreements concluded in 1915, the United States carefully avoided, even to the extent of side-stepping the technicality of reservation, any action that might be construed as recognizing Japan's special interests in China.

Having proclaimed the Monroe Doctrine denying the whole of the Western Hemisphere—a distance of five thousand miles to the southern extremity of South America—to any further extension of foreign control, it is hardly likely that the United States could not understand Japan's deep concern over the destiny of China, separated only by a narrow strip of water from Japan.

The United States Government appears to have been

swayed by the views of American financial and commercial interests which foresaw the unlimited possibilities of investment and trade in China. In addition, President Wilson had a personal dislike for any system such as the establishment of spheres of influence in China, and was strongly determined not to allow the principles of the Open Door and Equal Opportunity to become a dead letter.

On May 12, 1917, Aimaro Sato, Japanese Ambassador to Washington, called on Robert Lansing, the Secretary of State, at the latter's request, and was informed that it would greatly contribute towards closer relations between Japan and the United States if Japan would despatch a special mission to the United States, similar to those of Russia and Italy which were following the example set by Great Britain and France.

The Secretary of State also told the Japanese Ambassador that there were a number of questions which called for an early settlement, namely, the question of an agreement on supply aimed at curtailing unnecessary expenses borne by the Allied Powers; an agreement on common action connected with the guarding of the Pacific Ocean; and the withdrawal at a later stage of the United States Pacific Fleet to the Atlantic Ocean. In the course of these negotiations on pressing general problems, the United States would also entertain the idea of discussing specific problems related to the Far East.

In response to this American invitation, the Japanese Government appointed Viscount Kikujiro Ishii to head the special Japanese war mission, including Vice-Admiral Takeshita and Major General Sugano in his suite. Besides the questions of adjustment of supplies of material to the Allied Powers and the defense of the Pacific Ocean area, both of which were directly related to the war, the Japanese Government intended to take advantage of the occasion to negotiate on the following issues, hoping thereby to remove all major obstacles to friendly relations between the two countries:

1. The question concerning the status of Japanese nationals in the United States.

2. The question of clarifying Japan's special position in China, and adjustment of future moves of the two countries.

Since the first question is outside the scope of the present study, reference shall be made only to the second question, on which Viscount Ishii received instructions as follows from the Government.

The instructions, among other things, confined Japan's concern to her special and urgent interests in China. The Japanese Government considered the interests of the United States to be primarily economic, and in whatever circumstances not of a nature that would affect the destiny of that country. In assessing the present relationship between Japan and China, Japan's capital investments and volume of trade in China were incomparably higher than those of the United States. Moreover from a political standpoint, Japan's special interests far outweighed those of the European powers, being of tremendous importance to her welfare.

Consequently, should any power attempt to establish its political influence in China in disregard of or harmful to Japan's position, the latter would naturally have to adopt measures of self-protection. In view of the sensitiveness of public feelings in Japan towards international relations affecting China, the Japanese Government felt that the United States Government could be brought to recognize this natural state of affairs.

Far from having any intention of obstructing United States policy in the Far East, the instructions indicated Japan's willingness to cooperate with the United States under certain conditions.

The Imperial Government, which had not acted contrary to the principles of respecting the independence and territorial integrity of China, was prepared, if necessary, to reaffirm in conjunction with the United States the repeated statements relating to these principles. Providing that her special interests were not infringed, Japan had no intention of hindering United States economic activities in China. The principles of unrestricted and equal opportunity would assure just and fair competition to peoples of all nations.

Judging from the present conditions in China, collaboration of Japanese and American capitalists would not only benefit both countries, but also contribute enormously to the development of China's vast natural resources. Japan, therefore, felt it advisable to encourage cooperation between the financiers of the two countries for the promotion of opportunities.

The instructions continued: "In areas like South Manchuria and Eastern Inner Mongolia in which Japan has been maintaining special interests, the Japanese Government cannot remain indifferent to any agreement which a foreign national may conclude with the Chinese authorities, without Japan's prior understanding, on such enterprises as railways and mines, including investments by foreign nationals in which they become the main constituent of rights and duties.

"However, the Japanese Government has no objection, in principle, to citizens of the United States making investments through Japanese nationals in the aforementioned enterprises if they are not direct parties to the contract with the Chinese authorities concerned."

*   *   *

When Viscount Ishii arrived in America in September, 1917, he was accorded an enthusiastic ovation by the United States Government and people. On meeting President Wilson, Viscount Ishii casually sounded out the views of the President on the China question. The President replied that the United States Government would not wish for anything better than that the principles of Open Door and Equal Opportunity be faithfully observed in China by the nations concerned. However, he said, it was regrettable that so-called spheres of influence which menaced these principles had been set up by the powers concerned in various fields in China.

Together with his brief report on his conversations with President Wilson, Viscount Ishii filed a representation with his Government concerning the abolition of the spheres of influence in China. It seems that Viscount Ishii felt that the preservation of the sphere of influence was an anachronism, and that Japan should take the initiative in its abolishment, thus dispelling the suspicions of the foreign powers.

The Japanese Government, on the other hand, thought it advisable not to take any action that would alter the status quo in China at a time when it was difficult to foresee the future course of the war. It, therefore, decided that the time was not yet ripe to formulate any action to conclude agreements relating to the existing spheres of influence.

Having received no reply or instruction to his representation, Viscount Ishii opened negotiations with Secretary of State Lansing on the question of China. The American Secretary of State in opening the discussions stated that Japan was alleged to be acting arbitrarily in the Far East, and seeking to establish a dominating position, and if she were allowed to continue such a course would turn the principles of Open Door and Equal Opportunity in China into a mere scrap of paper.

In order to refute these allegations and vilifications, Secretary Lansing suggested that the United States and Japan issue a joint declaration, emphasizing their firm attachment to the principles of Open Door and Equal Opportunity and respect for the territorial integrity of China. The declaration would also serve as a guidance to the peoples of both countries.

Replying to Secretary Lansing, Viscount Ishii stated that since Japan did not object to the principles of Chinese territorial integrity, Open Door and Equal Opportunity, she would not object to their reaffirmation, but saw little purpose in issuing such a declaration if it were only confined to the principles mentioned above.

From Japan's viewpoint, her predominating interests in the whole of China, to say nothing of the region adjacent to Japan, were similar in certain respects to American interests in the Western Hemisphere, especially with regard to Mexico and Central America. Hence it was his country's opinion that the declaration upholding China's territorial integrity, Open Door and Equal Opportunity as proposed by the United States should be accompanied by a statement defining Japan's special relationship with respect to China, a step that would strike at the root of false propaganda, allay misunderstanding about Japan's intentions and clarify the actual circumstances existing in the Far East.

Recognizing the gravity of their conversations, the two statesmen agreed to temporarily suspend their talks to have time to consider the various problems involved. Viscount Ishii then proceeded to New York where he outlined Japan's policy towards China and its relation to the principles of Open Door and China's territorial integrity. He declared that an idea resembling an Asian Monroe Doctrine existed not only in the Western Hemisphere, but also in the Far East.

Returning to Washington after a week's stay in New York, Viscount Ishii resumed his negotiations with Secretary of State Lansing. When the Viscount paid a courtesy call on President Wilson, he found him much more friendly than on an earlier occasion. Discarding his previous attitude of aloofness, Secretary Lansing told Viscount Ishii that after studying the latter's suggestion he had found an idea on which they could reopen their negotiations afresh.

Secretary Lansing questioned Viscount Ishii on the exact wording to be employed in describing the "predominating interests" which he had referred to in their initial talks, in the event the term was included in a treaty. When Viscount Ishii suggested the words "paramount interest" as a fitting description of Japan's interests in China, the American Secretary immediately questioned the appropriateness of the words, describing them as much too strong. Once such interests were recognized by any of the countries concerned, it would have to acquiesce to any Japanese action in China. Thus, it was hardly possible that the United States Government would ever consent to recognize such a paramountcy by Japan.

In answer to Secretary Lancing, Viscount Ishii adopted a very flexible attitude, declaring that the Japanese Government was not particular about adhering to the words "paramount interests" and that, therefore, the United States was at liberty to select any other term which would effectively express Japan's intentions. During subsequent negotiations, when the United States showed some reluctance to accept the words "special interests and influence," Japan omitted the last two words. Agreement was finally reached between Japan and the United States on the adoption of the term "special interests."

* * *

Having overcome the obstacle of wording Japan's interests in China, the two countries affixed their signatures to a joint declaration, the so-called Lansing-Ishii Agreement, the official notes of which were exchanged between Secretary Lansing and Viscount Ishii at the State Department on November 2, 1917.

The full text of the notes is as follows:

EXCHANGE OF NOTES REGARDING CHINA
(THE LANSING-ISHII AGREEMENT)

From the Secretary of State to Viscount Ishii.

Excellency:

I have the honor to communicate herein my understanding of the agreement reached by us in our recent conversations touching the questions of mutual interest to our Governments relating to the Republic of China.

In order to silence mischievous reports that have from time to time been circulated, it is believed by us that a public announcement once more of the desires and intentions shared by our two Governments with regard to China is advisable.

The Governments of the United States and Japan recognize that territorial propinquity creates special relations between countries, and, consequently the Government of the United States recognizes that Japan has special interests in China, particularly in the part to which her possessions are contiguous.

The territorial sovereignty of China, nevertheless, remains unimpaired and the Government of the United States has every confidence in the repeated assurances of the Imperial Japanese Government that while geographical position gives Japan such special interests they have no desires to discriminate against the trade of other nations or to disregard the commercial rights heretofore granted by China in treaties with other Powers.

The Governments of the United States and Japan deny that they have any purpose to infringe in any way the independence or territorial integrity of China and they declare furthermore that they always adhere to the principle of the so-called "open door" or equal opportunity for commerce and industry in China.

Moreover, they mutually declare that they are opposed to the aquisition by any Government of any special rights or privileges that would affect the independence or territorial integrity of China or that would deny to the subjects or citizens of any country the full enjoyment of equal opportunity in the commerce and industry in China.

I shall be glad to have Your Excellency confirm this understanding of the agreement reached by us.

ROBERT LANSING

From Viscount Ishii to the Secretary of State.
Sir :

I have the honor to acknowledge the receipt of your note of to-day, communicating to me your understanding of the agreement reached by us in our recent conversations touching the questions of mutual interest to our Governments relating to the Republic of China.

I am happy to be able to confirm to you, under authorization of my Government, the understanding in question set forth in the following terms:

In order to silence mischievous reports that have from time to time been circulated, it is believed by us that a public announcement once more of the desires and intentions shared by our two Governments with regard to China is advisable.

The Governments of Japan and the United States recognize that territorial propinquity creates special relations between countries, and, consequently the Government of the United States recognizes that Japan has special interests in China, particularly in the part to which her possessions are contiguous.

The territorial sovereignty of China, nevertheless, remains unimpaired and the Government of the United States has every confidence in the repeated assurances of the Imperial Japanese Government that while geographical position gives Japan such special interests they have no desire to discriminate against the trade of other nations or to disregard the commercial rights heretofore granted by China in treaties with other Powers.

The Governments of Japan and the United States deny that they have any purpose to infringe in any way the independence or territorial integrity of China and they declare furthermore that they always adhere to the principle of the so-called "open door" or equal opportunity for commerce and industry in China.

Moreover, they mutually declare that they are opposed to the aquisition by any Government of any special rights or privileges that would affect the independence or territorial integrity of China or that would deny to the subjects or citizens of any country the full enjoyment of equal opportunity in the commerce and industry of China.

I take etc., etc., etc.

K. Ishii

The exchange of the foregoing notes affirmed (1) Japan's special interests in China; (2) the territorial integrity of China; and (3) the principles of Open Door and Equal Opportunity for commerce and industry in China.

Whereas the second and third points added nothing new to the United States' traditional policy since the Republican Administration's Secretary of State John Hay first enunciated them in 1899, the chief importance of the agreement lay in the first point under which the United States recognized Japan's "special interests" in China. However, the words "special interests" gave rise to many conflicting interpretations.

Answering a question from a senator in the Foreign Relations Committee of the United States Senate, Secretary Lansing said that the so-called "special interests" mentioned in the Lansing-Ishii Agreement had no political or other significance. Furthermore, United States recognition of Japan's special interests in China did not mean an endorsement of the so-called "Twenty-One Demands" of 1915, nor approval of the secret treaty concerning the final settlement of German rights in Shantung concluded between Japan and the four European powers of Great Britain, Russia, France, and Italy. He went on to declare that United States recognition of Japan's special interests had no political significance either to Manchuria or to any other region of China.

On the other hand, Viscount Ishii insisted that the Agreement was significant in that it recognized Japan's political as well as economic "special interests." If this were not so, there would have been no reason for the agreement inasmuch as the Root-Takahira Agreement had already upheld the principles of the Open Door and territorial integrity of China.

*   *   *

Positively asserting that the essence of Japan's special interests in China was primarily political, Viscount Ishii pointed to its indirect significance to economic, commercial, and industrial relations. "Even if China were to fall into ruins as a result of mighty natural upheavals, or sufferers from plague should crowd the city streets, or even if she should be in a constant state of rebellion with the specter of bolshevism haunting the land, these factors alone, however catastrophic," declared Viscount Ishii, would not necessarily "threaten the existence of the Western Powers.

"But the same could not be said of Japan, which could not stand singly without China. Any internal disturbance, plague or diabolical religion in China could easily affect Japan, making her also suffer from the same ill effects. This relationship existing between Japan and China is the basis of Japan's special interests in China. In other words, Japan and China are bound to stand or fall together. Geography has given the two countries a common destiny. Japan cannot escape from this fundamental truth, a truth which even the Western Powers can neither efface nor change.

"One may well question what is the consequence of this incontestable, inherent fact. In endeavoring to provide against natural calamity by construction works and flood control, preventing the outbreak of epidemics by improving sanitation facilities, improving government administration to remove restlessness among the people, and promoting Chinese culture to preclude the invasion of paganism, the Western Powers can only assist China from the standpoint of furthering the general interests of world civilization and within its limits.

"On the contrary, Japan is in a position to give every assistance to China not only from the standpoint of universal interests and within its limits, but also from her own self-defense requirements. As Japan's interests in China, compared with those of the Western Powers, became greater, her responsibility regarding questions affecting China grew proportionately, as did her voice in international matters concerning China. All of these factors constituted Japan's 'special interests' in China. Her special interests could only become meaningful within the context of political interpretation, without which the Lansing-Ishii Agreement would lose its major importance."

Viscount Ishii's exposition may generally be regarded as

the Japanese Government's interpretation of the "special interests" in China. It would be illogical if the United States tried to strike out the political meaning of special interests, and confined it only to an economic meaning. At the same time, there is evidence that the United States had not only interpreted the Lansing-Ishii Agreement as a tacit approval of the Asian Monroe Doctrine, but had also attached to it a comprehensive political meaning. When handing over the draft of the Japanese-American joint declaration to Viscount Ishii, Lansing, who had earlier conferred with President Wilson, declared that he believed that the official document was as good as the recognition of Japan's Monroe Doctrine, having in addition quite an important meaning in the Asian political situation.

The Nine Power Treaty, defining the principles and policy to be followed in matters concerning China, was signed at the Washington Conference on February 6, 1922. Among the most important provisions of the Nine-Power Treaty was the Hughes Open Door Resolution, giving a new and broader interpretation and containing stipulations which, for all intents and purposes, practically nullified the Lansing-Ishii Agreement.

The provisions in question were the following: "To refrain from taking advantage of conditions in China in order to seek special rights and privileges which would abridge the rights of subjects or citizens of friendly States, and from countenancing action inimical to the security of such States" (Article I [4]); and to refrain from seeking "any agreement which might purport to establish in favor of their interests any general superiority of rights with respect to commercial or economic development in any designated region of China" (Article III [a]).

Following the Washington Conference, President Harding, in a statement given to the United States Senate Foreign Relations Committee on March 7, 1922, affirmed that the Nine Power Treaty on China was the formal declaration of United

States policy towards China and that this should be substituted for any understanding or declaration of the United States which might be construed by any other power as having a meaning different from that of the Nine-Power Treaty. The above statement was also considered to be an official interpretation of the Lansing-Ishii Agreement.

No protest was lodged by the Japanese Government against this American interpretation. From a practical point of view, Japan attached very little weight to the Lansing-Ishii Agreement in the light of the quickly shifting situation in the Far East following the Washington Conference. Although Japan had no intention of repudiating the Agreement on her own volition, she also appears to have had no idea of rejecting any United States demand for the abrogation of the said Agreement.

*　　*　　*

Referring to the statement made by President Harding, Secretary of State Charles Evans Hughes on April 14, 1922, informed Saburi, Chargé d'Affaires of the Japanese Embassy in Washington, that both the United States and Japan were obliged to communicate the whole of the promises concerning China to the executive office of the Conference in accordance with the resolution of the Washington Conference.

If the Exchange of Notes Regarding China (Lansing-Ishii Agreement) was to be considered effective, it would be necessary to communicate not only the Exchange of Notes, but also the understanding, though unofficial and unsigned, which was reached when the official Notes were exchanged between Secretary Lansing and Viscount Ishii to the effect that "Japan and the United States agree to refrain from taking advantage of the present stage of affairs in order to seek special rights or privileges which would abridge the rights of subjects of other nations," to the executive office for the purpose of making them public.

The Japanese diplomat was further informed that the

United States Government desired to know whether the Japanese Government wished to have the Lansing-Ishii Agreement continued by communicating it to the executive office or intended to join the United States in mutually agreeing to its termination in view of the conclusion of the Nine-Power Treaty.

It should be noted here that Secretary Hughes in his negotiations with Viscount Ishii disclosed that he favored the termination of the agreement at this juncture. After giving serious consideration to the satisfactory settlement of this issue, the Japanese Government, on the basis of the decisions of the Foreign Relations Research Committee and the Cabinet, finally agreed to accept the United States recommendation.

Japan's decision not to insist on the continuation of the Agreement was based on the fact that Article I of the Nine-Power Treaty stipulated that "the Contracting Powers, other than China, agree to refrain from countenancing action inimical to the security of friendly nations," and Japan was given a general assurance by Great Britain, the United States, and France, who recognized Japan's special interests in Manchuria and Mongolia, that the new China Consortium formed in October, 1920, would not do anything in these regions to interfere with Japan's interests.

Japan held firmly to the view that her "special interests" in China, clarified in the Lansing-Ishii Agreement, arose from the territorial propinquity of Japan and China, and could not be altered either by elucidations in diplomatic documents or by any declaration of nullifying an agreement. Therefore, Japan's willingness to renounce the Lansing-Ishii Agreement should not by itself be construed as indicating a change in Japan's position in China. Japan did not fail to communicate the purport of her attitude to the United States.

Taking the international situation into due consideration, the two Governments did not formally terminate the Lansing-Ishii Agreement until the exchange of Notes was carried out on April 14, 1923, between Ambassador Hanihara and Secretary Hughes. Public announcement of the termination took place simultaneously in Tokyo and Washington on April 16, 1923.

CHAPTER 16

Termination of Anglo-Japanese Alliance and Formation of Four-Power Pacific Treaty 1920-1923

WHEREAS the Third Anglo-Japanese Alliance was to have expired on July 13, 1921, the question of the treaty revision had been frequently raised prior to the Washington Conference. While the British Prime Minister and Foreign Minister impressed upon Sutemi Chinda, the Japanese Ambassador at London, during a farewell call, that their Government would necessarily have to consider the views of their colonies and the United States concerning the revision of the Anglo-Japanese Alliance, Britain regarded the prolongation of the Treaty as a logical conclusion.

Meanwhile, in Tokyo, Sir Charles Norton Eliot, the British Ambassador, visited Foreign Minister Uchida on May 19, 1920, to inquire whether Japan intended to renew the Alliance. In reply, stating that he personally as well as a large majority of the Japanese people were favorably disposed towards continuing or renewing the Alliance, Uchida asked the British Ambassador what attitude the British Government and people held on this question.

The British envoy replied that most of the well-informed people in Great Britain were not opposed to its renewal. Touching on the relationship between the Anglo-Japanese Alliance and the League of Nations, he appeared to entertain the idea that the Alliance should become operative if and when the League of Nations failed to come up to expectations

259

or was unable to discharge its functions in the future. On May 21, the Japanese Government notified Great Britain of the Cabinet's decision to renew the Alliance.

On June 6 the British Ambassador called on Foreign Minister Uchida to clarify the British position regarding the Alliance. Drawing Mr. Uchida's attention to the relationship between the Anglo-Japanese Alliance and the League of Nations, the British Ambassador declared that it might be advisable, if the Alliance was to be renewed beyond July 13, 1921, for the two Governments to notify the League of Nations that the form of the said Alliance was not contradictory to the Covenant of the League of Nations.

In any event, the final decision would not be made until the British Government had conferred with the representatives of the British Commonwealth Governments in the autumn.

On the following day, the draft of the Anglo-Japanese Declaration to the League of Nations was communicated to the Japanese Foreign Office by the British Ambassador. This document was referred to the Japanese Foreign Relations Research Committee, and after slight modifications had been made in the wording in consultation with the British Government, it was forwarded to the League of Nations by the Japanese Government. This Declaration was subsequently published by the League of Nations on July 14, by the House of Commons on July 15, and by the Japanese Government on July 23.

Full Text of the Declaration

THE Governments of Japan and Great Britain have come to the conclusion that the Anglo-Japanese Agreement of July 13th, 1911, now existing between the two countries, though in harmony with the spirit of the Covenant of the League of Nations, is not entirely consistent with the letter of that Covenant, which both Governments earnestly desire to respect.

They accordingly have the honor jointly to inform the League that they recognize the principle that if the said Agreement be continued after July 1921, it must be in a form which is not inconsistent with that Covenant.

Although the Japanese Government was prepared to open negotiations on the revision of the Agreement with the British Government, the latter insisted that it could not begin the talks until the Prime Ministers of the British Dominions had been consulted. Owing to Britain's domestic situation, this conference did not take place until June, 1921, and the two countries were obliged to despatch a second Declaration relating to the Anglo-Japanese Agreement to the League of Nations on July 7. The text of this Declaration was made public by the Japanese Government on July 13, 1921.

Text of the Second Declaration

WHEREAS the Governments of Great Britain and Japan informed the League of Nations in their joint notification of July 8th, 1920, that they recognized the principle that if the Anglo-Japanese Alliance Agreement of July 13th, 1911, is continued after July 13th, 1921, it must be in a form which is not inconsistent with the Covenant of the League, they hereby notify the League, pending further action, that they are agreed that if any situation arises whilst the Agreement remains in force in which the procedure prescribed by the terms of the Agreement is inconsistent with the procedure prescribed by the Covenant of the League of Nations, then the procedure prescribed by the said Covenant shall be adopted and shall prevail over that prescribed by the Agreement.

Earlier, on July 4, 1920, on the occasion of an official call, the Japanese Ambassador in London, Hayashi, was informed by Foreign Secretary Lord Curzon of the British Government's view that as a result of the submission of the joint notification to the League by Japan and Great Britain, an early settlement of the question of revising the Alliance had become less urgent. Moreover, since the Alliance would continue after July 13 in a form not inconsistent with the spirit of the Covenant of the League, Great Britain desired to solve existing problems in the light of the present circumstances. Lord Curzon frankly told Ambassador Hayashi that the Alliance was now operating in conditions radically different from those at the time of the conclusion of the Alliance. In reference to India, for example, there now existed no threat or danger whatever.

Although no misunderstanding existed between Japan and Britain, explained Lord Curzon, certain quarters in the United States and China regarded the revision of the Alliance with lurking suspicions. Accordingly, Great Britain hoped not only to continue the Agreement in its present form but to call a Pacific Conference attended by Japan, Britain, the United States, and possibly even China if this was desirable, to discuss the entire range of pending questions. Britain suggested that the venue of the conference should be somewhere in the United States, and the date should be either at the end of 1920 or the beginning of 1921.

One of the major factors contributing to Britain's change of stand on the revision of the Alliance may be ascribed to the Canadian Prime Minister, Arthur Meighen, who was firmly against any revision of the pact.

Despite the widespread support for the Alliance in Great Britain, the Canadian leader contended that revision of the Agreement would be construed as tacit approval of Japan's aggression in the Far East. This same notion was shared semiconsciously by the average Canadian, who also supported the policy of Anglo-American amity. The Canadian Government also feared that in the event of a war between Japan and the United States, her territory would not remain unaffected. In addition, Canada could hardly favor an alliance between Britain and Japan which she considered to be an obstacle to Anglo-American friendship and American-Canadian friendship. It was a cardinal principle of Canadian policy to rely on America's goodwill for the maintenance of her own security.

On the other hand, why did Prime Minister Hughes, known for his energetic opposition to the principle of racial equality at the Versailles Peace Conference, loudly support the Anglo-Japanese Alliance? For a year or two following the outbreak of the Great War, Hughes and his party were disinclined to curry Japan's friendship towards the "White Australia" policy, preferring to applaud President Wilson's naval program as ushering in a new balance of power in the Pacific Ocean.

It began to become apparent, however, that Australia, hit hard by a depressive fall in commodity prices, could not expect relief from Great Britain which was then experiencing a severe depression. Disappointment was also felt in Australia at the size of Britain's naval base in Singapore which was far below the anticipated scale, and there was a growing realization that the country could not rely on Great Britain in case of a naval race in the Pacific area. Faced with the urgent need to cultivate the friendship of a strong power in the Pacific, Hughes finally decided to seek common understanding with Japan.

It will be recalled that the Anglo-Japanese Alliance originally had the objectives of countering Russian aggression, protecting India and Manchuria, and curbing the growing influence of Germany in the Far East. The existence of this Alliance was always a source of grave anxiety for the United States, particularly after the Russo-Japanese War. To allay such an anxiety, the Governments of Japan and Great Britain had agreed in Article IV of the Alliance of 1911 that:

"Should either High Contracting Party conclude a treaty of general arbitration with a Third Power, it is agreed that nothing in this Agreement shall entail upon such Contracting Party an obligation to go to war with the Power with whom such treaty of arbitration is in force." This was an official affirmation that Great Britain would not be entailed to give assistance to Japan in case Japan went to war with the United States.

With Russia and Germany temporarily eliminated from the power struggle as a result of World War I, the United States feared that she had the greatest chance of becoming Japan's enemy under the objectives of the original Alliance. Thus, the Alliance became the object of increasing unpopularity and distrust in the United States.

Soon after the commencement of negotiations for the renewal of the Alliance, public opinion in the United States stiffened sharply. American interest in the progress of the negotiations was unusually keen.

In this mounting tension, Ambassador Shidehara felt it necessary to issue the following statement on July 4, 1921, in an effort to remove the misunderstanding:

"From the very outset, the Anglo-Japanese Alliance has never regarded the United States as an enemy. While the Japanese Government has all along desired to strengthen its relations with Great Britain, it has at the same time possessed a firm hope of furthering the traditional friendly ties with the United States. Moreover, it firmly believes that these two policies are not incompatible.

"The continuation of the Anglo-Japanese Alliance has been criticized in some quarters as likely to foster Japan's aggressive designs towards China. Japan, however, is well aware that such an aggressive policy is not only a violation of the provision stipulated in the preamble of the Alliance, but this would destroy her own security and happiness."

In view of the momentous changes in international relations and Japan's new status on the international scene, the Japanese Government and opinion at home felt that it would not be prudent to abrogate the Alliance for the following reasons:

1. In the postwar years of Anglo-Saxon domination, if the

Anglo-Japanese Alliance was extended, Japan would be able to utilize the role of Great Britain in the event of a dispute with a third power.

2. Abrogation of the Alliance would lead to the inevitable increase of Britain's naval strength in the Far East, an eventuality which would be disadvantageous to Japan in many respects.

3. Japan being the only major power whose people were of a different racial stock there was danger that the abolition of the Alliance might result in heightened anti-Japanese feelings among the other foreign powers.

4. The British Far Eastern policy was primarily economic, benefiting from the maintenance of the status quo. The continuation of the Alliance with Great Britain which was pursuing a sound policy would ensure peace in the Far East.

Although it was under these circumstances that the Japanese Government favored the renewal of the Anglo-Japanese Alliance, it was aware that if the Alliance was harmful to Japanese-American friendship it would not be able to fulfil its objective in view of the existing ties of friendship between Britain and the United States.

It may, thus, be assumed that the statement issued by Ambassador Shidehara was intended to reassure the United States of Japan's friendship as a prerequisite to the renewal of the Anglo-Japanese Alliance.

Essentially, Japan's fundamental policy in revising the said Alliance was to prevent Japan becoming isolated from the international arena, and the Government had every desire to maintain its policy of understanding and cooperation with the United States.

Should it become difficult for any reason to achieve the above objectives in the circumstances arising from the Washington Conference, or should the renewal of the pact obstruct their realization, Japan was not necessarily averse to conceding on the question of the pact's renewal and to formulating a treaty or understanding among Japan, Great Britain, and the United States at the Washington Conference.

However, at the Washington Conference the participants decided to respect the decision of the British Empire Conference to allow the Anglo-Japanese Alliance to lapse and as an alternative to arrive at a common understanding among the powers with interests in the Pacific region. In line with America's wish, the Four-Power Pacific Treaty was announced at a conference on December 10, 1921, bringing to an end the alliance between Japan and Great Britain.

At the Washington Conference the Japanese delegation awaited an opportunity to exchange views with the British delegation on the best course to follow after the Anglo-Japanese Alliance had gone out of existence. The British delegation also appeared eager to discuss the new situation with the Japanese delegation. Hence, when he met the Japanese delegate to the Washington Conference, Tomosaburo Kato, on November 22, 1921, the British delegate, Arthur J. Balfour, solicited the former's views on the renewal or revision of the Alliance in relation to the Conference, stating:

"Although the collapse of Russia and Germany has nullified for the time being the primary reason which gave rise to the conclusion of the Anglo-Japanese Alliance, the Alliance which has greatly benefited Japan and Great Britain should not be lightly discarded. There is no assurance that a similar circumstance which does not now exist may not arise in the future. It is also essential to consider the present situation."

Mr. Balfour then presented his personal plan, a draft based on a three-power treaty of Japan, Great Britain, and the United States—a treaty that would be acceptable to the United States. It reserved the right to revive the Anglo-Japanese Alliance should the necessity arise in the future. Although the British plan envisaged the treaty to be limited to the three powers, the British delegate believed that it would be difficult to reject the application of China or any other power to participate in the treaty. He urged that due consideration be paid to this matter.

Taking into account the general situation and the related circumstances, the Japanese Government concluded that there was no other course open but to adopt the three-power treaty formula in the place of the Anglo-Japanese Alliance. When this decision was communicated to the British delegate, steps were soon taken to hold a conference between Japan, Great Britain, and the United States to work out an alternative plan.

To initiate discussions, Japan forwarded the tentative plan of the Japanese delegate Mr. Shidehara to Mr. Balfour who acknowledged that he fully shared the principles embodied in the plan. After suggesting certain amendments, he desired that the Japanese Government transmit the plan to the United States delegate, Charles Hughes.

In these circumstances, Charles Hughes in his meeting with Arthur Balfour on November 28, 1921, expressed his satisfaction with Shidehara's tentative plan, as modified by Balfour, but emphasized that there was still a strong body of opinion at home which was anti-British and anti-Japanese. In order to overcome this opposition, Hughes suggested the inclusion of France in the negotiations. On the other hand, he fully appreciated Japan's desire to avoid enfeebling the treaty by having too many participants. He, therefore, hoped to limit the additional participant to France. The American representative hoped to confine the purpose and scope of the treaty to the Pacific Ocean region, and to conclude a separate agreement on China with the powers concerned.

On December 6, 1921, the Japanese delegation informed the United States delegation that Japan had no objection to French participation in the proposed treaty relating to the Pacific area. After the "Big Three" delegates, Kato, Hughes, and Balfour, had come to a practical agreement on December 7, the French delegate, René Viviani, was invited to join the talks on December 8, at which time the draft treaty presented by Charles Hughes formed the basis of discussions.

When Hughes invited opinions from the delegates regarding the United States draft, the Japanese delegate inquired whether the wording "insular possessions" stipulated in the draft included Japan's home islands. To Hughes' affirmative reply, the Japanese delegate pointed out that Japan proper formed the main part of the Japanese Empire and did not fall within the category of Japan's possessions.

In reply, Hughes made it clear that he was not in favor of excluding the mainland from the wording of "insular possessions," but was prepared to clarify Japan's position in a supplementary agreement.

After a series of heated and bitter debates by the delegates on the question of excluding Japan Proper from the insular possessions, Shidehara, Balfour, and Hughes finally came to an understanding on December 9, as a result of which the United States, Great Britain, France, and Japan initialed the Treaty between the Four Powers Concerning Their Insular Possessions and Insular Dominions in the Region of the Pacific Ocean, in Washington on December 13, 1921.

The four powers were pledged in Article I "to respect their rights in relation to their insular possessions and insular dominions in the region of the Pacific Ocean" and in case of any controversy arising among them out of any Pacific question which could not be solved by diplomacy and which might affect the existing harmonious relations between the contracting parties, to invite the other parties "to a joint conference to which the whole subject will be referred for consideration and adjustment."

If their rights were "threatened by the aggressive action of any other Power," they agreed in Article II "to communicate with one another fully and frankly in order to arrive at an understanding as to the most efficient measures to be taken, jointly or separately." Article III regulated that the Treaty was to remain in force for ten years, and to continue in force, subject to termination upon one year notice.

Upon ratification in Washington, Article IV affirmed, "the agreement between Great Britain and Japan, which was concluded in London on July 13, 1911, shall terminate." Moreover, the four signatory powers declared that the Treaty was to apply to the Mandated Islands in the Pacific Ocean.

The text of the Treaty follows.

Treaty between the four Powers concerning their insular possessions and insular dominions in the region of the Pacific Ocean

I.

The High Contracting Parties agree as between themselves to respect their rights in relation to their insular possessions and insular dominions in the region of the Pacific Ocean.

If there should develop between any of the High Contracting Parties a controversy arising out of any Pacific question and involving their said rights which is not satisfactorily settled by diplomacy and is likely to affect the harmonious accord now happily subsisting between them, they shall invite the other High Contracting Parties to a joint conference to which the whole subject will be referred for consideration and adjustment.

II.

If the said rights are threatened by the aggressive action of any other Power, the High Contracting Parties shall communicate with one another fully and frankly in order to arrive at an understanding as to the most efficient measures to be taken, jointly or separately, to meet the exigencies of the particular situation.

III.

This Treaty shall remain in force for ten years from the time it shall take effect, and after the expiration of said period it shall continue to be in force subject to the right of any of the High Contracting Parties to terminate it upon twelve months' notice.

IV.

This Treaty shall be ratified as soon as possible in accordance with the constitutional methods of the High Contracting Parties and shall take effect on the deposit of ratifications, which shall take place at Washington, and thereupon the agreement between Great Britain and Japan, which was concluded at London on July 13, 1911, shall terminate. The Government of the United States will transmit to all the Signatory Powers a certified copy of the *procès-verbal* of the deposit of ratifications.

The present Treaty, in French and in English, shall remain deposited in the Archives of the Government of the United States, and duly certified copies thereof will be transmitted by that Government to each of the Signatory Powers.

DECLARATION.

1. That the Treaty shall apply to the Mandated Islands in the Pacific Ocean; provided, however, that the making of the Treaty shall not be deemed to be an assent on the part of The United States of America to the mandates and shall not preclude agreements between The United States of America and the Mandatory Powers respectively in relation to the Mandated Islands.

2. That the controversies to which the second paragraph of Article I refers shall not be taken to embrace questions which according to principles of international law lie exclusively within the domestic jurisdiction of the respective Powers.

Shortly thereafter, on January 24, 1922, the four contracting powers agreed on the stipulations supplementary to the
Quadruple Treaty signed at Washington on December 13,
1921, that the Treaty should not include Japan Proper and
the Bonin Islands (not to be fortified) as a part of Japan. The
Supplementary Agreement was read out by Henry Cabot
Lodge, the United States Plenipotentiary, at the general meeting on February 4, 1922, as follows:

"The term 'insular possessions and insular dominions' used
in the aforesaid Treaty shall, in its application to Japan, include only Karafuto (or the southern portion of the island of
Sakhalin), Formosa and the Pescadores, and the islands under
the mandate of Japan."

The Supplementary Agreement was signed by the respective plenipotentiaries of the United States of America, the
British Empire, France, and Japan on February 6, 1922, and
each signatory power of the Quadruple Treaty notified the
Netherlands and Portugal of their resolutions by an identical
note on February 4 and 6 that, neither country being a signatory of the said Treaty and their possessions in the region of
the Pacific Ocean therefore not being included in the Agreement, "the Governments of the Signatory Powers of the said
Treaty desire to declare that they are firmly resolved to respect the rights of the Netherlands and Portugal in relation
to their insular possessions in the region of the Pacific Ocean."

It should be noted that the geographical extent of the
Quadruple Treaty was confined within narrow limits. It did
not apply to continental territories of the signatory powers in
the region of the Pacific Ocean such as the Kwantung Province,
Korea, and French Indo-China. The sphere of obligation of
each signatory power was also circumscribed within narrow
bounds of "consideration and adjustment," and there was no
stipulation on the use of armed forces and military sanctions.
The four powers participating in the negotiations had, nevertheless, attained their respective objectives.

It may safely be assumed that Japan escaped international

isolation by joining the Four-Power Treaty which had replaced the Anglo-Japanese Alliance, and greatly strengthened her security under Article XIX of the treaty restricting fortifications and naval bases in the Pacific Ocean. The United States, the British Empire, and Japan agreed under this stipulation to maintain status quo with regard to fortifications in their respective regions.

The emergence of the Quadruple Pacific Entente and the abrogation of the Anglo-Japanese Alliance, in the view of the United States, greatly contributed to easing her sense of insecurity in the Far East. In Great Britain, the Treaty was warmly welcomed as having secured the friendship of both Japan and the United States. The Anglo-Japanese Alliance formally came to an end when ratifications of the Quadruple Treaty were deposited in Washington on August 17, 1923.

CHAPTER **17**

Nine-Power Treaty Relating to China 1921 - 1922

THE Nine-Power Treaty relating to China, concluded at the Washington Conference on February 6, 1922, became an object of public attention with the outbreak of the Manchurian Incident. Japan's recognition of the independence of Manchoukuo was strongly denounced as being in contravention to the Nine-Power Treaty. Certain quarters abroad also reacted strongly against the so-called Amau statement, emphasizing Japan's "special position" and "special responsibilities" with regard to China, issued in April, 1934, as being a violation of the said Treaty. Criticisms of Japan's attitude towards the self-government movement in North China made it growingly imperative that the Nine-Power Treaty should be more fully understood and recognized.

At the opening of the sixth general assembly, the last session of the Washington Conference, on February 4, 1922, Elihu Root, the United States delegate, read the text of the Nine-Power Treaty which was unanimously adopted. The Treaty comprised resolutions adopted by the Far Eastern Committee which could be modified into treaty form. A special characteristic of this Treaty was that in each case the provisions were the result of coordinated resolutions, rather than diplomatic negotiations and mutual concessions.

Without understanding the origin of each article and the statements made by the delegates of the Contracting Powers

273

during the deliberations, it would be very difficult, if not impossible, to make a correct interpretation of the Treaty. The following is a detailed explanation of each of the Articles:

ARTICLE I

The Contracting Powers, other than China, agree:

1. To respect the sovereignty, the independence, and the territorial and administrative integrity of China;

2. To provide the fullest and most unembarrassed opportunity to China to develop and maintain for herself an effective and stable government;

3. To use their influence for the purpose of effectually establishing and maintaining the principle of equal opportunity for the commerce and industry of all nations throughout the territory of China;

4. To refrain from taking advantage of conditions in China in order to seek special rights or privileges which would abridge the rights of subjects or citizens of friendly States, and from countenancing action inimical to the security of such States.

The so-called Root resolution, or the "Root Principles" as it later became known, put forward by the American delegate Elihu Root at the third session of the Far Eastern Committee on November 21, 1921, was later incorporated into Article I of the Nine-Power Treaty. Full particulars concerning the circumstances under which the Root resolution was incorporated into Article I may be summarized as follows:

Firstly, the said resolution was formulated by Root himself on the basis of the common features of the "ten points" presented by the Chinese delegate at the first session of the Far Eastern Committee and of the various opinions on the question of China as expressed by the delegates of the powers at the second session of the Far Eastern Committee.

In his inaugural address before the first session of the Far Eastern Committee on November 16, Chairman Charles Hughes stressed the importance of China in the problems of the Pacific and the Far East. After referring to the difficulties which faced the United States during its early years of independence as a result of national disunity, Hughes sympathized with China's difficulties and hoped that that country would enjoy a promising future. He also touched upon Japan's position in the world and the universal respect for Japan's remarkable development. In conclusion, Hughes voiced his desire to see the realization of the principle of the Open Door for all nations in China, at the gate of which stood Japan.

As the proceedings were about to commence, Shih Chao-chih, the Chinese delegate, suddenly presented China's "ten points" as the basis for discussion. China's proposition, however, was not formally adopted, but was submitted to a committee together with other similar propositions for discussion.

Aside from China herself, Japan was more vitally involved in the problems of China than any other power represented at the Washington Conference. As soon as China had presented her ten points, the Japanese delegation submitted a memorandum through Tomosaburo Kato at the second session of the Far Eastern Committee on November 19, outlining the fundamental principles of Japan's policy towards China. In that memorandum, Japan stated:

1. that "existing difficulties in China lie no less in her diplomatic situation than in her external relations" and that the Conference should confine itself to adjusting China's foreign relations, leaving her domestic situation to be worked out by the Chinese themselves;

2. that Japan was "solicitous of making whatever contributions" she was capable of "toward China's realization of her just and legitimate aspirations," as Japan was "entirely uninfluenced by any policy of territorial aggrandizement in any part of China," adhered "without condition or reservation to the principle of the open door and equal opportunity in China," looked to China in particular for the supply of raw materials essential for her industrial life and for foodstuffs as well, and did not claim in her trade relations with China any special rights and privileges but welcomed fair and honest competition with all nations; that Japan was ready to cooperate with other powers in an endeavor to arrive at an arrangement with regard to extraterritoriality in China in a manner which was fair and satisfactory to all parties concerned;

3. that Japan was participating in the Conference, "not to advance her own selfish interests," but "to cooperate with all nations interested for the purpose of assuring peace in the Far East and friendship among nations." Furthermore, the Japanese delegation warned against "protraction of the discussions by detailed examination of innumerable minor matters" as Japan believed that "the principal object of the Conference is to establish in common accord policies and principles which are to guide the future actions of the nations represented."

Thereupon, the French delegate, Aristide Briand, declared that while China's demands as manifested in the "ten points" were generally justifiable by the attending representatives, in order to achieve substantial results it was essential to have them thoroughly examined. The British delegate, Arthur Balfour, then expressed Britain's desire to leave the principle of the Open Door, territorial integrity, the question of China's relief, and other issues relating to that country to be worked out by the Chinese themselves. When an opportunity afforded, extraterritoriality should be abolished and a legal system of justice should be enforced. Balfour pointed out that this policy had repeatedly been voiced by Great Britain.

Statements were also delivered by the delegates of Italy, the Netherlands, Belgium, and Portugal.

In order to agree on the fundamental principles for dealing with the problems of China, the United States delegate Elihu Root proposed to draft a resolution if the Committee had no objection. Root, who was entrusted with the task by Chairman Hughes, submitted a draft resolution on November 21 to the third session of the Far Eastern Committee. Following an exchange of views on the meaning of certain words and phrases, the resolution was unanimously adopted.

1. Concerning the first principle as well as the other principles incorporated into Article I of the Nine-Power Treaty, needless to say they were recognized by the powers in the past, but what is worth noting is that the principle of administrative integrity was injected into the text of the international agreement. Respect for China's territorial and administrative integrity was expressed in the phrase the "maintenance of territorial and administrative entity" in the notes concerning American policy towards China which the U.S. Secretary of State, John Hay, sent to various nations on July 3, 1900.

In discussing this point in the Committee, Tomosaburo Kato, the Japanese delegate, questioned whether "administrative integrity" meant respect for China's political independence, or whether it was intended to affect the acquired rights and interests of the powers. In his reply, Root maintained that any special rights vested by China in the past would not be affected by this resolution. It is highly significant that the rights already acquired by the various powers were excluded.

2. Under the second principle, the Contracting Powers, deeply concerned about China's internal disorders, desired to express their dissatisfaction with the Governments in Peking and South China which relied on military force and their wish to see the appearance of an effective and stable government truly reflecting the will of the people. In the attainment of this objective, the powers frowned upon intervention, emphasizing that the problem should be worked out by the Chinese themselves. At the same time, if requested by China, the powers concerned were willing to render assistance in removing obstacles and offering financial support. This was quite an entirely new principle.

3. The third principle hardly requires any elaboration. While the equality of opportunity in China has been an immutable principle, the powers did clarify that the principle of equal opportunity extended not only to the eighteen provinces of China's mainland, but also to her outlying territories.

4. Concerning the meaning of the word and the category of "rights" stipulated in the fourth principle, over which there was disagreement between the Italian and British delegates, the Committee finally decided to interpret the wording of the fourth principle to read: "to refrain from taking advantage of conditions in China . . . which would abridge the rights vested to any private company or nation by China. . . ."

At the time the Root principles were formulated, the consensus of world opinion was that Japan had shown a conciliatory attitude that exceeded all expectations and that these four principles should override all existing treaties concerning China.

Views were also expressed that the principles should be treated as principles, and that the questions of China could be truly solved in the future by applying these principles to each practical case. It was inevitable, therefore, that doubts were entertained on the exact interpretation of the Root principles which were incorporated into Article I of the Nine-Power Treaty.

ARTICLE II

The Contracting Powers agree not to enter into any treaty, agreement, arrangement, or understanding, either with one another, or, individually or collectively, with any Power or Powers, which would infringe or impair the Principles stated in Article I.

This Article was based on the Geddes resolution concerning the conclusion of an international agreement relating to

China adopted at the fourteenth session of the Far Eastern Committee on December 8, 1921.

In the third clause of the ten points concerning the general principle of the Far Eastern questions, China suggested that: "the Powers agree not to enter into any treaty or agreement directly related to China with one another without giving prior notice to China or without the participation of China."

In this connection, Ku Wei-chun (Dr. Wellington Koo) of China delivered the following statement when referring to this paragraph at the fourteenth session of the Committee: "China considers that she has a justifiable right to be invited to negotiations on agreements which deal with or are intended to deal with the general affairs of the Far East."

Although treaties might be signed with friendly sentiments towards China, the results of such pacts, such as stipulating the sphere of influence, showed every indication of affecting China politically and economically, even restricting her freedom of action. In these circumstances, China's actions and interests even within her own territory would no doubt be governed by the actions of other countries which could subject to their influence the supreme interests of China.

In rebuttal, Arthur Balfour of Britain declared that although the most important part of Dr. Wellington Koo's speech was devoted to the question of spheres of influence, Great Britain regarded the question as a thing of the past. Since she had discarded the practice, Britain had not the slightest intention of reviving the issue.

Now that the Root resolution, respecting China's sovereignty and territorial and administrative integrity had been adopted, Balfour believed that if the resolution were to be faithfully implemented it would be able to satisfy the proposals made by Dr. Wellington Koo.

In order to avoid confusion in the ensuing debate, the British delegate Sir Auckland Campbell Geddes submitted the following draft resolution to be incorporated as the fifth principle in addition to Root's four principles, namely "The

Contracting Powers agree not to enter into any treaty, agreement, or arrangement, either with one another, or, individually or collectively, with any Power or Powers, which would infringe the principles stated above."

Arthur Balfour in supporting the suggestion stated that the additional clause as proposed by Mr. Geddes was advisable, otherwise a secret agreement could easily exist in violation of the rule that all treaties should be widely publicized.

After Mr. Root had expressed his approval of the Geddes proposition, the Japanese delegate Masanao Hanihara maintained that, although the Japanese Government approved the spirit of the Geddes resolution, it felt that this form of principle was already adequately taken care of in Clause 1 of the Root principles. Its inclusion being superfluous, the Japanese Government desired that it be adopted as a separate resolution from that of the Root principles.

In the subsequent debates, René Viviani of France and Carlo Schanzer of Italy agreed with the Geddes proposal, while Robert L. Borden of Canada spoke in favor of Hanihara's proposition. As the result of the repeated proposals by the Japanese delegate Hanihara to draft the Geddes resolution separately from the Root resolution, the former was finally incorporated into Article II of the Nine-Power Treaty.

ARTICLE III

With a view to applying more effectually the principles of the Open Door or equality of opportunity in China for the trade and industry of all nations, the Contracting Powers, other than China, agree that they will not seek, nor support their respective nationals in seeking—

(**a**) any agreement which might purport to establish in favour of their interests any general superiority of rights with respect to commercial or economic development in any designated region of China;

(**b**) any such monopoly or preference as would deprive the nationals of any other Power of the right of undertaking any legitimate trade or industry in China, or of participating with the Chinese Government, or with any local authority, in any category of public enterprise, or which by reason of its scope, duration or geographical extent is calculated to frustrate the practical application of the principle of equal opportunity.

It is understood that the foregoing stipulations of this Article are not to be so construed as to prohibit the acquisition of such properties or rights as may be necessary to the conduct of a particular commercial, industrial, or financial undertaking or to the encouragement of invention and research.

China undertakes to be guided by the principles stated in the foregoing stipulations of this Article in dealing with applications for economic rights and privileges from Governments and nationals of all foreign countries, whether parties to the present Treaty or not.

This Article III consists of the first and second clauses of the Hughes resolution relating to the question of the Open Door in China which was adopted at the twentieth session of the Far Eastern Committee on January 18, 1922.

The subject of the Open Door came up for discussion time and again after adopting the draft to raise China's import tariff. Charles Hughes of the United States explained the consistent policy of his Government on the issue of the Open Door in China since Secretary of State John Hay first enunciated it and insisted on the abolition of the so-called spheres of influence in China. He then presented a draft resolution to ensure a more effective application of the four Root principles towards China under which the powers would agree not to seek any position of superiority in China.

Arthur Balfour of Britain did not feel that the resolution would offer any special problem as its principle had been widely acknowledged by the powers, but he expressed his doubts whether it could prevent future world disputes. However, the British delegate assured the conference of Britain's wholehearted support for the resolution.

After a brief discussion, Hughes submitted a revised draft of the resolution to the Far Eastern Committee on the following day.

1. With a view to applying more effectually the principles of Open Door or equality of opportunity in China for trade and industry of all nations, the Powers other than China represented at this Conference agree:

(**a**) Not to seek or to support their nationals in seeking any arrangement which might purport to establish in favor of their interest any general superiority of rights with respect to commercial or economic development in any designated region of China.

(**b**) Not to seek or to support their nationals in seeking any such monopoly or preference as would deprive other nationals of the right of undertaking any legitimate trade or industry in China or of participating with the Chinese Government in any category of public enterprise or which by reason of its scope, duration or geographical extent is calculated to frustrate the practical application of the principle of equal opportunity.

It is understood that this Agreement is not to be so construed as to prohibit acquisition of such properties or rights as may be necessary to the conduct of a particular commercial, industrial or financial undertaking or to the encouragement of invention and research.

2. The Chinese Government takes note of the above Agreement and declares its intention of being guided by the same principles in dealing with applications for economic rights and privileges from governments and nationals of all foreign countries whether parties to that Agreement or not.

3. The Powers including China represented at this Conference agree in principle to the establishment in China of a Board of Reference, to which any question arising on the above Agreement and Declaration may be referred for investigation and report.

(A detailed scheme for the constitution of the board shall be framed by the special conference referred to in Article I of the convention on Chinese customs duties.)

A fourth clause proposed that provisions of other agreements might be submitted by the parties concerned to the board of reference for the purpose of endeavoring to arrive at a satisfactory adjustment on equitable terms.

In clarifying the substance of the revised draft of the resolution, Hughes emphasized that his objective was to affirm the meaning of the Open Door principle. Although it was impossible to predict all the contingencies, it should nonetheless be possible to define the principle in more concrete terms. With the aim of settling all kinds of problems as practically as possible, Hughes pointed to the stipulation in the third clause for the establishment of an appropriate board. The object of the board, which would have no power to make decisions, should be investigation and reporting, as provided for in the final clause.

Furthermore, it was explained that no nationals would be placed under restraint by the report of the board of reference. No countries would lose their rights to maintain what they thought beneficial nor would any nationals be threatened with the loss of their rights or what they had acquired. The stipulations could at least have the effect of reducing unnecessary disputes, should they occur, by affording an opportunity to have them generally considered by an appropriate machinery.

After Hughes had faced a volley of questions on his proposition from the various delegates and replied to the French delegate Albert Sarraut on measures for enforcing the decisions of the board of reference, the Japanese delegate Kijuro Shidehara declared that the principles formulated in the resolution were of an entirely different scope from the policy of the Open Door as it had been enunciated in 1899, and that the draft resolution gave, in a certain sense, a new definition of that policy.

As it appeared that the concessions already granted by China would be subject to examination in the light of this new stipulation, he maintained that this new definition should not have any retroactive force and offered an amendment to the fourth clause to that effect. Visibly embarrassed by this proposal, Hughes replied that it was not a new statement, but rather a more precise elaboration of the principle that had long been acknowledged and to which the powers concerned had given their unqualified adherence for twenty years.

It was finally agreed to strike out the fourth clause after the Canadian delegate Robert Borden proposed its elimination from the resolution and the Chinese delegate Shih Chao-chih favored its retention. Finally, the Hughes resolution was adopted without the fourth clause in compliance with Shidehara's support for Borden's proposition along with the delegates of France and Italy.

Thus, Clauses I and II of the Hughes resolution were incorporated in Article III of the Nine-Power Treaty, the backbone of the said Treaty, while Clause III was adopted as a separate resolution after repeated discussions at the thirty-first session of the Far Eastern Committee on February 3, 1922. In this manner, the so-called policy of the Open Door with respect to China received "a more precise, and, at once, more binding international legal status than it had ever possessed previously."

ARTICLE IV

The Contracting Powers agree not to support any agreements by their respective nationals with each other designed to create Spheres of Influence or to provide for the enjoyment of mutually exclusive opportunities in designated parts of Chinese territory.

The resolution concerning "the limitation of any exclusive agreement relating to China among the third nationals" adopted at the twenty-third session of the Far Eastern Committee on January 21, 1922, was incorporated into Article IV of the Nine-Power Treaty.

China's first reaction to Japan was the attempt by the Chinese delegate Wang Chung-hui to place the question of spheres of influence before the Far Eastern Committee on December 12, 1922. The Chinese delegate in his speech referred to the sense of vagueness inherent in the term "spheres of influence," which denoted nothing else than a special status in commerce and other rights and privileges whose origin was ambiguous, to say the least. It was Germany which had first used this term in asserting her rights in Shantung.

China, generally speaking, found the term taking two separate forms. In the first instance, it appeared in treaties between certain nations wherein China was excluded. In the second, reference was made to the spheres of influence in treaties or agreements concluded by third powers with China, e.g., the Sino-Japanese Treaties and Notes of 1915 resulting from the "Twenty-One Demands."

At the same time, China welcomed the views of both Great Britain and the United States opposing the spheres of influence, and hoped that other nations would do likewise, thereby removing misunderstanding on the part of the people of China and the restriction on her sovereignty.

In order to accelerate discussions, Elihu Root urged the Chinese delegation to submit a list of stipulations which China desired to abrogate. Complying with Root's request, Wang Chung-hui on December 14 laid before the Far Eastern Committee a list of so-called "restrictive stipulations," consisting of fourteen treaties and five nonalienation agreements.

On this occasion, he took pains to single out the Sino-Japanese Treaties and Notes of 1915, pointing out that "never before has China experienced such an infringement on her sovereignty as the 'Twenty-one Demands.'" China also claimed that she was forced to sign the Sino-Japanese Treaties and Notes of 1915 under pressure of an ultimatum. Being engaged in World War I, China affixed her seal to these Treaties in the interests of peace in the Far East, he asserted. Accordingly, China desired, in the common interest of the powers as well as of China and in conformity with the principles relating to China already adopted by the Committee, that the said Treaties and Notes be reviewed and annulled.

Assuring the Chinese delegation that Japan would reply after a careful study of the subject, Masanao Hanihara made it clear that Japan could not agree to discuss the question of the validity, revision, or abrogation of the Treaties and Notes of 1915 at the Conference. If it was to be taken up at all, stated the Japanese delegate, it would have to be a matter concerning only Japan and China. The subject was subsequently shelved.

Then, the question of publicizing the treaties and notes relating to China was taken up for discussion at the twenty-third session of the Far Eastern Committee on January 21, 1922, at which the American delegate Root introduced a resolution to the effect that: "in order to eliminate the Chinese Government's anxiety in connection with the treaties and notes relating to China, the contracting Powers agree not only to publicize these treaties and notes, but also not to support any agreements by their respective nationals designed to create spheres of influence or to provide for the enjoyment of exclusive interests in Chinese territory."

In the course of the discussions on the said resolution, Kijuro Shidehara again reminded Root that the gist of the resolution might have been contained in the resolution on the Open Door which had been adopted earlier. However, after the British delegate Charles Balfour had expressed the belief that overlapping would produce no ill effects, the said resolution was unanimously adopted and incorporated into Article IV of the Nine-Power Treaty.

ARTICLE V

China agrees that, throughout the whole of the railways in China, she will not exercise or permit unfair discrimination of any kind. In particular there shall be no discrimination whatever, direct or indirect, in respect of charges or of facilities on the ground of the nationality of passengers or the countries from which or to which they are proceeding, or the origin or ownership of goods or the country from which or to which they are consigned, or the nationality or ownership of the ship or other means of conveying such passengers or goods before or after their transport on the Chinese railways.

The Contracting Powers, other than China, assume a corresponding obligation in respect of any of the aforesaid railways over which they or their nationals are in a position to exercise any control in virtue of any concession, special agreement or otherwise.

The first and second clauses of the Geddes resolution, concerning the standardization of Chinese railway charges adopted at the twenty-first session of the Far Eastern Committee on January 19, 1922, were put in statuary form as Article V of the Nine-Power Treaty.

During the discussion of the question of the Chinese Eastern Railway at the twentieth session of the Far Eastern Committee on January 18, Chairman Hughes had queried if any of the delegates had any intention of presenting a resolution on the Chinese railway charges against which bitter complaints had been made by foreign nationals about the unfair discrimination practiced by the foreign-operated railways in the past ten years.

Assuming that "it is a matter of common interest for the Powers concerned that their nationals should be given parity of treatment in respect of their commerce in relation with the railways in China," Auckland Geddes, the British delegate, presented a resolution on the question of the standardization of Chinese railway charges.

After an exchange of views as to the meaning of certain words and phrases, the resolution, with minor corrections, was unanimously adopted at the twenty-first session of the

Far Eastern Committee on January 19, and later incorporated into Article V of the Nine-Power Treaty at the fifth General Committee meeting on February 1, 1922.

ARTICLE VI

The Contracting Powers, other than China, agree fully to respect China's right as a neutral in time of war to which China is not a party; and China declares that when she is a neutral she will observe the obligations of neutrality.

The eighth clause relating to respect for China's neutrality, contained in China's "ten points" adopted at the thirteenth session of the Far Eastern Committee on December 7, 1921, as well as the principle that China would observe the obligations of neutrality were incorporated into Article VI of the Nine-Power Treaty.

Following a discussion in the Far Eastern Committee of the question of stationing foreign troops in Manchuria, Wang Chung-hui, the Chinese delegate, summarized his country's proposition as follows:

"While the question of respecting China's neutrality is the natural consequence of the Root resolution, warring nations have often violated her neutrality in the past. A striking example was the Russo-Japanese War which was conducted entirely on China's territory, as was the Japanese landing in a neutral zone, 150 miles from Tsingtao, during Japan's military operations against Germany. In order to avoid such outrageous occurrences in the future, China desires to uphold the principles of neutrality."

It was only after prolonged discussions that the Chinese proposition was finally adopted as a reaffirmation of the principles of international law and her observance of neutrality obligations were additionally incorporated into Article VI of the Nine-Power Treaty.

ARTICLE VII

The Contracting Powers agree that, whenever a situation

arises which in the opinion of any one of them involves the application of the stipulations of the present Treaty, and renders desirable discussion of such application, there shall be full and frank communication between the Contracting Powers concerned.

This Article VII was the stipulation based on the American proposition concerning the action which would be taken whenever any dispute arose involving the application of the stipulations of the Nine-Power Treaty.

ARTICLE VIII

Powers not signatory to the present Treaty, which have Governments recognized by the Signatory Powers and which have treaty relations with China, shall be invited to adhere to the present Treaty. To this end the Government of the United States will make the necessary communications to non-signatory Powers and will inform the Contracting Powers of the replies received. Adherence by any Powers shall become effective on receipt of notice thereof by the Government of the United States.

ARTICLE IX

The present Treaty shall be ratified by the Contracting Powers in accordance with their respective constitutional methods and shall take effect on the date of the deposit of all the ratifications, which shall take place at Washington as soon as possible. The Government of the United States shall transit to the other Contracting Powers a certified copy of the procès-verbal of the deposit of ratifications.

The present Treaty, of which the French and English texts are both authentic, shall remain deposited in the archives of the Government of the United States, and duly certified copies thereof shall be transmitted by that Government to the other Contracting Powers.

Article VIII, stipulating the procedure of adherence by

any power to the Nine-Power Treaty, and Article IX, relating to ratifications of the said Treaty, were both unanimously adopted.

From the analytical explanations of each of the Articles of the Nine-Power Treaty, it is abundantly clear that the backbone of the Treaty was Article I and Article IV upholding the Open Door principle. The Japanese Government, as a matter of principle, wholeheartedly endorsed the spirit of these articles as being in line with Japan's fundamental policy of respecting the principles of Open Door and equal opportunity in all parts of China.

The so-called Open Door policy in China was historically proclaimed by John Hay, the United States Secretary of State, in 1899. When the original pronouncement of this policy was made, American representatives were directed to obtain from the Governments of the powers concerned a formal assurance on the following three points, namely, noninterference with equitable administration of the Chinese treaty tariff, nondiscrimination in railway charges, and nondiscrimination in harbor dues—all within the "spheres of influence" claimed by the powers in China.

Until the policy was reaffirmed at the Washington Conference, the powers had observed the Open Door as it related to China. At the same time, the United States which had originally pronounced this policy did not wish to have it construed in a narrow sense, as revealed in the diplomatic negotiations between Japan, the United States, and Russia on the question of Manchuria before hostilities had broken out. Since its proposition for the neutralization of the railways in Manchuria in 1907, the United States had consistently endeavored, in the name of the Open Door, to eliminate spheres of influence and special interests.

However, the Nine-Power Treaty provided the legal basis for declaring that the Open Door policy was opposed to spheres of influence and special interests. By affixing their signatures to the document, the powers had for the first time officially agreed to bind themselves to the principles of the Open Door, principles which they were now honor-bound to respect under international law.

By signing the Nine-Power Treaty, China did not gain any specific interest due to the fact that the Open Door was only "an effective measure not only for the powers themselves, but also for their nationals to protect their interests in China." The advent of the Treaty removed fears that certain powers would monopolize China's economy or damage the interests of other powers. Furthermore, China's sovereignty and her territorial and administrative integrity were assured.

On the other hand, since China was a disunited country there was always the danger that her sovereignty might be infringed, or that the interests of other powers might be exposed to danger. This situation existed alongside the principle of the Open Door in China even after the signing of the Nine-Power Treaty.

The Treaty no doubt restricted the actions of the various powers, but it did not appear to have much effect on the disturbed local conditions and disunity on the Chinese mainland.

CHAPTER **18**

New Relationship under the
Soviet-Japanese Treaty
1921 - 1925

~~~~~~

1

IT is problematical whether or not the basic treaty and the annexed protocols relating to the restoration of diplomatic relations between Japan and the Soviet Union, signed at Peking in January, 1925, can be included in the scope of the Japanese treaty negotiations. However, it is undeniable that the Soviet-Japanese Treaty not only contributed to the settlement of pending questions, but also bore an important political significance.

Commenting on the Soviet-Japanese Treaty, the Soviet Foreign Minister G. V. Chicherin remarked: "It is a manifestation of Japan's desire to escape from the dominating policy of the Entente Powers." Although it was ironical that the Treaty was not an alliance in a statutory form, but rather a spiritual alliance, Chicherin declared, "as for the effect of this treaty, it will no doubt be strongly reflected in all aspects of international relations."

Moreover, on the occasion of the signing of the Soviet-Japanese Treaty, Chicherin, in a review of the past, present, and future relations between Japan and his country, said: "While eagerly waiting for the good news that the Soviet-Japanese Treaty would be signed, I read the memoirs of the late Count Hayashi, former Japanese Ambassador to London.

His memoirs vividly relate Japan's efforts to initiate negotiations with Tsarist Russia during the tenure of the foreign ministry of both Lobanoff and Muraviev. On the other hand, the Japanese Government adopted an aggressive attitude towards the Soviet regime during the early days of the Russian revolution. Nevertheless, the warm and friendly welcome extended to Mr. R. R. Joffe, the Soviet representative to the Tokyo Conference, by the people of Japan was an eloquent testimony of the importance which they attached to the friendly relations between Japan and the Soviet Union, representing at the same time a most auspicious beginning for the signing of the Soviet-Japanese Treaty."

Welcoming the conclusion of the Treaty, Baron Shimpei Goto, then Mayor of Tokyo, who had invited R. R. Joffe to Tokyo, emphasized that the Treaty had not only contributed towards the solution of pending questions, but was also of great international political significance. Mayor Goto in his address said:

"The restoration of Soviet-Japanese relations has brought the first ray of hope for the settlement to some extent of the thorny questions that had hitherto plagued the relations between the two countries. Consequently, should the peoples of Japan and the Soviet Union deepen their friendly relations, they will advance the welfare of the peoples of the two countries and demonstrate the righteousness of the coexistence of the races in Europe and Asia, permitting Japan to establish a Pacific policy and elevating the position of the Soviet Union in a world based on peace in the Far East.

"However, we should not overlook the fact that the restoration of Soviet-Japanese relations is bound to gravely affect Anglo-American policy towards the Soviet Union, Japan and China. For one thing, the quadruple relations between Japan, the Soviet Union, the United States and China will become more complicated and delicate.

"While Japan has succeeded in establishing an advantageous footing in the world arena, I feel that she must be increasingly vigilant in her policy towards China and other major international issues. It is my intense desire that Premier Kato or whosoever shall hold the office of Japanese premier in the future will not fail to pay due consideration to this delicate trend of international relations."

A careful examination of the treaty documents relating to the restoration of Soviet-Japanese relations will reveal that the Treaty can be construed neither as an alliance nor an agreement in the strict sense of the word. They broadly stipulated a modus vivendi, paving the way to solutions of long outstanding questions between the two countries, i.e., in particular, the question of mutual recognition and matters relating to North Sakhalin.

In making a further study of the Japanese treaty negotiations, it may be helpful if reference is made here to the Soviet-Japanese Treaty and the annexed protocols which had a profound effect on the political situation not only of the Far East but also of the world, as has been earlier stressed by both Baron Goto and Mr. Chicherin.

2

NOTHING can better illustrate Japan's political philosophy and her practical strategy in foreign affairs than her diplomatic maneuvers vis-à-vis Russia between 1921 and 1925. In order to restore diplomatic relations between Japan and the Soviet Union, severed since 1917, Japan never tired in her persistent negotiations over a period of five years, conferring variously in Dairen, Changchun, Tokyo, and Peking. These negotiations may have established a kind of a diplomatic record, not only from the point of view of time but in the number of different negotiators appointed to attend the talks. This fact alone amply demonstrates the serious and difficult nature of the negotiations.

The first Soviet-Japanese Conference was held in Dairen

on August 26, 1921. Earlier in the fall of 1920, as a result of an agreement between political parties representing various districts of Eastern Siberia, the Far Eastern Republic was established with its capital in Chita, Siberia. Its independence was recognized by the Soviet Union in February, 1921.

The Far Eastern Republic on more than one occasion approached the Japanese Government with the proposal to open up diplomatic and commercial ties. Japan was, however, uncompromisingly opposed to the Bolshevik regime until the spring of 1921 when public opinion began to soften its views, favoring the evacuation of Japanese troops from Siberia and reopening of diplomatic relations with the Russians.

Faced with these circumstances, the Japanese Government formulated at a Cabinet meeting a general policy to be followed in the negotiations with the Soviet Union. At the opening talks in Dairen, Japan was represented by Hajime Matsushima, Consul-General at Vladivostok, and the Chita Government by its Minister for Foreign Affairs, Mr. Yourin. These talks were also attended by an unofficial observer from Moscow.

At the outset, Mr. Yourin presented twenty-nine terms as the basis for concluding the Soviet-Japanese Treaty, proposing that the questions of commercial relations and the evacuation of Japanese troops be discussed simultaneously. Insisting that the question of Japanese evacuation should not be a subject of discussion, Matsushima submitted seventeen amended terms to Yourin. The principal demands approved by the Japanese Cabinet were as follows:

1. The Far Eastern Republic should at least refrain from imposing the Communist system on Japanese nationals;

2. Communist propaganda should not be carried out;

3. Military installations built by Tsarist Russia which were considered a threat should be dismantled;

4. The principle of equal opportunity for the commerce and industry of all nations in Siberia should be observed.

Motivated by a desire to come to an early settlement, the

Japanese Government accepted Russia's double formula relating to commercial and military agreements and agreed to the establishment of a committee with the Soviet Union participating to revise the fishery agreement.

Furthermore, Japan accepted Russia's demand to open negotiations for the settlement of the Nikolaievsk Affair as soon as the basic agreement was concluded. Japan also decided to withdraw her troops from North Sakhalin upon the settlement of the Nikolaievsk Affair, and had no intention of violating Russian sovereignty and territorial integrity to reach an acceptable solution.

As the negotiations began to drag on, progress appeared negligible. Suddenly on April 8, 1922, Yourin was replaced by Petrov who abruptly requested that Japan announce a definite date for withdrawing her troops and allowing the troops of the Chita regime to enter Vladivostok.

Adopting a conciliatory attitude, Japan agreed to comply with the first demand by announcing that the Japanese troops would be completely withdrawn within three months, but she could not acquiesce to the second demand. Dissatisfied with Japan's concessions, Petrov declared that he would return to Chita as it would be futile to continue negotiations. Thus, on April 16, 1922 the conference broke up without having reached any decision.

3

AFTER the abortive Dairen Conference, the Soviet Union, through Antonoff, a Darita correspondent in Peking, communicated in the middle of June its wish to resume negotiations with Japan.

The chief cause for the failure of the Dairen Conference has been attributed to Russian suspicions about Japan's intention to withdraw her troops from Siberia. To remove such suspicions, the Japanese Government on July 1 issued a statement which it transmitted to the Chita Government on July 19, declaring its decision to evacuate all Japanese troops from the Maritime Province, including Nikolaievsk in Siberia, by November 1. Japan having agreed to the reopening of the negotiations, the Changchun Conference was convened on September 4.

At the resumed conference, Japan was represented by Tsuneo Matsudaira, Director of the European and American Affairs Bureau, the Soviet Union by R. R. Joffe, and Chita by Yanson. Before the conference got underway, a dispute arose over the status of Joffe. It had been Japan's understanding that the conference was to be confined to Japan and the Chita regime, who would discuss questions of the Far East as proposed at the Dairen Conference. Soviet participation would be invited only on such broad issues as fisheries and navigation as well as the Nikolaievsk Affair.

Giving a lead to Yanson, Joffe attempted to steer the conference to matters which concerned the whole of Russia, including recognition of the Soviet Union, and even opposed any discussion of basic understanding touched upon at the Dairen Conference.

Thus, as the Conference progressed, the gap between the Japanese and Russian attitudes became wider, finally reaching an impasse when Russia insisted on separately discussing the Nikolaievsk Affair and the evacuation of North Sakhalin —a position which Matsudaira rightfully rejected, maintaining that the two questions were inseparable. With neither side willing to compromise, the conference was adjourned on September 26, 1922.

4

HAVING failed to achieve any success at the Changchun Conference, R. R. Joffe began laying the groundwork for negotiating a Sino-Soviet Treaty of Friendship in Peking. Anxious to restore diplomatic relations between Japan and the Soviet Union, Shimpei Goto, the Mayor of Tokyo, sought and obtained approval from Prime Minister Tomosaburo Kato to invite Joffe to Tokyo. Accepting the official invitation after seeing Dr. Sun Yat-sen in Shanghai, Joffe arrived in Atami, Japan, on January 29, 1923, ostensibly to receive medical attention.

On September 27, Japan honored her evacuation pledge by pulling out her troops from Nikolaievsk. When the Japanese forces evacuated the Maritime Province of Siberia on October 25, the troops of the Far Eastern Republic entered Vladivostok. In the wake of the major shift in the Far Eastern political situation, the Chita Government was dissolved. Its request to be amalgamated into the Soviet Union on November 14 was approved the next day, giving Moscow direct administrative control over the entire region of Siberia with the exception of North Sakhalin.

The conversations which Joffe had with the Japanese authorities from February 1 to April 24 were unofficial and unbinding. However, on the last day of the conversations, Goto informed Joffe that the Japanese Government had decided on April 20 that it would be prepared to hold the third Soviet-Japanese Conference if the two parties could reach a preliminary agreement on the following two questions:

1. The Nikolaievsk massacre.

2. Sakhalin.

On the latter issue, the Japanese Government intimated its desire to solve the Sakhalin question through its purchase of North Sakhalin. Countering these demands, Joffe put forward his own preliminary conditions:

1. Equality in negotiations.

2. Fixing of date of evacuation of North Sakhalin.

3. De jure recognition.

To further clarify Japan's position, Viscount Goto wrote to Joffe on May 6, explaining that his Government desired Russia to confirm the validity of her old debts to Japan, to pay reparations for Japanese losses sustained during the Russian Revolution, and to honor all former treaties.

In reply, Joffe informed the Japanese Government by letter on May 10 that the Soviet Government categorically refused to recognize old debts or old treaties, but deeply regretted the unfortunate incidents in Nikolaievsk. While recognizing its material responsibility over the affair, the Soviet Government felt that Japan should express the same sentiments over similar incidents which had occurred in Russia.

On the question of Sakhalin, Joffe made it clear that since Russia had no intention of relinquishing the island except for a very high price, he would suggest the formation of joint Russo-Japanese enterprises to exploit the oil, coal, and forests of North Sakhalin. Finally, he reiterated Russia's demand that Japan evacuate the upper half of Sakhalin Island.

Convinced that unofficial negotiations by unofficial persons had reached their limits, Japan suggested that the officials of the two countries should continue talks at an unofficial level. Consequently, Joffe and Toshihiko Kawakami, Japanese Minister to Poland, received their accreditations from the respective governments to open the so-called First Tokyo Conference, held in a Japanese restaurant named Tsukiji Seiyoken, Tsukiji, Tokyo, on June 28, 1923.

The Kawakami-Joffe conversations which were held on twelve separate occasions covered all pending fundamental issues, particularly the questions of North Sakhalin and the Nikolaievsk Affair.

To Japan's proposal to purchase the Russian half of Sakhalin Island for 150,000,000 yen, Russia demanded 1,000,-000,000 gold rubles, later arbitrarily raised to 1,500,000,-000 gold rubles. Then Japan proposed that she be granted a 55 to 99 year lease to exploit the Island's oil, coal, and lumber, but Joffe refused to be drawn into making any definite commitment.

Responding to Japan's insistence that Russia apologize and pay indemnity for the settlement of the Nikolaievsk Affair,

Joffe termed as totally unacceptable any solution of the Niko-laievsk Affair which attempted to use the military occupation of Sakhalin as a bargaining condition. If such an attempt were made, Joffe warned, he would immediately withdraw from the negotiations.

The Japanese delegate then announced his country's read-iness to settle the Nikolaievsk claims in a manner agreeable to Russia, but requested an early settlement of the problem of North Sakhalin. With disagreements outweighing agree-ments at the Conference, Joffe announced in the session of July 31 that he had been instructed by his Government to discontinue the discussions. So ended another unsuccessful round of Soviet-Japanese talks.

5

As soon as he arrived in Peking early in September, 1923, Karakhan, the Far Eastern representative of the Soviet Union, took the initiative in approaching Minister Yoshizawa to resume the Russo-Japanese official conversations as an exten-sion of the unofficial negotiations held by Kawakami and Joffe. But the Yamamoto Cabinet, preoccupied with the task of reconstruction and rehabilitation in the wake of the dev-astating earthquake in Tokyo in September, 1923, could not give any definite reply to Karakhan. Views were also split within the Cabinet on how these negotiations should be conducted.

Soon after the Kiyoura Cabinet was inaugurated in Jan-uary, 1924, the anti-Japanese immigration law was enacted in Washington in April. With the international position of the Soviet Union improving, the view began to gather strength in the Japanese Government that further delays in negotia-tions would only harm Japan's bargaining position.

The Japanese Government, therefore, decided to reopen official negotiations with the Soviet Union. Following the exchange of credentials between the Japanese and Soviet delegations, the Peking Conference was formally opened on May 14, 1924.

However, a political crisis in Japan caused the downfall of the short-lived Kiyoura Cabinet and the subsequent formation of the Kato Cabinet on June 9, bringing Baron Kijuro Shidehara to the helm of the Foreign Office. In the meantime, the Sino-Soviet agreement had been concluded in March and Great Britain had officially recognized the regime in Moscow.

Minister Yoshizawa was immediately recalled to Tokyo for an important conference at which the Kato Cabinet defined its new Soviet policy based on Baron Shidehara's general policy of conciliation. As a matter of general principle, the conferees decided to continue the conversations in Peking and to reach a Soviet-Japanese agreement by offering reasonable solutions to pending questions.

Specifically, the Japanese proposals at the Peking Conference were to include the following basic issues: the restoration of Soviet-Japanese relations; Japanese interests in North Sakhalin and evacuation of Japanese troops; apology for the Nikolaievsk Affair; banning of Soviet propaganda activities; recognition of all old treaties and old debts; most-favored nation treatment in commerce; and the restoration of the Japanese Legation.

Nevertheless, North Sakhalin proved to be the most troublesome issue. Although the Japanese Government required Russian apology for the sake of national prestige and for justifying its occupation of Sakhalin as a retaliation for the so-called Nikolaievsk Massacre, a massacre which had taken place before the Red Army had advanced into the region, Moscow was willing to tender an apology because it attached little importance to formalities such as "national honor" and desired an early establishment of normal relations with Japan.

Little interest was shown in the discussions on old debts. Both Japan and Soviet Russia appeared to attach only minor importance to this question. Japan's demand for the recognition of old debts did not prove to be a stumbling block to the negotiations. Although Moscow generally rejected this demand, it did consent with some reservations to recognize the Portsmouth Treaty. In a conciliatory mood, Japan no longer even insisted on an official apology for the Nikolaievsk Affair. This left North Sakhalin as the only real issue.

Before agreement was finally reached, after many months of drawn-out negotiations, the officials of the two sides had met on sixty-one occasions, or a total of seventy-seven times if the preliminary discussions between Minister Yoshizawa and Karakhan are included. The Soviet-Japanese Treaty and its annexed protocols were signed on January 20, 1925. Throughout the parleys, Minister Yoshizawa's patience and prudence were beyond all praise, but Japanese diplomacy glaringly exhibited its drawbacks of indecision and instability.

While negotiations were proceeding, Karakhan aired his thoughts in a letter to Dr. Sun Yat-sen, saying: "Japan is showing irresoluteness and is wavering. On the one hand, she will not back down on her claims, but on the other she is afraid to show resoluteness, knowing that in such an event the negotiations will be terminated. Thus, they prefer to procrastinate, to put off the moment of decision as long as possible. Yet this is a short-sighted policy as time is on our side, not the Japanese."

6

THE Soviet-Japanese Treaty and the annexed protocols signed at Peking between Yoshizawa and Karakhan on January 20, 1925, were ratified by the Japanese Government, on the advice of the Privy Council, on February 25 and promulgated on February 26. They were also ratified by the Soviet Government on February 20, and both Governments exchanged instruments of ratification on April 25 in Peking.

The Treaty consisted of a convention, two protocols, and various notes and declarations. According to the First Article of the convention, there was to be mutual de jure recognition and exchange of diplomatic and consular representatives. Under the Second Article, previous treaties and agreements between Russia and Japan, prior to 1917, were to be revised or canceled at a future conference, except the Treaty of Portsmouth of 1905. The Third Article said the Fishery Convention of 1907 was to be revised, and in the meantime the temporary procedure in regard to fishery bases established in 1924 was to be maintained.

It might be relevant here to refer briefly to the revision of the Fishery Convention of 1907. Japanese fishing right in the northern waters was recognized by Russia for the first time in the Treaty of 1875 concerning the exchange of Sakhalin and the Kurile Islands between Japan and Russia. Ever since, Japanese fishing activities in that part of the world grew with the years.

Under the first Russo-Japanese Fishery Convention of July 27, 1907, the conclusion of which was paved by the Portsmouth Treaty, Russia agreed to grant to Japanese subjects "the right to capture, gather, and manufacture marine products along the Russian coast facing the Japan Sea, the Okhotsk Sea, and the Bering Sea." The Convention was to have been in force for twelve years, but in 1919 the Russo-Japanese diplomatic relations were severed as a result of the 1917 Bolshevik Revolution and the question of the revision of the Convention was held in abeyance. Then followed Japan's ill-fated Siberian expedition which further delayed formal recognition of Soviet Russia.

The conclusion of the 1925 Treaty meant the recognition of the Soviet Union, and the two Governments agreed to revise the 1907 Convention, "taking into consideration such changes as may have taken place in the general conditions since the conclusion of the said Fishery Convention" and, pending the revision, the Soviet Union agreed "to maintain the practices established in 1924 relating to the lease of fishery lots to Japanese subjects."

The task of revising the 1907 Convention was officially started in December, 1925, and required over two years of protracted negotiations before the final accord was reached. Japan was guided in her negotiations by her desire to remedy all inconveniences and disadvantages borne by Japanese enterprises, to clarify and amend vague regulations, and to revise regulations which were made void by the changed conditions, especially by the improvement in fishery devices. The negotiations were closed at Moscow by the signing of a new Fishery Convention on January 23, 1928, and by its ratification in May in Tokyo.

The Fourth Article stated that a treaty of commerce was to be concluded on a most-favored-nation basis. Meanwhile, certain general rules regarding individual liberty of residence and travel, protection of life and property, and free, unhampered, and unrestricted permission to trade were accepted as binding on both parties.

The Fifth Article exchanged a mutual pledge for restraining all persons in official capacity and all organizations receiving Government financial assistance from engaging in any propaganda likely "to endanger the order and security" of either country. The Sixth Article stated that the Soviet Government, realizing "the needs of Japan with regard to natural resources," agreed to grant to Japanese subjects and corporations concessions for the exploitation of minerals, forests, and other natural resources in all the territories of the Union of Soviet Socialist Republics. The Seventh Article provided for the exchange of ratifications at Peking.

Protocol A consisted of five articles, of which the First Article related to the return of Embassies and Consulates. Article II left all debts due to the Government or subjects of Japan by the former Russian Government to be adjusted by subsequent negotiations, with a proviso that in this adjustment the Government and subjects of Japan should not, other things being equal, be placed in any position less favorable than that of the Government and nationals of any country. Article III provided for the withdrawal of all Japanese troops from North Sakhalin by May 15, 1925, and for the full restoration of the evacuated territories to the Soviet Government. In Article IV both parties declared that there existed no treaty or agreement of military alliance or any other secret agreement constituting an infringement upon or menace to the sovereignty, territorial rights, or national safety of either. This stipulation had very important significance politically. Article V provided that the protocol should be considered as ratified on ratification of the convention.

Protocol B consisted of provisions regarding oil and coal concessions in North Sakhalin. In other words, Protocol B was to be a basis of an agreement on concessions to be concluded within five months from the date of complete evacuation of all Japanese troops from North Sakhalin according to the stipulation of Article III of Protocol A. The period of oil and coal concessions was fixed at forty to fifty years. Royalties were to be payable to the Soviet Government at the rate of 5 to 8 per cent on coal, and 5 to 15 per cent on oil; in the case of a gusher the royalty might be raised to 45 per cent.

Other documents consisted of a declaration by Karakhan that the recognition of the Treaty of Portsmouth did not imply that the Government of the Soviet Union shared with the former Tsarist Government the political responsibility for its conclusion; an exchange of notes making interim arrangements for the continued working of coal and oil fields by Japanese in North Sakhalin; and a note of apology by Karakhan for the Nikolaievsk incident of 1920.

In accordance with the Treaty thus concluded, the evacuation of the Japanese troops from North Sakhalin and the official transfer to the Soviet Union were duly completed on May 15, 1925, as previously arranged, and at the end of June, Tokichi Tanaka, the first Japanese Ambassador to the Soviet

Union, left for Moscow, accompanied by members of the Sakhalin Oil Company, for the purpose of negotiating the details of the concessions. In December, agreements for the concession for forty-five years of coal and oil fields in North Sakhalin to certain firms recommended by the Japanese Government were signed. Thus, there existed a fair chance for political and economic cooperation between Japan and the Soviet Union. The agreement enabled Japan to secure such natural resources as oil, coal, lumber, and marine products from North Sakhalin, East Siberia and its waters which were of vital importance for Japan's defence and industry as well as for the solution of her population problem. Notwithstanding, the solid results of the Treaty did not prove very satisfactory to Japan—the anticipated expansion in trade failed to materialize.

7

SOVIET publicists endeavored to represent this Treaty as a treaty of alliance between Japan and the Soviet Union, since both countries were internationally isolated at the time of the conclusion of the pact. In Japan, Baron Shidehara, the Foreign Minister, took great pains to clarify Japanese views on the Treaty, stating before the Diet on January 22, 1925, that "it was simply clearing the ground preparatory to the resumption of diplomatic relations between the two nations which shared many common interests.

"If all pending questions were not settled before the re-establishment of diplomatic relations, embarrassing friction would immediately result and would compromise the future relations of the two countries. Nothing has been further from our minds than the idea of bargaining for the recognition of the Soviet in exchange for coal and oil concessions. We have simply tried to foresee and eliminate sources of future differences."

It should be noted that on February 9, 1925, the Chinese Government protested against Article II of the Soviet-Japanese Treaty which, by recognizing the Treaty of Portsmouth, endorsed several matters prejudicial to the territorial sovereignty, rights, and interests of China (i.e. the provisions relating to Kwantung in South Manchuria), and which was also diametrically opposed to Article IV of the Sino-Soviet Treaty of May 31, 1924. In the light of these circumstances, it is presumptuous to assume that the Soviet-Japanese Treaty presented an answer to the quest for a "modus vivendi." The Treaty itself, however, was of deep significance in the realm of Far Eastern politics.

PART II
Historical Survey

CHAPTER 19

Aftermath of the Sino-Japanese War
1895-1898

~~~~~~

1

HAVING amply demonstrated her military prowess in the Sino-Japanese War, Japan quickly won recognition as one of the major countries of the world. Consequently, Japan's continental policies may safely be said to have sprouted in the mid-1890's.

Prior to Japan's ascendancy, Great Britain, in order to defend her sprawling interests in India and the Far East, maneuvered to conclude an alliance with China to offset Russia and France. Britain also envisaged in the years before the outbreak of the Sino-Japanese War a triple alliance of Britain, Japan, and China, but Japan's adherence was regarded as secondary.

While China revealed her frailty, contrary to general expectations, Japan surprised the world by scoring a decisive victory over her giant neighbor and, at the same time, upset the power position in the Far East. Even during the progress of the war, Great Britain began to show signs of desiring closer relations with Japan at the sacrifice of China.

The *Times* of London frankly admitted that Japan's military successes deserved honorable recognition and that there was every reason to regard Japan as an important power in the Far East. The paper, moreover, declared that all Englishmen worthy of the name should not entertain the slightest feeling of petty jealousy towards the rising island nation with which Britain had so much in common and with whose people Britons would, sooner or later, have to come into close relationship.

The *Pall Mall Gazette* went so far as to state that formerly the British had guided the Japanese, but the time had now come when Japan would give a lead to Great Britain. On the European Continent, a French newspaper remarked "a house garlanded with flowers and trees attracts a crowd of people. Japan has won a greater victory in Europe than in the battles of the Sino-Japanese War. The nation is now able to rely on her own strength and steer an independent course in the days ahead."

The progress of the Sino-Japanese War was decisively tragic for the Celestial Empire in all respects. Foreign military observers in the Far East were astonished by Japan's overwhelming victory. Just as the world had overestimated China's strength in the past twenty years before her dismal defeat, so, too, it had woefully neglected the advances made by Japan.

The Japanese Chargé d'Affaires ad interim in London, Yasuya Uchida, stated during the war that the Japanese people could act in a similar manner as other peoples who could realize their own strength. Even if the objectives were regarded as empty dreams, the European nations should not be afforded the slightest avenue to intervene in the conduct of the Japanese.

Although the above statement was exaggeratedly spoken, it cannot be denied that the result of the Sino-Japanese War was the "upgrading of the fame of one Empire and the downgrading of the reputation of another," as was observed by the British international jurist, Mr. Holland.

The actual state of Japan's foreign policy during the Sino-Japanese War is vividly described in Count Mutsu's reminiscences. The Japanese statesman admits that the Government did nothing to effectively counter the powers' intervention which had already been foreshadowed during the conflict.

Alluding to the same subject, Baron Rosen, the Russian Minister in Tokyo, wrote in his memoirs, *Forty Years of Diplomacy,* that European diplomatic circles regarded the conduct of the Japanese Government in risking a military clash with China without prior consultations with European powers as foolhardy and fraught with grave dangers. He likened Russia's advantageous position as somewhat similar to that of Austria-Hungary when Russia was preparing for war with Turkey in 1877.

The Japanese Government did not begin to adopt countermeasures until the powers had already decided on intervention. Under the terms of the Treaty of Shimonoseki which formally ended the Sino-Japanese War, China was to have ceded the Liaotung Peninsula to Japan, but Russia, France, and Germany demanded that in the interest of peace in East Asia the Liaotung Peninsula should be restored to China. This fatal blow was delivered only six days after the signing of the Treaty of Shimonoseki and just three days after the ratification of the Treaty by Japan.

To cope with the grave situation, an emergency meeting was convened in Hiroshima in the presence of the Emperor, at which it was decided to refer the issue to an international conference. The tentative decision of the Hiroshima Conference was vigorously opposed by Count Mutsu who urged that the question of the Triple Intervention be clearly separated from the question of the Peace Treaty.

Thus, Japan decided to negotiate with flexibility, willing to listen to the views of the three powers but to adhere to a policy of no concession towards China. In view of subsequent events, it was a prudent policy. Had an international conference taken place at the time, it is apparent from diplomatic documents released to date that not only would Russian interests have been ensured in Manchuria, but France would have attempted to secure interests in the direction of Taiwan and the Pescadores.

By failing to place China under treaty obligation not to lease the Liaotung Peninsula which Japan had renounced, the latter committed a grave diplomatic blunder. Notwithstanding, the small island nation of Japan had rightly won her place as an equal among the major powers in the Far East. Although Japan acceded to the Triple Intervention, she was able to exact from her remarkable military victories an indemnity of 230,000,000 taels (30,000,000 of which was in compensation for the restoration of Liaotung); the full independence of Korea; the cession of Formosa and the Pescadores to Japan; commercial and navigational interests, not to mention consular jurisdiction and the most-favored-nation treatment, by the Treaty of Shimonoseki signed on April 17, 1895.

Notable is the fact that Lord Kimberley, the British Minister for Foreign Affairs, had twice remonstrated with Japan on the question of territories. This British stand appears to have strongly influenced Japan's counterplan towards the *Dreibund* as well as her continental policy. The first remonstrance was made on April 23, 1895, when Minister Kato turned to Great Britain for assistance in connection with the Triple Intervention.

In reply, Lord Kimberley emphasized that Great Britain regarded Japan's demand for the dismemberment of China as undesirable. Speaking frankly, the British Foreign Minister urged that both Japan and China shelve the question of territories. Insofar as Liaotung Peninsula was concerned, his Government had no direct interests.

Three days later, when Minister Kato attempted to ascertain British intentions regarding the Triple Intervention, Lord Kimberley informed him that the British Government had decided not to intervene in the affair, feeling that the act of interceding in behalf of Japan would also be regarded as an intervention. Lord Kimberley then went on to strictly warn

Japan of the consequences entailed in the possession of Liao-tung Peninsula.

He felt that future benefits accruing from the possession of Liaotung Peninsula were highly doubtful. Owing to their similar geographical features and their sound national strength, both Japan and Britain had no fear of foreign invasion by sea. By securing a toehold on the Chinese mainland, Japan would be jeopardizing her own national security. Since any attempt to invade Japan would be fraught with countless dangers, Britain could envisage no such possibility. However, any nation possessing a powerful navy could with relative ease isolate Liaotung from Japan. In that event, with the said territory in a state of siege, Lord Kimberley questioned the wisdom of dispossessing China of Liaotung Peninsula.

2

In the aftermath of the Sino-Japanese War, there were increasing indications of the approaching collapse of China and her dismemberment by the European powers. In their book, *Far Eastern International Relations,* Hosea B. Morse and Harley F. McNair described the situation as follows:

"In the war with Japan, China was not merely defeated—she was humbled. Her armies never once scored a victory, but fled from every field of battle, and surrendered one strong position after another. Her fleet, on which many hopes had been based, was driven ignominiously to the shelter of fortified ports. Her commanders showed themselves all incompetent, and many, cowards. Her administration was as inefficient and as corrupt in the hour of the nation's peril as it notoriously was in time of peace; and her people, while they had acquired some sense of nationality, were still an inchoate mass, in which self-interest was the only motive power and blind fury replaced patriotic endeavor. During the war her most energetic efforts were directed, not to defeating the enemy, but to invoking the intervention of foreign powers, which, her rulers hoped, might save her from the results of her own weakness, without the necessity of making any serious efforts to remedy the causes of that weakness.

"It was the duty of foreign powers, and not any part of the duty of China, to save China from aggression and dismemberment. . . . To all experienced observers—experienced in the ways of the West but not in those of the East—it seemed clear that dismemberment was impending and was inevitable."

Of all the powers who laid covetous eyes on China at the close of the Sino-Japanese War, Russia was by far the most aggressive. Taking advantage of the Triple Intervention, Russia quickly acquired the right to construct a railway across North Manchuria to Vladivostok as a reward from China. This Russian advance into Manchuria was a signal for a mad scramble by the Western Powers to seize concessions in the Celestial Empire. The first power to follow the Russian leadership was Germany which acquired the lease of Kiaochow for ninety-nine years.

Having opened the floodgates, Russia compelled China to lease the southern tip of Liaotung Peninsula, including Port Arthur and Talienwan, the very territory which Russia forced Japan to restore to China in the name of peace in the Far East. This lease, consummated in the convention of March 27, 1898, was to run for twenty-five years, and provided also for the extension of the Chinese Eastern Railway from Harbin to Talienwan and Port Arthur. Finally, France, the third party of the *Dreibund,* seeing that naval bases in China could be had for the asking, demanded and received from China the lease of Kwangchow Bay for ninety-nine years.

As soon as Russia leased Port Arthur and Germany acquired Kiaochow, Great Britain, although initially opposed to the partitioning of Chinese territory, felt that she could no longer remain an idle spectator. She not only obtained the lease of Weihaiwei under the treaty of July 1, 1898, but secured from China a solemn undertaking not to cede to any power the nine provinces along the Yangtze Valley. At the same time, Japan, a cautious bystander, was able to secure from China a promise not to cede Fukien Province opposite Formosa to any power.

By these actions, Great Britain and Japan showed their displeasure at the partitioning of China, which appeared impossible to check. They regarded the Chinese assurance as an indemnity against the interests acquired by the other powers. Even the United States was considering the lease of Santuao in Fukien Province.

Japan's foremost concern, however, was Korea rather than China, and she regarded the reaching of an understanding with Russia over Korea as absolutely necessary to avoid an impending Russo-Japanese clash. Therefore, after the Sino-Japanese War, Japan's policy towards the Chinese mainland was based on the Exchange Policy, as it was popularly known in Japan, proposing that if Russia recognized Japan's freedom of action in Korea, Japan in return would regard Manchuria as lying outside of Japanese interest.

This policy of compromising with Russia, it will be remembered, constituted the crux of Marquis Ito's Russian policy in 1898, warmly supported by the leading Russophile diplomats of "Kasumigaseki," including Foreign Minister Nishi. At this juncture, while the theory of joining Great Britain in a common cause to halt the Russian juggernaut found wide support among people outside of Government circles, those inside the Government did not declare their support outwardly. Eventually, the trend of opinion tipped in favor of the group supporting the Anglo-Japanese alliance, but at the beginning it was the Russophiles who formed the main current of opinion in the Japanese Government.

The reason was simple. The pursuance of a successful compromising policy towards Russia was regarded as more feasible than the formation of an Anglo-Japanese alliance. In addition, from the point of view of Japan's security, the former policy was regarded as being more beneficial. In other words, it was forcefully argued that even if Japan did succeed in entering into such an alliance with Great Britain, this very act might endanger Japan's position in the Far East, even to the extent of provoking the Russians into hostilities with Japan—an eventuality for which Japan was ill prepared.

In spite of difficulties, Japan continued perseveringly to negotiate with Russia on the principle of the Exchange Policy, but Russia was not prepared to countenance the loss of Korea. Her intention was to approve only the commercial and economic interests in the southern part of Korea, reserving the interests in the north for herself. In addition, she wanted to place many limitations on Japan's political and military actions in the Korean Peninsula, not to speak of her design to lease Bazampo, an important port in the south. Japan could not tolerate these further indications of Russian subtlety and all her attempts to arrive at a conclusive settlement came to nought.

Hence, whether it was the Waeber-Komura Memorandum, the Yamagata-Lobanoff Protocol, or the Nishi-Rosen Protocol, the two sides failed to touch the heart of the question because of the Russian evasive tactics and lack of sincerity. Deeply disappointed in her failure to conclude a satisfactory agreement with Russia, Japan decided to conclude an alliance with Great Britain.

CHAPTER **20**

Origins of the Russo-Japanese War
1898-1904

~~~~~~

1

GRAPPLING with the grave situation which made Great Britain's traditional foreign policy of "glorious isolation" no longer tenable in the Far East and throughout the world, her statesmen, in 1898, began to seek alliances with other powers. At this juncture, however, Great Britain found herself in a very difficult situation, not unlike that which faced Japan. For over half a century, Great Britain had been successfully maintaining her national prestige in China, developing her vast commercial interests and giving the lead to the policies of the Western powers towards China.

The Triple Intervention and the consequent aggressive policy of Russia towards China were a blow to Britain's prestige and her interests in China, and at the same time indirectly jeopardized the security of India and Britain's far-flung colonial empire. In view of the fact that Britain was incapable of forestalling the tripartite interventionists, Russia, France, and Germany, she found it imperative to adopt a "policy of compensation."

Although Britain did acquire certain interests during the successive grabs staged by the European powers, these acquisitions did not reflect the motivation of her policy towards China. Regarding her interests as chiefly commercial, the

British Government favored the Open Door, and the maintenance of China's independence and territorial integrity. Having failed to block the demands of the powers against China, Britain had no alternative but to adopt the policy of compensation. Ironically, each compensation denoted a failure rather than a success of British diplomacy. It was not only her commercial interests that were gravely endangered, but her prestige in the Far East suffered badly.

The year 1898 marked an important turning point in Russia's Far Eastern policy and for Britain, too, it was a year of decision, a decision to abandon her traditional policy of so-called glorious isolation. In place of this traditional policy, three choices were open to Britain in the Far East; (1) to ally herself with Japan; (2) to ally herself with Germany and win the adherence of either Japan or the United States to the alliance; and (3) to reach a friendly understanding with Russia. It was the third alternative which Britain initially attempted to attain: a satisfactory understanding with Russia.

In the early days of 1898, the British Government secretly negotiated with Russia for the achievement of friendly understanding. In these negotiations, Great Britain made it unmistakably clear that the prerequisite to understanding was not territorial partition, but the partition of preponderance, embracing the principles of respect for existing treaties and noninfringement of territorial sovereignty. Britain suggested that Russian preponderance in China could be a line drawn by the Yellow River Valley and the region to the north, while her own preponderance would be in the area of the Yangtze River Valley.

Disappointed at Russia's negative attitude regarding her proposals for reaching a broad understanding, Britain moved in the direction of concluding the Anglo-German alliance. Talks were opened by Joseph Chamberlain, Secretary of State for the Colonies, with the German Minister in London,

Hatzfeldt, but the talks dragged on to the following year without making any notable headway.

It was during this stage of the negotiations that Anglo-Japanese relations took on a new significance when Joseph Chamberlain drew Japanese Minister Kato's attention to the urgency of Japan entering into negotiations with Great Britain for the realization of an Anglo-Japanese alliance. Minister Kato lost no time in reporting Chamberlain's overture to Count Okuma, Minister of Foreign Affairs, and recommending that negotiations with Britain be held without delay. The Ito Cabinet was unable to come to any decision on the Chamberlain proposal, but Britain in the meantime succeeded in concluding a special partial agreement relating to China with Russia and Germany.

In 1899 an Anglo-Russian Agreement dividing the spheres of railway construction interests was concluded, assigning the area north of the Great Wall to Russia and the Yangtze Valley to Britain. In view of Russia's aggressive conduct during the Boxer Uprising, an Anglo-German Agreement relating to the Yangtze, upholding China's territorial integrity, was signed on October 6, 1900.

In reply to an inquiry whether the principles embodied in the agreement were acceptable to her, Japan expressed her readiness to participate in the Anglo-German Agreement in the same capacity as the contracting parties. It was in accordance with the principles of this Agreement that Germany, acting independently of Japan and Britain, made a protest against the Russian occupation of Manchuria. Shortly thereafter Germany reversed her stand, asserting that Manchuria was outside the sphere of the said Agreement and should not, therefore, come within the purview of the treaty. This change in German attitude was disappointing to both Japan and Great Britain.

Realizing that any fundamental agreement, either general or specific, with Germany and Russia was unattainable,

Great Britain was left with only one alternative, the conclusion of an alliance with Japan. It was with unusual seriousness that Britain embarked upon her policy of allying herself with Japan.

With the dismemberment of China assuming ominous proportions, the United States moves in the Far East became increasingly positive. As soon as John Hay, former Ambassador to London, became Secretary of State on September 30, 1898, he quickly foresaw the danger which American interests were bound to face as a result of the militant policy being pursued by the European powers. To meet this deplorable situation in China, Hay revised United States policy. He was not slow to appreciate the real motive behind the British House of Commons' passage of a resolution supporting the principle of free trade at Chinese treaty ports.

Addressing notes to Great Britain, Germany, and Russia on September 6, 1899, to Japan on November 13, and to Italy and France on November 17 and 21 respectively, John Hay directed American representatives to obtain from the Governments concerned "formal assurance" regarding the principle of equal opportunity for trade in all parts of the Chinese Empire.

Recognizing that the enunciated doctrine was aimed at assuring equal treatment in commerce and navigation of the powers within any leased territory or within any so-called "sphere of interest" they might possess in China, and that it would check to some extent the impending dismemberment of China by Russia, Germany, and France and contribute to China's safety, Foreign Minister Aoki replied that the Japanese Government was willing to accept the United States proposal, providing all powers concerned accepted the same. It should be noted here that the doctrine of China's "territorial and administrative entity," associated with the Open Door doctrine, was evolved independently of the original Open Door proclamation.

Ever since America enunciated the Open Door policy,

Japan and Great Britain have strongly supported this principle. During this period, the United States' interests, insofar as the Far Eastern questions were concerned, were similar to those of Japan and Great Britain, but, owing to the Monroe Doctrine and with due regard to Senate opinion, her Government was unable to negotiate a treaty of alliance with European powers or Japan.

In the spring of 1901, Baron von Eckardstein, Chargé d'Affaires of the German Embassy in London, advocated an Anglo-German-Japanese alliance as a measure to accelerate the negotiations on the Anglo-German alliance. This, in turn, paved the way for the negotiations of an Anglo-Japanese alliance between Hayashi, Japanese Minister in London, and Lord Lansdowne, the British Foreign Minister. Thus, the first Anglo-Japanese Alliance was concluded in January, 1902.

Clearly designed to oppose Russia's ambitions, the Anglo-Japanese Alliance affirmed that Great Britain and Japan were actuated solely by a desire to maintain the status quo and general peace in the Extreme East, to uphold the independence and territorial integrity of the Empire of China and the Empire of Korea, and to secure equal opportunities in those countries for the commerce and industry of all nations. The two powers defined their respective special interests, those of Great Britain relating principally to China while those of Japan related to both China and Korea.

Moreover, in case either Great Britain or Japan, in defence of their respective interests, should become involved in war with another power, the other "will maintain a strict neutrality, and use its efforts to prevent other Powers from joining in hostilities against its ally"; but, should any other power or powers enter the war, the other "will come to its assistance, will conduct war in common, and will make peace in mutual agreement with it." Neither party, without consulting the other, would enter into separate arrangements with other powers to the prejudice of the interests above described.

In the secret note exchanged between Great Britain and

Japan, both nations declared that "at the present moment Great Britain and Japan are each of them maintaining in the Extreme East a naval force superior in strength to that of any third Power."

It was not the intention of the Japanese Government to fight against Russia with the backing of the Anglo-Japanese Alliance. Japan desired only that the Alliance would make Russia compromise in a rational manner on her demands and would facilitate an amicable settlement of the questions of Manchuria and Korea.

Parallel with the negotiations on an Anglo-Japanese alliance, Marquis Ito, a champion of the so-called Exchange Policy affecting Manchuria and Korea, conferred in St. Petersburg on the Korean and other questions with Count Lamsdorff, Minister for Foreign Affairs, and Count Witte, Minister of Finance. He appealed to the Japanese Government to postpone the conclusion of the Anglo-Japanese Alliance until the completion of the Russo-Japanese discussions. While Witte was quite receptive to Marquis Ito's proposals, Lamsdorff offered many amendments, including the imposition of various restrictions on Japan's freedom of action and Japanese recognition of Russia's freedom of action in Manchuria.

Even if the Russo-Japanese negotiations had been successfully concluded on the basis of Marquis Ito's cherished plan, the agreement could hardly have been acceptable to the Katsura Cabinet. The Japanese Government and people were fully aware of the fact that a Russo-Japanese understanding would be impossible without Japan scoring a military victory over Russia.

2

AFTER the conclusion of the Anglo-Japanese Alliance, Japan's pressing need was the adjustment of Russo-Japanese relations.

for the settlement of the questions of Manchuria and Korea. The Cabinet as well as the *genro* went into every aspect of Japan's policy before the opening of the Imperial Conference on June 23, 1903, at which Japan decided to consider Russo-Japanese relations in the light of new developments in the Far East. Minister Kurino in St. Petersburg received his instructions in July to begin direct negotiations with Lamsdorff, the Russian Minister for Foreign Affairs.

The Japanese proposals, presented by Minister Kurino on August 12 to Lamsdorff, consisted of six articles. With the aim of averting future disputes, these articles, comprising the Japanese proposals, attempted to define the special interests of Japan and Russia in regions of the Far East where they came into direct contact.

While Russian interests in Manchuria were extensive, the interests of Japan in Korea were paramount over those of other powers, due mainly to Japan's propinquity to Korea and her special geographical position. Moreover, for reasons of national security, Japan could not consent to surrender those paramount interests and influence to, or share them with, other powers.

Thus, Japan entered into consultations with the Russian Government for the conclusion of a bilateral agreement concerning the question of Manchuria in an effort to replace the latter's unilateral declaration. Once Russia had occupied Manchuria, the independence of Korea, it was felt, would exist in name only. Korean independence, therefore, was indispensable for Japan's safety and closely allied to the question of Manchuria's future. Prior to these negotiations, the course of Japan's fundamental policy towards Russia had already been charted at a meeting attended by two *genro,* Marquis Yamagata and Marquis Ito, and two leading members of the Cabinet, Prime Minister Katsura and Foreign Minister Komura, as follows:

1. In case of Russian failure to evacuate from Manchuria, particularly from Liaotung Peninsula, Japan should seize this opportunity to satisfactorily solve the question of Korea.

2. Korea should not, under any circumstances, transfer any part of her territory to Russia.

3. Japan was prepared to entertain a certain amount of concession in Manchuria.

The points deserving the greatest attention in the Japanese proposals to Russia were, firstly, the Japanese demand for complete control over Korea and, secondly, the agreement that the troops sent for suppressing insurrection or disorder would in no case exceed the actual number required, and would be forthwith recalled as soon as their mission was accomplished.

The express aim of these provisions was to prevent Russian administrative policy from extending over Manchuria and Korea. Although it was now Russia's turn to suggest her basis of negotiations with Japan, she not only neglected the Japanese proposals but made several of her own modifications on the question of Korea. She did not present her counterproposal to Japan until October 3, 1903.

Russia sought to impose on Japan several intolerable conditions regarding Korea, i.e., "not to use any part of the territory of Korea for strategical purposes" and "not to fortify the southern coast which would threaten the free navigation of the Korean Straits," and to consider the territory lying north of the 39th Parallel as a neutral zone into which neither country should introduce troops. In short, the Russian counterproposal excluded the question of respecting Chinese territorial sovereignty and the question of Manchuria from the field of discussion, and demanded that Manchuria and its littoral should be recognized by Japan as in all respects outside her "sphere of interest."

As earlier stated, the Japanese proposals should have been acceptable to any power which desired to maintain justifiable interests in China. But Russia's counterproposal was a conspicuous manifestation of Russian ambition that was inconsistent with Japan's policy, not to speak of the policies of Great Britain and the United States.

There was a complete lack of progress in the continued exchange of views between Japan and Russia. The Russian proposal appeared, in essence, to have no other aim but to diminish Japan's freedom of action in Korea. Having made the maximum possible concession, the Japanese Government was at a loss to understand why Russia was not able to commit herself with a third power on the question of China, while at the same time agreeing to conclude an understanding relating to Korea.

In short, throughout the Russo-Japanese negotiations, Russia displayed no sincerity, nor any desire for compromise or conciliation. Adopting such dilatory tactics as removing the seat of negotiations from St. Petersburg to Tokyo, Russia wilfully chose to delay the talks while augmenting her military and naval preparations in the Far East. It is not surprising, therefore, that the Japanese Government had as early as December, 1903, come to a firm conviction that war with Russia was unavoidable.

CHAPTER **21**

Agreements Resulting from the Russo-Japanese War 1904-1908

1

THERE were several vital rights and interests which the Japanese Government desired to acquire on the Asian continent on the conclusion of the peace treaty with Russia. Anticipating Japanese victories at Liaotung and Port Arthur, they were drawn up in the autumn of 1904, and consisted of:

1. THE QUESTION OF KOREA

Russia should acknowledge that Japan possessed Korea within her paramount influence, and engage not to obstruct or interfere with any measures of protection, guidance, and control which Japan found it necessary to take in Korea.

2. THE QUESTION OF MANCHURIA

In view of Japan's repeated unequivocal statements that she adhered to the principle of equal opportunity in Manchuria and, even in the event of victory, had no intention of territorial gains at the expense of China, both Japan and Russia should restore Manchuria to China as far as circumstances warranted, subject to guarantee of reform and improved administration capable of maintaining peace, order, and adequate protection of life and property.

3. THE LEASE OF KWANTUNG PROVINCE

Russia should transfer to Japan the leased territory in the

Liaotung Peninsula, and all rights and privileges connected thereto.

4. THE QUESTION OF PEACE

While moderation was to keynote Japan's demands even in the event of a sweeping military victory, she should not accept any peace terms which were confined to a temporary suspension of hostilities or prevented the attainment of her primary objective: the establishment of permanent peace.

The foregoing Japanese peace terms were generally approved by Great Britain, Japan's ally, and the United States. On assuming the role of peacemaker, President Roosevelt in January, 1905, expressed his belief that not only did Japan have the right to possess Port Arthur, but also had the right to place Korea under her sphere of influence. As for Manchuria, the American President felt that it should be restored to China and become a neutral zone under the guarantee of powers, a proposal which he had already made in letters to Great Britain, France, and Italy. Although no reply had been received from any of the countries, he did not expect a negative response from Great Britain.

The difference of views between Japan and Great Britain and the United States on the peace terms hinged on the Japanese Government's view that Manchuria should be restored to China, subject to the guarantee of reform and improved administration capable of maintaining peace and order and adequately protecting life and property, and the view of President Roosevelt that the administration of Manchuria should be based on the principle of international neutrality.

In keeping with the traditional American policy of keeping aloof from foreign entanglements, President Roosevelt, while supporting the Japanese view for the restoration of Manchuria to China, strongly felt that an internationally guaranteed neutrality of Manchuria would be in the best interest of the Japanese people.

Japan's reason for opposing the suggested neutrality of

Manchuria was based on the fear that it would invite joint intervention by undesirable powers, thereby seriously restricting Japan's freedom of action in negotiating with Russia at the peace conference. This Japanese stand later won the approval of President Roosevelt who, in March, 1905, gave up his suggestion for the neutralization of Manchuria. However, it cannot be overlooked that this neutrality plan preceded Harriman's plan to purchase the South Manchurian Railway and Knox's neutralization plan for the Manchurian railways.

The most controversial issues facing the peace conference were the amount of indemnity and the transfer of territory. Having subscribed a billion yen for emergency war bonds, the interest of which amounted to almost 100 million yen annually, it was natural that Japan should demand indemnification.

Russian reaction to Japan's demands was not unexpected. Witte accepted certain modifications, but vehemently objected to the cession of Sakhalin. In fact, the Tsar had earlier instructed Witte that the conference be peacefully concluded, but that not a ruble be paid as war indemnity nor an inch of Russian territory be ceded.

There were fears that Russian rejection of the terms would lead to a rupture of the conference and a fresh flare-up in the hostilities. However, progress was quickly made on the outstanding questions related to Japan's position in Manchuria and Korea.

Before attempting to analyze the various questions stipulated in the Portsmouth Treaty, reference should be made to the two major questions—the renewal of the Anglo-Japanese Alliance and the Japanese-American understanding concerning their Far Eastern policies—which emerged between the opening of the Russo-Japanese War and its termination.

Firstly, Japan and Great Britain, mutually desirous that the First Anglo-Japanese Alliance should be extended to strengthen the existing close understanding between them, concluded the Second Anglo-Japanese Alliance in August,

1905, just prior to the ratification of the Portsmouth Treaty. The new agreement, which was defensive as well as offensive, broadened the application of the treaty to extend as far as India.

As compensation, Great Britain now specifically recognized that Japan, possessing paramount political, military, and economic interests in Korea, had the right to take any necessary measures of guidance, control, and protection. Significant was the abandonment of the neutrality clause which animated the first alliance, and the contracting parties agreed that, in case either contracting party was attacked, the other contracting party would come to the assistance of its ally and conduct the war in common, and make peace in mutual agreement.

While the foremost aim of the First Anglo-Japanese Alliance was to forestall Japan from surrendering and to enable her to effectively resist the attacks which Russia might make singly or in concert with her allies, the Second Alliance had the objective of diverting Russia's attention from India and East Asia towards Europe and to create conditions for her cooperation with the allied powers. This scheme was notably successful. Only after this conversion of Russian policy did it become possible to attain Japanese-Russian and Anglo-Russian agreements.

Secondly, Japan and the United States concluded the so-called Taft-Katsura Agreement signed on the occasion of the visit to Tokyo on August 25, 1905, of United States Secretary of War Taft who was accompanied by more than eighty Senators and Congressmen on their way to the Philippines for an inspection tour. The agreement followed a long talk between Secretary Taft and Prime Minister and concurrently acting Foreign Minister Katsura on a wide range of current problems.

An American press report at the time quoted Premier Katsura as having assured Secretary Taft, a private emissary of President Roosevelt, that Japan harbored no aggressive design on the Philippines and regarded the maintenance of general peace in the Extreme East as a cardinal principle of her international policy. To achieve this objective, the Japanese Premier believed that the best, in fact the only, means was for the three Governments of Japan, the United States, and Great Britain to reach a common understanding.

Taft replied that while the United States President had no power to conclude a secret treaty without the approval of the Senate, the Government could, whenever it deemed it necessary for the maintenance of peace in the Extreme East, lend proper cooperation to Japan and Great Britain whose views it shared in this regard. In such circumstances, Taft asserted, the United States would act no differently than if bound by treaty obligations.

With regard to the question of Korea, Premier Katsura observed that, being the direct cause of the war with Russia, it was a matter of absolute importance for Japan to seek a complete solution of the peninsular problem as a logical consequence of the war. If she were left to herself in the postwar period, Korea would revert to her old habit of imprudently entering into agreements or treaties with other powers, thereby reviving the same international complications that existed before the war, explained Premier Katsura.

On hearing the Premier's statements, Taft frankly admitted the justness of Katsura's observations. Expressing his own personal opinion, Taft admitted that it would be a logical outcome of the war for Japan's military forces to establish suzerainty over Korea and that Korea should not enter into any agreement with an external power without Japan's consent as a measure of contributing to the maintenance of permanent peace in the Extreme East.

These privately expressed views, exchanged between Katsura and Taft, were confirmed by cable by President Roosevelt on September 21, 1905. The Taft-Katsura Agreement, though not by any means a treaty of alliance, was described in some quarters as essentially a formation of a Japanese-

Anglo-American Alliance. Nonetheless, due importance should be attached to the understanding as a moral backing by the United States President that the United States would join in a common action with Japan and Great Britain for the preservation of peace in the Extreme East.

The Portsmouth Treaty, terminating the Russo-Japanese War, was signed on September 5, 1905, soon after the two important questions described above were settled. By the terms of the Treaty, Japan succeeded in defining her vital interests in various stipulations relating to Manchuria and Korea.

By virtue of Article II, Russia acknowledged that Japan possessed in Korea paramount political, military, and economic interests and undertook not to obstruct or interfere with any measures of guidance, protection, and control which Japan found it necessary to take in Korea. Both Japan and Russia mutually engaged "to evacuate completely and simultaneously Manchuria except the territory affected by the lease of the Liaotung Peninsula" and "to restore entirely and completely to the exclusive administration of China all portions of Manchuria," and Russia declared that she had in Manchuria "no territorial advantages or preferential or exclusive concessions or franchises in impairment of Chinese sovereignty or inconsistent with the principle of equal opportunity." This latter declaration, however, was not observed despite the fact that Japan, prior to the Russo-Japanese War, was most eager to see it materialized. Together with Great Britain and the United States, Japan attached great importance to this obligation from the standpoint of her own security.

Japan and Russia agreed in Article IV not to obstruct any general measures, commonly affecting all countries, which China might take for the development of commerce and industries in Manchuria. This stipulation, as another form of expressing the principle of Open Door, was highly significant. Under Article V, Russia pledged to transfer and assign to Japan, subject to the consent of the Chinese Government, the lease of Port Arthur, Talien, and adjacent territory and territorial waters and all rights, privileges, and concessions connected with or forming part of such lease, together with all public works and properties.

Moreover, Russia engaged in Article VI to assign and transfer to Japan, without compensation and subject to the consent of the Chinese Government, the portion of the railway south of Changchun and all its branches together with all rights, privileges, and properties appertaining to it in that region, as well as all coal mines in that region belonging to or worked for the benefit of that railway.

In formulating this article, Japan initially demanded the entire section of the railway south of Harbin, but had to be satisfied with the portion of the railway south of Changchun under actual occupation by Japanese troops. Under Article VIII, Japan and Russia mutually concurred to operate their respective railway lines in Manchuria exclusively for commercial and industrial purposes and in no wise for strategic purposes. Japan and Russia also pledged, with a view to promoting and facilitating intercourse and traffic, to conclude a separate convention for the regulation of their connecting railway services in Manchuria.

During the construction of the Chinese Eastern Railway, Russia posted railway guards for the protection of her railway lines against attacks by lawless elements. Even in the absence of treaty stipulations on railway guards between Russia and China, Russia had, after the Boxer Uprising, been expanding her special rights, substantially reinforcing the number of guards for the occupation of Manchuria.

Under Article I of the Additional Agreement of the Portsmouth Treaty, Japan and Russia retained the right to maintain railway guards for due protection of their respective Manchurian railway lines. The two Governments, however, reciprocally engaged that the guards to be so maintained should not in any case exceed five for each kilometer of railway.

By the Additional Agreement Japan secured certain additional rights which strengthened her special position in Manchuria. Among them may be mentioned the opening of sixteen new cities and towns for "international residence and trade," the reconstruction of the military railway between Mukden and Antung, and the organization of a Sino-Japanese joint stock company for the purpose of developing the lumber interests along the Yalu River.

Article II of that historic document dealt with the question of the withdrawal of Japanese troops and railway guards, in which Japan consented "to take similar steps" with Russia "in the event of Russia agreeing to the withdrawal of her railway guards or in case other proper measures are agreed to between China and Russia," with, however, a now-famous proviso: "When tranquillity shall have been re-established in Manchuria and China shall have become herself capable of affording full protection to the lives and property of foreigners, Japan will withdraw her railway guards simultaneously with Russia."

This provision later became the basis of the Japanese right to continue to maintain railway guards in Manchuria. It should be remembered that the Evacuation Protocol of October 30, 1905, authorized the employment by Japan of railway guards in Manchuria, the number being fixed at fifteen per kilometer "on the average."

With the conclusion of the Portsmouth Treaty, the Russo-Japanese War passed into the pages of history as an event which propelled and magnified the presence of Japan on the Asiatic Continent. By expelling Russian power in Korea and South Manchuria and by taking over the lease of Kwantung Province from Russia, Japan acquired the basis of prosperity for her special interests in Korea and Manchuria.

However, the transfer of the Russian leases of Kwantung Province and the Manchurian Railway was subject to China's consent. Immediately after the Portsmouth Conference, therefore, the Japanese Government took steps to initiate negotiations with China. At the Sino-Japanese Conference opened at Peking on November 17, 1905, Foreign Minister Komura, assisted by Minister Yasuya Uchida, then at the Court of Peking, headed the Japanese delegation, while Prince Ching and Yuan Shih-kai represented the Celestial Empire. After twenty sessions, the Sino-Japanese Treaty—the so-called Peking Treaty—was agreed upon on December 18 and signed December 22.

By agreeing to the Peking Treaty, China approved the Russo-Japanese transactions contained in the Portsmouth Treaty. In the Protocol attached to the Treaty, China affixed her signature upon this important agreement which, however, contained the seeds of future Sino-Japanese difficulties over their respective railway policies in Manchuria. "The Chinese Government engage, for the purpose of protecting the interests of the South Manchuria Railway," read the celebrated Protocol, "not to construct, prior to the recovery by them of the said railway, any branch line in the neighborhood of and parallel to that railway, or any branch line which would be prejudicial to the interests of the above-mentioned railway."

There is ample evidence to support the statement that the Russo-Japanese War ranks among the most decisive wars in world history. By concluding the Second Anglo-Japanese Alliance, the Taft-Katsura Agreement, the Portsmouth Treaty, and the Peking Treaty, Japan for the first time assumed an undisputed position among the foremost powers.

As a result of her unbroken record of military triumphs and the peace treaty, Japan succeeded in expelling Russian influence from Korea and from the south of Manchuria, and by acquiring a strong foothold on the Asiatic Continent through the Peking Treaty was also able to look forward to trade expansion in North China.

In other words, by demonstrating her national strength, Japan ushered in a new era of equal relations with the Western powers in China. Japan also succeeded in concluding the

Franco-Japanese Agreement in June, 1907, the Russo-Japanese Agreement in July, 1907, and the Root-Takahira Agreement in November, 1908. It can doubtlessly be said that these agreements had not only contributed to the adjustment of all Japanese interests vis-à-vis the Western powers, but also served to inaugurate a new and happy era of cooperation for Japan.

2

ALTHOUGH it was mutually agreed at the time of the conclusion of the Portsmouth Treaty that the details would be worked out at a future date, negotiations on the Russo-Japanese fisheries agreement, the Russo-Japanese treaty of commerce and navigation, and the treaty connecting the Chinese Eastern Railway with the South Manchuria Railway failed to produce any visible results. Japan and Russia held prolonged negotiations from December, 1905, but the lack of any progress greatly annoyed Japan. A favorable turn in the diplomatic talks on an Anglo-Russian Agreement, however, provided a stimulus to the Russo-Japanese talks in which Great Britain and France played the mediatory role.

France, in particular, took the initiative in promoting closer ties with Japan, extending to the latter a five per cent loan of 300 million francs in Paris in March, 1907. Furthermore, shortly after commencing negotiations in Paris on the conclusion of a political agreement, the French Minister for Foreign Affairs, M. Pichon, and the Japanese Ambassador to France, Kurino, signed the Franco-Japanese Agreement in June, 1907.

In this agreement, France not only confirmed the principles of the Anglo-Japanese Alliance with regard to China, but in it France also recognized the results of the Russo-Japanese War, and succeeded in having Japan agree to respect her territorial rights in French Indo-China. Worth noting, too, was the fact that Japan and France confirmed their respective spheres of influence in China. In the exchange of official documents, France designated the three provinces of Kwantung, Kwangsi, and Yunnan as her regions of special interests, and, in return, Japan stipulated Fukien Province, Manchuria, and Mongolia as her regions of special interests.

The Franco-Japanese Agreement was undoubtedly one of the primary factors influencing Russia to adopt a more conciliatory attitude. It also expedited the talks between Japan and Russia over the details of the Portsmouth Treaty, despite the serious collision of views relating to the question of Mongolia. On July 30, 1907, the two countries at long last inked the documents of the First Russo-Japanese Agreement (the Motono-Iswalsky Agreement).

The Russo-Japanese Agreement, together with the Anglo-Japanese Alliance, decisively influenced the Far Eastern political situation until the outbreak of the Russian Revolution. There were not a few advocates of the policy of cooperation with Japan among the Russians before the Russo-Japanese War. The war liquidated the question of the "Exchange Policy" involving Manchuria and Korea, leaving only the issues of how to divide the spheres of influence of the two countries in Manchuria and Mongolia.

A detailed study of each stipulation of the historic Portsmouth Peace Treaty, signed on September 5, 1905, reveals that the foundation of future cooperation between Japan and Russia rested on the clarification of the rights and interests of both nations in East Asia. In the secret convention of the First Russo-Japanese Agreement of 1907, Japan and Russia agreed on the line of demarcation in Manchuria, and to mutually respect each other's interests.

In exchange for Russia's acknowledgment of Japan's freedom of action in Korea, Japan recognized Russia's special interests in Outer Mongolia. This important fundamental agreement formed the basis of several agreements and secret conventions which were concluded with the object of reinforcing the Russo-Japanese Agreement. That no diplomatic furor arose over Japan's annexation of Korea was attributable to the existence of the Taft-Katsura Agreement, Article III of the Second Anglo-Japanese Alliance, and Article II of the secret convention of the Russo-Japanese Agreement.

As outcome of the Anglo-Japanese Alliance, the Franco-Japanese Agreement, and the Russo-Japanese Agreement, fear of encirclement or *einkreisung* which had haunted Germany became a reality as far as her policy in the Far East was concerned. To reassert German influence, the Kaiser began nursing a fantastic notion of concluding a triple alliance of Germany, the United States, and China.

Meanwhile, the goodwill and sympathy which the United States had earlier shown to Japan turned to suspicion as the Far Eastern power balance shifted in favor of Japan, following her victory in the war against Russia. The world became increasingly aware of the growing strain in Japanese-American relations stemming from stern measures adopted by the United States against the rising tide of Japanese immigration, the exclusion of Japanese students from schools in California, and the despatch of America's main naval units to the Pacific area. Until the conclusion of the Japanese-American Agreement in 1908, the Kaiser feverishly attempted to exploit the situation to his own advantage.

President Roosevelt, however, paid scant attention to the formation of the Triple Alliance, describing it as the Kaiser's daydream. What President Roosevelt desired first and foremost was to obtain Britain's cooperation on questions of Japanese immigration and of the Far East.

The United States Government, while dismissing any possibility of a war between Japan and Anglo-America, nonetheless felt that, if any risk of war did arise, it could only be averted through concerted joint warnings by the two Governments.

Great Britain held the opinion that anything like joint action between Great Britain and the United States in this matter would only antagonize Japan, and declared that it was unwise at this stage to issue any warning to Japan since only harm could result from such an action. Having branded the German proposition for a triple alliance as Utopian and unrealistic and having realized that common action with Great Britain was unattainable as a result of British commitments to Japan and Russia, the United States singly had no other alternative but to adopt a conciliatory policy towards Japan. Aided by these circumstances and Japan's unchanging desire to remain on friendly terms with the United States, Baron Takahira and Elihu Root, the Secretary of State, formalized an understanding by an exchange of notes on November 30, 1908.

These notes, commonly known as the Root-Takahira Agreement, constituted "a frank avowal" of the common aim, policy, and intention in the region of the Pacific Ocean by Japan and the United States, and defined that: "it is the wish of the two governments to encourage the free and peaceful development of their commerce on the Pacific Ocean; the policy of both governments is directed to the maintenance of the existing status quo in the region above-mentioned and to the defence of the principle of equal opportunity for commerce and industry in China; should any event occur threatening the status quo as above described or the principle of equal opportunity, it remains for the two governments to communicate with each other, in order to arrive at an understanding as to what measures they may consider it useful to take."

At the time of the conclusion of this Agreement, critics charged Japan with having fallen into a trap set by herself. Yet it is undeniable that the Agreement did help to dispel all major doubts that had contributed to the strained relations between Japan and the United States ever since the end of the Russo-Japanese War. Together with the Anglo-Japanese, the Franco-Japanese, and the Russo-Japanese Agreements, it may be safely assumed that the Japanese-American Agreement also constituted one of the props guaranteeing the general peace in the Far East.

CHAPTER 22

Development of Japanese
Continental Policy
1905-1914

1

WHILE Japan and Russia were mutually bound by Article III of the Portsmouth Treaty to evacuate completely and simultaneously Manchuria except the territory affected by the lease of the Liaotung Peninsula, their representatives signed a protocol on the battlefield on October 30, 1905, in order to put the agreement into effect. In conformity with this protocol, both Japan and Russia in April, 1907, completely withdrew their troops from Manchuria, except the leased territory and the land attached to the railways.

In spite of her bloody sacrifices in the Russo-Japanese War, the only tangible assets Japan was able to gain were the Russian leased territory in South Manchuria and the railway between Talien and Changchun. In essence, although Japan's profit and loss account showed nothing more than these acquisitions, insidious moves were already afoot to deprive the country of even these costly gains.

This move was heralded by the arrival in Japan in August, 1905, of Edward H. Harriman, a great American railway tycoon, at the invitation of the American Minister in Japan, Lloyd C. Griscom. In his interviews with Premier Count Katsura and the *genro,* Harriman described his grandiose plan for the joint Japanese-American control of the South Manchuria Railway as a vital link in a global transportation network.

This fabulous proposal so impressed Marquis Inouye, the Finance Minister, who had been experiencing almost insuperable difficulties in putting Japan's postwar financial house in order, that he quickly became fascinated by the plan, even to the point of declaring that it would be the height of folly for Japan to throw away this golden opportunity. By jointly operating the enterprise, Marquis Inouye foresaw the possibility of utilizing the railway as a buffer zone against any Russian attempt to launch a war of vengeance. Consequently, on October 12, 1905, Count Katsura and Mr. Harriman affixed their signatures to the provisional memorandum concerning the "Joint Japanese-American Control of the South Manchurian Railway."

Uncompromisingly opposed to the very idea of a joint management, Foreign Minister Komura charged the Government with grave indiscretion, and tried to persuade the Premier, the Cabinet Ministers, and the *genro* to nullify the provisional agreement. Baron Komura's forceful protestations finally swayed Premier Katsura and his Cabinet to decide in favor of renouncing the Katsura-Harriman provisional memorandum.

This incident itself did not necessarily cause anti-Japanism among the American intellectuals. Even those who were anti-Japanese did not regard the Japanese action as a proof that Japan was excluding all other trade rivals in China and flouting the principle of the Open Door. The fact was that the Katsura Cabinet had no definite policy that could be described as continental imperialism.

The beginning of 1906 saw the formation of the Saionji Cabinet which undertook the responsible task of making a special study of the entire situation in Manchuria and of drawing up appropriate recommendations. As soon as Premier Marquis Saionji returned from his private tour in Manchuria, he recommended to an important council meeting in the Imperial Presence on May 24, 1906, three fundamental principles:

"To respect China's sovereignty and maintain equal commercial opportunity; to adopt a policy that will win the friendship of the Manchurians and their understanding of Japan's mission and, insofar as possible, avoiding the use of Japanese troops; to encourage Sino-Japanese joint enterprise, in other words, to pay the closest attention to avoid Japan's Manchurian policy becoming a cause of anti-Japanese movement in South China, and not to accord any opportunity to the movement for the recovery of rights."

These fundamental principles were carefully weighed and adopted.

The first postwar case involving a protest from foreign countries, especially Great Britain and the United States, pointing out that Japan was not faithfully adhering to the principle of Open Door, was made in early 1906 in relation to Manchurian trade.

Having been barred from any profitable commercial activity in Manchuria during the Russo-Japanese War, the foreign businessmen naturally expected trade to resume unhindered with the termination of the war. Feeling, however, that their economic activities were being seriously hampered by military orders of the Japanese Army Commander, they appealed to their respective Governments, charging Japan with infringement of the principle of the Open Door.

The United States Government protest against the Japanese Government stated that the United States Government had received a report from its Commissioner in China that the conduct of the Japanese military authorities in Manchuria during and until the end of evacuation of Japanese troops was so strict that it left almost or absolutely no doors open to foreign trade, and that Japan was only aiming to promote her commercial interests. The United States regretfully informed the Japanese Government that her anxiety over the principle of the Open Door in Manchuria had become an issue.

Endorsing the American protest, the British Government also demanded that the Japanese Government should lift restrictions imposed on British trade at the time of evacuation of Russo-Japanese troops, "to benefit the British nationals."

The Japanese Government, replying to these protests, declared that those restrictions were a passing phenomenon, necessitated by military reasons, and that Japan solemnly pledged that she would strictly adhere to the principle of Open Door in Manchuria. This Japanese statement appeared to have satisfied both the British and the United States Governments that Japan intended to faithfully abide by the policy of Open Door in Manchuria. Their merchants in China, however, were not content with these assurances.

The depressed state of trade in Manchuria, acutely felt by the Anglo-American nationals, was due, however, in large measure to the unsettled regional situation and not, as they insistently charged, to a closed-door policy by Japan. As soon as Japan completed the Manchurian evacuation in April, 1907, she proclaimed that she would promptly establish a customhouse in Talien, a move which automatically dispersed all doubts as to whether Japan was observing her Open Door policy in Manchuria.

2

LOOMING large in the international disputes in Manchuria was the question of railways, which replaced trade in importance. Assuming that prior to the Sino-Japanese and Russo-Japanese Wars the powers' struggle in China was for acquisition of concessions and the establishment of the so-called spheres of influence, it may equally be said that during the period from the Russo-Japanese War to World War I, the powers were competing in the field of railway investments.

Consequently, the focal point of foreign pressure against Japan's policy towards China was on questions relating to the railways, such as the question of a short line between Hsin-mintun and Fukumen which had given rise to a controversy after the Russo-Japanese War.

The Chinese Government in November, 1907, secretly granted a concession to Pauling and Company, a British construction firm, to construct the so-called Hsinmintun-Fukumen Line. Japan reacted immediately, warning Peking through the Japanese Minister in China that the said scheme was totally unacceptable on the basis of the protocol annexed to the Peking Treaty of 1905, in which China agreed, "for the purpose of protecting the interests of the South Manchuria Railway, not to construct any branch line in the neighborhood of and parallel to that railway, or any branch line which would be prejudicial to the business of the above-mentioned railway."

At the same time, Great Britain, who as an ally of Japan was deeply interested in the controversy, supported the Japanese contention and instructed the British Minister in China that Great Britain regarded the construction of the new line as unjustifiable and improper. On the other hand, the British nationals in China, not to speak of the Newchuang Chamber of Commerce, joined in a drive to oppose Japan's attitude.

Soon after the contract on the said new line was reached, Tang Shao-i, newly appointed Military Governor of the Mukden Province, granted concessions on railways and mines especially to Anglo-American nationals and adopted a policy of curbing Japan. His ambitious scheme was to extend the Hsinmintun-Fukumen line, connecting it with Tsitsihar, a scheme which he believed would make it possible to develop the vast stretch of fertile plain through a network of railways and Tientsin port, thus circumventing Japan's South Manchuria Railway and Talien port.

The Japanese Government, naturally considering that the realization of such a Chinese scheme would adversely affect the management of the South Manchuria Railway, proposed a compromise that could possibly lead to an amicable settlement of the issue.

To meet this development, the Japanese Government suggested to China that she would forego the concession of laying a railway between Hsinmintun and Fukumen and, in its place, construct a new line from Fukumen to a certain station along the South Manchuria Railway, giving Pauling and Company the contract to lay the said line. Confronted by the refusal of the Chinese Government, the Japanese Government conceded a step further by recognizing the construction of the Hsinmintun-Fukumen line, but, at the same time, demanded as compensation the right to lay a branch line from one of the stations of the South Manchuria Railway to Chengkiatun.

The Chinese Government not only vetoed this plan, but also insisted that the question should be brought before the International Court of Justice at The Hague. The Japanese Government flatly rejected this Chinese proposal and the project for the new line was temporarily stalled without having reached any satisfactory solution.

The subject of the Hsinmintun-Fukumen line was part of the question of Chientao as well as the five items relating to Manchuria of 1909. The negotiations between Ishuin, the Japanese Minister to China, and Liang Tun-yen, finally led to the signing of the Sino-Japanese Agreement on September 4, 1909. Article I of the five items relating to Manchuria stipulated that: "the Chinese Government agrees to negotiate beforehand with the Japanese Government in case it undertakes the construction of the Hsinmintun-Fukumen line." Thus, an outstanding problem was tentatively settled.

Meanwhile, Mr. French, a representative of Pauling and Company, called on Japanese Minister Ishuin in June, 1909, to inquire whether, in the event Japan could not agree to the Hsinmintun-Fukumen line, she would entertain the idea of an alternative line from Chinchow to Tsitsihar. The Japanese Government, at a Cabinet meeting in July, agreed to Japan's participation in the construction of the said line on condition that she would join in the supply of capital and technicians required for the new line, and that China would construct a connecting line from a certain station of the South Manchuria Railway to the said line. Japan communicated her decision to the Chinese Government, and informally notified the Governments of Great Britain and the United States of these terms.

It was during this series of negotiations between Japan and Great Britain that French became intimately associated with Willard Straight, the United States Consul-General in Mukden. With Straight's cooperation, French was able to secure from China, on October 2, 1909, a provisional concession for the construction of a railway from Chinchow on the Gulf of Pechihli to Aigun on the Amur River.

On December 18, 1909, the United States Government transmitted a memorandum to the Japanese Government, inviting Japan as an interested power to participate in the financing and construction of the said railway. The Japanese Government, after expressing sincere appreciation for the American invitation, replied that, while the Government agreed in principle to the joint participation in the said enterprise with the other interested powers, it reserved its final decision pending a full study of the details.

It would be entirely misleading to place the blame for the miscarriage of the Chinchow-Aigun line on Japan's shoulders. While it is true that Japan had not approved of the said line as a branch line parallel to the South Manchuria Railway, it was Russian opposition that was the overriding factor in obstructing the Chinchow-Aigun line.

In an official notification to the United States Government, the Russian Government made no secret of its opposition, stating that it was displeased with the scheme for the construction of a main line, such as the Chinchow-Aigun line, which was injurious not only to the Chinese Eastern Railway but was also a threat to Russia's vested position in Manchuria. It further charged that the purpose of the railway was more political and military than commercial.

Russia specifically accused the British Government of infringing the Anglo-Russian Agreement of 1899 by lending its support to the said scheme. Recognizing the validity of the Russian complaint, British Foreign Minister Grey in a statement to Parliament declared that, in consideration of the existence of the Anglo-Russian Agreement, the British Government was not able to positively assist in the construction of the new line until the Chinese Government had arrived at an agreement with Russia on the issue.

*　　*　　*

The United States Government invitation to Japan to take part in the construction of the new line mentioned above was accompanied by the Knox proposal to neutralize the Manchurian railways. Following a frank exchange of views with the Russian Government, Japan decided to join in the rejection of the Knox plan.

The Japanese Government interpreted the Knox plan as a clear infringement of the Portsmouth Treaty and the Peking Treaty, and could find no justifiable reason in the present state of affairs in Manchuria for adopting a new system of railway administration differing from that of the other parts of China.

As for the question of Open Door, its significance was greater than elsewhere in China because the South Manchuria Railway was strictly designed for commercial and industrial purposes. With this view in mind, Japan considered that the common railway administration system of the powers was apt to be governed by political rather than economic requirements. This arrangement, it was keenly felt, was not only harmful to public interest, but impaired the enterprise and obscured responsibility.

Apprehensive lest the internationalization of the railway administration would inflict incalculable damage to Japan's commercial and industrial development in Manchuria, Japan firmly maintained that she could not possibly accept the forfeiture of the South Manchuria Railway.

The Chinese Government, on the other hand, opined that if it could induce Great Britain and the United States to invest in Manchuria, the relations between Japan and Anglo-America would become exceedingly strained. In China's view the best scheme to check Japan's continental development was to involve Anglo-America with the question of railways in Manchuria at the expense of Japan. International opinion at the time regarding the problem was substantially identical. This Chinese policy succeeded to a certain extent.

Upon reconsidering the whole question of railways in Manchuria, at the height of the controversy over the Hsinmintun-Fukumen line in 1907 to 1908, Willard Straight, the United States Consul-General in Mukden, viewed the turn of events as a golden opportunity to realize the Harriman project. Before long, concrete plans began to emerge for the establishment of the Manchurian Bank, the Chinchow-Aigun line and the neutralization of the Manchurian Railways. In other words, it was a typical example of American dollar diplomacy in which economic interests played the predominant role in Manchuria during the years from 1907 to 1910.

Strictly speaking, however, this development was not the result of the national policy of the United States. As earlier stated, the prime movers of American investments in Manchuria were Harriman and Straight. There is hardly any room to doubt that China's diplomacy was instigated by purely political motives. Although China had hoped to put the value of the Anglo-Japanese Alliance to the test, she failed in her ultimate aims. Great Britain, in supporting Japan's stand concerning the question of concluding a railway line parallel to the South Manchuria Railway, appealed to the British firms to exercise self-restraint and, at the same time, urged the United States to invite Japan's participation in the Chinchow-Aigun line.

Insofar as the Knox Neutralization Plan for Manchurian Railways was concerned, Great Britain, acquainted with the views of the Japanese Government, felt unable to agree with the plan in the absence of the Japanese Government's approval of the proposal. It was apparent that the British Government tried to fully respect Japan's special interest in Manchuria. However, the fact should not be overlooked that Great Britain had adopted such a policy in lieu of the protection of her special interests in the region of the Yangtze Valley.

Around February, 1913, the Japanese Government informed the Chinese Government of its willingness to provide the necessary funds for the construction and administration of the Ning-Hsiang Railway. In reply, the Chinese Government stated that, while a number of senior officials, including Yuan Shih-kai, desired to cooperate with the Japanese Government in the economic sphere, and welcomed its investments, the Chinese Government would be more favorably disposed to consider Japan's proposal if the funds were to be furnished in cooperation with Great Britain since the said railway was to be constructed along the Yangtze River where the latter held the dominant interests.

Receiving his instructions from the Japanese Government, Ishuin, Minister to China, opened negotiations with the Chinese Government, during which he discovered that China had no objection if the Ning-Hsiang line was to be undertaken by Great Britain and the Kiukiang-Fukien line by Japan. Moreover, Japanese technicians were to be used for the construction of the line between Nanchang and Pinghsiang in order to respect Japan's interests in the Pinghsiang coal mine. China was also agreeable to the placing of the cargo and passenger divisions of the whole line under the same system.

Later, however, British Minister Jordan told Ishuin that while he had no objection to the project, he personally felt the necessity of fundamentally solving the question of the

Chinese railways. Asserting that there was no scope for British capital in railways in regions where Japan's influence was paramount, such as Manchuria, in Shantung where Germany was supreme, and in Yunnan, an area in which French influence predominated, if Great Britain had to cooperate with other powers in investments in the Yangtze Valley which fell in her sphere of influence, a number of questions which could not be ignored would inevitably arise. This point had lately been raised by a number of British nationals, and since the matter could not be overlooked it would have to be referred to the British Government for final action.

The Japanese Government then explained its attitude on the Ning-Hsiang line to the British Government, notifying the latter that while Japan could gladly accept any future cooperation of British financiers it would be prudent to begin negotiations immediately in order to forestall moves by third powers.

On October 11, 1913, the British Government, in its reply to the Japanese Government, pointed out that Great Britain had special and paramount interests in the Yangtze Valley, of which the Japanese Government was well aware, just as Japan had her special interests in the region of South Manchuria. Hence, Great Britain regarded the granting of the concession on the Ning-Hsiang railway to a British organization and control of the railway as logical since the said railway would not only be operating in the region where Great Britain maintained her sphere of influence, but the line would also be connected with the two lines operating on British capital. It was the British stand that, if placed in a similar position in South Manchuria, the Japanese Government would undoubtedly wish to acquire control of such a line.

Although it was up to Great Britain to consider, after final plans were made, to what extent Japan should be allowed to participate in the construction of the Ning-Hsiang line, Japan should be seriously prepared on her part to give adequate facilities to British enterprises in South Manchuria if her Government expected to receive concessions in the Yangtze Valley.

Japan was reluctant, however, to place Manchuria on the same footing as the Yangtze Valley. The Japanese Government in a strong protest against Great Britain stated that: "while the British Government appeared to measure Japan's interests in South Manchuria by her interests in the Yangtze Valley, the British Government should have been fully informed of the fact that Japan has been holding special interests politically and strategically in South Manchuria by her treaty rights and her adjacency to the region, and that these interests were the result of two wars. Accordingly, the Japanese Government, as an ally of Great Britain, deeply regrets that the latter seems to apply a rule similar to that of the other regions of the Chinese Empire to the situation in South Manchuria."

The British Government, however, firmly rejected Japan's contention. Considering it inadvisable from Japan's overall position to engage in a controversy with an ally on such a regional issue as the Ning-Hsiang railway, the Japanese Government finally retracted its demand relating to the new railway, but persisted in upholding its principle in Manchuria.

The loan for the Ning-Hsiang line was finally concluded between the Anglo-Chinese Corporation and the Chinese Government on March 31, 1914. Applying the provisions of the Anglo-Russian Agreement of 1899, which divided the spheres of interests in railway construction in China—Russia north of the Great Wall and Great Britain in the Yangtze Valley—Great Britain seemingly approved Japan's maintenance of her sphere of influence in South Manchuria after the Russo-Japanese War, conditioned, of course, by Japan's recognition of the Yangtze Valley as Britain's sphere of influence.

The Japanese Government, however, could not gloss over the fact that Japan's interests in the Yangtze Valley were equal, if not superior, to those of Great Britain, and, accordingly, was not in a position to treat Britain's special interests in the Yangtze Valley in the same light as Japan's special interests in Manchuria.

CHAPTER 23

Adjustment of Sino-Japanese
Relations
1905-1914

1

In pursuing its policy on the Asiatic continent, Japan necessarily had to adjust Sino-Japanese relations. While the Peking Treaty and its Additional Agreement contributed towards the settlement of the fundamental issues between Japan and China in the aftermath of the Russo-Japanese War, there still remained many knotty problems which awaited solution through concrete negotiations between these two Asiatic powers.

As stated earlier, Japan was successful in defending her justifiable interests in South Manchuria against the aggressive railway policies of the Western powers. In addition to this singular success, she also reached a number of other amicable arrangements with the Chinese Government on such outstanding questions as the following:

1. THE QUESTION OF THE PEKING-MUKDEN RAILWAY

The first pending issue relating to the question of Manchuria to be resolved after the Russo-Japanese War concerned the Hsinmintun-Mukden Railway. The Peking-Mukden line, constructed with British capital, was owned and operated by China, but was actually under the control of a British officer. During the construction of this railway, a bridge over the Liao River was contemplated in order to extend the line to

Mukden, but Russia, regarding Manchuria as within her influence, opposed not only the extension of the said line to the east of Hsinmintun, but from a strategic point of view also the construction of the Liao River railway bridge.

The Japanese military headquarters had during the war with Russia ordered the army railway construction corps to build a temporary railway between Mukden and Hsinmintun. Some years later in April, 1907, when the South Manchuria Railway Company was established to assume the administration of the railway formerly owned by the Japanese Government in South Manchuria, the Chinese Government addressed a request to the Japanese Government as well as to the said company for the transfer of the Hsinmintun-Mukden line to its jurisdiction. The transfer was effected in accordance with the Sino-Japanese Convention of April 15, 1907, signed at Peking, stipulating the payment of 1,600,000 yen, and the provision by the South Manchuria Railway of one-half of the funds necessary for the construction of the line east of the Liao-ho. (Article I of the Agreement concerning the Hsinmintun-Mukden and the Kirin-Changchun lines.) The details of the loan agreement, including the provision that China was to borrow 320,000 yen, equivalent to one-half of the cost of construction of the line east of the Liao-ho, at an annual interest rate of five per cent, were settled by a Supplementary Agreement of November 12, 1908, signed at Peking. (Article I and Article II.)

2. THE QUESTION OF THE KIRIN-CHANGCHUN RAILWAY

China agreed, under the provisions of the Sino-Japanese Convention of April 15, 1907, to borrow from the South Manchuria Railway Company one-half of the fund necessary for the construction of a railway line between Changchun and Kirin. (Article II of the Agreement concerning the Hsinmintun-Mukden line and the Kirin-Changchun line.) In November, 1908, agreement was reached on the details relating to the loan necessary for the new line, in which China was to borrow one-half of the construction cost, or 2,150,000 yen, at an annual interest of five per cent.

Construction of the said line was initiated in May, 1909, and it was opened to traffic at the end of October, 1911. However, when it became apparent that the Kirin-Changchun line was being mismanaged and was in serious financial difficulties, the Japanese Government secured possession of the administrative rights of the said line under an agreement with the Peking Government in 1919.

3. THE QUESTION OF THE ANTUNG-MUKDEN RAILWAY

Article VI of the Additional Agreement of the Peking Treaty stipulated the future development of the Antung-Mukden line, and its reconstruction from a light traffic railway into a commercial line to be completed by December, 1908. However, unforeseen engineering difficulties and other causes hampered its scheduled completion. Russia's sudden decision to reconstruct the Amur Railway and at the same time to double-track the Siberian Railway awakened Japan to the full realization that any further delay in the reconstruction of the Antung-Mukden line would be fraught with grave consequences.

The situation became even more crucial when the Chinese Government, declaring that it could not approve Japan's proposal to widen the track gauge to standard gauge, began making unreasonable demands regarding the withdrawal of police and guards in the railway zone.

In a determined move, the Japanese Government instructed Minister Ishuin in Peking to deliver an ultimatum to the Chinese Foreign Office in August, 1909, informing the Peking Government that Japan, reserving the right of freedom of action, had decided to undertake the reconstruction work on the line on the basis of the survey conducted by the Sino-Japanese joint commission.

The Japanese Government, furthermore, ordered President Nakamura of the South Manchuria Railway Company to promptly begin reconstruction work on the Antung-Mukden line. In taking this firm action, Japan clarified her true intentions by stating that:

"Providing that reconstruction is not obstructed, the Japanese Government would gladly enter into any negotiations relating to the question of the Antung-Mukden line, and would always be prepared to discuss any other pending question in a spirit of compromise and conciliation." In the face of Japan's firm stand, the Chinese Government conceded, resulting in the detailed agreement concerning the reconstruction of the Antung-Mukden line being signed between Koike, the Japanese Consul-General in Mukden, and Hsi Liang, the Governor-General of the Three Eastern Provinces (Manchuria), and Cheng Te-chuan, the Governor of Mukden Province.

Although Japan is vulnerable to criticism as aggressive for having attained her objective by an ultimatum, her actions were prompted by strategical necessity. As provided for in the Portsmouth Treaty, Japan and Russia undertook to construct railways in Manchuria only for purely commercial purposes. The obvious motive of this provision, which was political, was designed to avoid a collision between Japan and Russia.

It was hardly surprising, therefore, that Japan took these decisive and unavoidable self-defensive measures in the face of Russia's clear intention to construct a military railway in Manchuria. The Russo-Japanese War strikingly testified to the strategic value of the Antung-Mukden line. In the light of the fact that the line also discharged an important function as a connecting link between Korea and Manchuria, the Japanese Government could hardly have been expected to ignore the strategic importance of the Antung-Mukden line.

*   *   *

In connection with the Antung-Mukden line, Japan negotiated with China in 1909 on the following six questions, namely:

(1) the question of the Fukumen line; (2) the question of the Tashihchiao branch line; (3) the question of the extention of the Peking-Mukden line; (4) the question of Fushun and Yentai coal mines; (5) the question of the coal mines along the Antung-Mukden line and the South Manchuria Railway; and (6) the question of the possession of Chientao.

Earlier, on December 28, 1909, the Japanese Minister to China, Ishuin, under instructions from Foreign Minister Komura, had explained the Japanese views on the pending questions between Japan and China to Na Tung, Chinese Foreign Minister, and Yuan Shih-kai at the Ministry of Foreign Affairs in Peking.

But in its memorandum of March, 1909, the Chinese Government, in a sweeping rejection of the Japanese demands, stressed the urgent need of settling the Chientao question. If Japan and China could not bridge their differences, the Chinese Government was of the view that there was no alternative but to appeal to the World Court at The Hague for the solution of all pending issues.

Although the Chinese Government eventually retracted its proposal to seek arbitration, the stalemate in the negotiations remained unbroken. It was in these circumstances that a sudden breakthrough was achieved by the Japanese ultimatum concerning the Antung-Mukden line. Having found a way out of the impasse, the two countries signed an agreement on the questions of Manchuria and Chientao on September 4, 1909.

Relevant background information on the important issues affecting Japan and China may be summarized as follows:

1. THE QUESTION OF THE TASHIHCHIAO BRANCH LINE

This line was in temporary service for the transportation of railway materials during the days of the Chinese Eastern Railway. With the recovery of rights in mind, the Chinese

Government attempted to take advantage of Japan's promise to remove this line in the future by demanding, on the pretext of an old agreement with Russia, either the removal of this line or the construction of the said line by China in accordance with the statement of the Chinese delegate as recorded in the minutes of the Peking Conference.

Ultimately, the Chinese Government not only approved the Tashihchiao line as the branch line of the South Manchuria Railway on the understanding that Japan would return the line to China at the time of the expiration of the loan agreement with the South Manchuria Railway Company, but also agreed to the extension of the said line to Yingkou as the terminus.

2. FUSHUN AND YENTAI COAL MINES

With the transfer of the Tashihchiao line to Japan, the Fushun and Yentai coal mines along the line came under the management of Japan in accordance with Russia's interpretation that the said mines were part and parcel of the railway rights, as in the cases of the Chiao Chi Railway (German) and the Peking-Mukden Railway (British).

Regardless of its unquestionable right to operate the Fushun and Yentai coal mines, Japan was about to negotiate with the Chinese Government on the rate of taxes. This Japanese approach was sharply repudiated by the Chinese Government with the claim that the Fushun coal mine was the private property of Wang Cheng-jao, a Chinese subject, and that no clear proof existed concerning the transfer of the Yentai coal mine to Russia.

After repeated negotiations, however, China finally consented to recognize Japan's right to mine coal at the Fushun and Yentai mines. At the same time, Japan acknowledged the payment of taxes on her mining activities. Both nations further agreed to conclude a separate agreement on tax rates which accorded with the most favored rates levied on other coal mines in China.

Having thus settled a vital issue, successive negotiations on other mines along the South Manchuria Railway and the Antung-Mukden line were amicably concluded. Japan and China also agreed to operate these mines as joint enterprises by nationals of the two countries.

*   *   *

The subject of Chientao, as previously mentioned, was settled simultaneously along with five other items relating to Manchuria. Chientao, situated between Paektusan and the Tumen River, had hitherto been regarded as undemarcated territory. The Korean Government, however, had frequently referred to it as part of Korea, basing its claim on the fact that Koreans had long been residing in the area. Korea believed that it should at least be regarded as a neutral zone between China and Korea.

China, on the other hand, asserting that the region was a Chinese possession, claimed that she had been administering the affairs of Chientao as part of Manchuria.

In seeking a solution to the Chientao question, Japan's Foreign Minister Komura laid great stress on the Government's desire to protect Korean residents. By intimating Japan's readiness to recognize China's territorial sovereignty Komura hoped to satisfactorily solve other outstanding questions. Japan's avowed intention was specifically focused on the settlement of the question of constructing the Kirin-Hoeryong line by linking it to the issue of Chientao.

The mere recognition of China's territorial sovereignty over Chientao, however, did not satisfy the Chinese Government, which was even opposed to Japan's consular jurisdiction, declaring that "the Korean immigrants are regarded and treated on the same footing as other Chinese nationals and are, moreover, under Chinese jurisdiction."

China went on to insist that the question of constructing the Kirin-Hoeryong line could not be a subject of discussion between Japan and China as it was irrelevant to the boundary dispute. Giving in to China's demands on the question of

Chientao, by not only recognizing her territorial sovereignty but also her jurisdiction, Japan obtained China's consent for the extension of the Kirin-Changchun line to Hoeryong in Korea. It was agreed at the same time that the entire management of the extended line was to be similar to that of the Kirin-Changchun line.

Note should also be taken of the fact that other questions, essential for adjusting Sino-Japanese relations, including the question of cables and telegraphs and lumbering rights along the Yalu River, were all amicably settled in subsequent talks.

2

It will be interesting to study the problems involving China from the standpoint of international politics. One such development of international significance was the American neutralization scheme for the Manchurian railroads, which proved abortive. The Japanese and Russian Governments, after holding several discussions on the American proposition, arrived at an identity of views. By their taking common action, to express their objections to the said plan, the Russo-Japanese Agreement became a living force for the first time.

Confronted with the concerted Japanese and Russian objections, not to speak of the lukewarm attitude of the British and French Governments, the United States was finally forced to withdraw the Knox Neutralization Plan, which found support only among the Germans.

In 1910, the Second Russo-Japanese Agreement, expanded and strengthened by a secret convention, was concluded with the mutually expressed purpose of adequately promoting and defending their respective special interests within the spheres of influence indicated in their previous agreement.

In the same year, the British Foreign Minister, Sir Edward Grey, informed the Japanese Government that the United States and Great Britain were contemplating the advisability of concluding a general and unlimited arbitration treaty, adding that his Government was ready to reply to the United States with the following two alternative propositions:

1. "to suggest to the United States the participation of Japan in the proposed arbitration treaty," or

2. "to detach the Anglo-Japanese Alliance from the effective sphere of the proposed treaty, but to revise the Treaty of Alliance at the time of its expiration so as to conform to the general principle of the arbitration treaty."

Foreign Minister Grey expressed a desire to be apprised of the Japanese Government's reaction to these propositions after due consideration. As a result of a series of deliberations on the full implications of the proposal, Japan rejected the first of the two alternatives of the British Government on the ground that it could not possibly accept an arbitration award on matters which might possibly affect the very existence of a nation, especially in view of the fact that Japan would be in an unfavorable position since most of the arbitrators would be Europeans and Americans who had different cultural, racial, and religious backgrounds.

The Japanese Government communicated its decision to Foreign Minister Grey, holding that the Anglo-Japanese Alliance should not be applicable in matters involving the United States, as it was clear that Great Britain would endeavor under all circumstances to avert war with the United States, if only out of economic necessity and her relations with Canada, as well as to avoid becoming entangled in any explosive issues between Japan and the United States.

It was against this background that the Third Anglo-Japanese Alliance was signed on July 13, 1911, containing a very important addition to meet the new situation arising from Japan's annexation of Korea and the proposed changes that had taken place in the Far Eastern situation, including the stipulation that the Alliance was to remain in force for ten years. It is undeniable that the effectiveness of the Third

Anglo-Japanese Alliance was seriously weakened by the revision that placed the United States outside the purview of the Alliance.

Although the Anglo-Japanese Alliance originally aimed at countering Russia, the situation in the Far East was radically altered by the Russo-Japanese Agreement and the Anglo-Russian Agreement. For all intents and purposes, the Anglo-Japanese Alliance lost its original significance since Russia could no longer be regarded as a potential enemy by both Japan and Great Britain.

As the value of the Anglo-Japanese Alliance diminished, Japan and Russia began to draw closer together. When the Imperial Chinese Government Five Percent Currency Reform and Industrial Development Sinking Fund Gold Loan was signed between the Peking Government and the Four Power Banking Group of Britain, the United States, Germany, and France, the Japanese and Russian governments drew attention to Article XVI of the said Four Power Agreement giving preference in loan operations, especially in Manchuria, to the participating banking group.

The two countries, after due consultation, demanded that Article XVI be either amended or expunged, claiming that "the arrangement appeared to be harmful to the development of their special interests in Manchuria." Russia followed up this action by notifying the Consortium Governments that "Russia maintains special interests and rights in North Manchuria, Mongolia and Western China under the provisions of treaties and agreements concluded with China," and that "Russia reserves the right to take any essential measure to protect her interests in the said regions."

Objecting naturally to the same Article, Japan made a similar declaration that, in view of the Russian pronouncement, "she reserves the right to take the same posture concerning South Manchuria and adjoining Inner Mongolia." This coordinated action led to the conclusion of the Third

Russo-Japanese Agreement in July, 1912, under which the two powers pledged to respect the regions of special interests of both nations, and confirmed the division of Inner Mongolia into eastern and western sectors as they had done earlier in Manchuria in 1907.

Just prior to this development, the Manchu dynasty which had ruled China for three hundred years was dramatically overthrown in the autumn of 1911 by the Chinese revolutionary forces led by Dr. Sun Yat-sen. Deeply shocked by this sudden turn of events, Japan was initially prepared to undertake unilateral intervention in case China should request assistance in preserving the imperial throne. At the same time, Japan was gravely concerned that such an action would not only be regarded with suspicion, but might precipitate an international dispute, leading eventually to anti-Japanese feelings among the revolutionary forces.

Japan, therefore, proposed to Great Britain that the two countries should jointly intervene in accordance with the Anglo-Japanese Alliance. As the Japanese Government conducted negotiations with Great Britain, it also attempted to mollify the revolutionaries by informally proposing a constitutional monarchy, as a compromise, to the leaders of the Chinese Revolution.

With the forces of Dr. Sun in control of the Yangtze Valley, Great Britain was reluctant to apply any pressure on the new rulers of China. In this fluid situation, even Yuan Shih-kai, the Chinese Government's representative, showed no determined inclination to stick to the principle of constitutional monarchy. Recognizing the absence of any compelling reason to unilaterally uphold the system of constitutional monarchy against the wishes of other powers, the Japanese Government decided to adopt a passive attitude.

With the outbreak of the Chinese Revolution, the Western powers became apprehensive lest Japan, seizing this opportunity, should despatch troops to China or otherwise extend her special interests in Manchuria and Mongolia. Far from having any such ambitions, Japan's primary concern was in the system of government in China.

Hoping to gain advantages from the Chinese upheaval, Russia made strenuous efforts to expand her vested interests in northern Manchuria, Mongolia, and Turkistan. Contrary to the policy of Japan and the other powers, which respected the independence and territorial integrity of China, Russia pursued a policy of instigating secessionist activities on the part of China's adjacent dependencies with the ultimate aim of amalgamating them into the Russian Empire.

In furtherance of these goals, Russia was not satisfied with the reservations she had attached to northern Manchuria, Mongolia, and Turkistan on the occasion of the materialization of the Reorganization Loan, but plotted to establish a four power banking group—separate from the Four Power Consortium—composed of Russian, Belgian, French, and British banking corporations under the supervision of the Russo-Asian Bank.

The disturbed conditions during and immediately after the Chinese Revolution afforded Japan an ideal opportunity for expansion on the Chinese Continent. Foreign aggrandisement being at its peak, Russia was pushing vigorously into Mongolia, and Great Britain into Tibet. In sharp contrast, Japan's action was so restrained that the German Ambassador felt obliged to report that the death of Emperor Meiji had possibly paralyzed the Japanese government machinery.

The massacre of several Japanese nationals by the Chinese in Nanking in 1913 finally awakened the Japanese Government to the need to adopt positive measures to settle the questions of Manchurian and Mongolian railways. After a series of negotiations, agreement was reached in the form of an exchange of notes dated October 5, 1913, known as the Five Manchurian and Mongolian Railways Loan Agreement.

On the same day, the Chinese Foreign Minister, in a statement to the Japanese Minister in China, referred to the oft-discussed question connected with the construction of railways in Manchuria in the following vein: "The Chinese Government desires to cooperate with the Japanese Government with regard to the railway loan." With the exchange of these notes, the Japanese Government obtained from China a provisional agreement concerning the Japanese right of financing the construction of the following three projected connecting lines of the South Manchurian Railway and the Peking-Mukden line:

1. The Ssupingkai-Chengchiatun-Taonan Railway
2. The Kaiyuan-Hailungcheng Railway
3. The Changchun-Taonan Railway

In addition, the Chinese Government also assured Japan that it would preferentially negotiate with the Japanese financiers should foreign capital be required for the construction of the Taonan-Jehol Railway and the Kirin-Hailungcheng Railway. Less than a year later, the world was embroiled in the Great War of 1914–1918.

CHAPTER 24

The Twenty-One Demands
1914-1915

SHORTLY following the outbreak of World War I, the Japanese Government decided in August, 1914, to comply with the British Government's request under the Anglo-Japanese Alliance to assume the role of a belligerent. Although it is not the purpose here to delve into the details surrounding Japan's decision to participate in the conflict, it is relevant to note that Sino-Japanese relations deteriorated from bad to worse as soon as Japan declared war against Germany and captured Kiaochow Bay which the Germans had leased from China.

In line with this stand, China demanded the withdrawal of Japanese troops from the zone along the old German railway between Tsingtao and Tsinan, but the Japanese Government officially replied that it would not evacuate from the zone until peace was restored. In retaliation, China canceled on January 7, 1915, her war-zone proclamation, implying thereby that Japan should at least retire within the original German leased territory. This act caused widespread resentment in Japan which found the proclamation absolutely unacceptable.

On the eve of World War I, there were not a few outstanding questions between Japan and China which were awaiting final solution. Foremost among them was the conclusion between these two nations of an agreement for the disposition of the ticklish question of Shantung if the two powers were to avoid controversial discussions over the vexed issue at the peace conference.

In addition, there were other questions that urgently needed settlement, such as the extension of the leases of the Kwantung territory, the South Manchuria Railway, and the Antung-Mukden Railway, all of which were due to expire within ten to twenty-six years. Japan eagerly desired to extend the terms of her vested rights in both Manchuria and Mongolia—rights which she hoped to perpetuate in view of her heavy sacrifices in two wars against China and Russia respectively.

It would be wrong to overlook the fact that Japan did not regard either the Peking Treaty or the successive Sino-Japanese agreements as a solid guarantee for the security of Japan's special footholds in China. Influential Japanese politicians, almost without exception, were gravely concerned about this state of affairs at the time of Japan's involvement in the global conflict.

It was natural, therefore, that Japan should wish to settle these pending questions with China at an opportune moment. Foreign Minister Kato devoted most of his attention towards the prompt solution of these questions, i.e., the extension of the leases of Kwantung Province, the South Manchuria Railway, and the Antung-Mukden Railway, as well as the clarification of Japan's vested rights in Manchuria and Mongolia.

The fall of Tsingtao on November 7, 1914, stirred Baron Kato into action. Having obtained the Cabinet's approval for commencing negotiations, he recalled Minister Eki Hioki to Tokyo on November 12, and entrusted him on December 3 with the important task of negotiating with China. Subsequent talks with the Chinese Government finally resulted in the direct presentation by Minister Hioki of the famous "Twenty-One Demands"—or more precisely, fourteen "demands" and seven "wishes" contained in five groups—to President Yuan Shih-kai at his official residence in Peking on January 18, 1915.

Group I, consisting of four articles, related to the disposition of German economic rights in Shantung.

Group II, consisting of seven articles, was aimed at strengthening Japan's position in South Manchuria and Eastern Inner Mongolia.

Group III, consisting of two articles, was intended to secure mining and railway concessions in Central China, and transform the Han-Yeh-Ping Company into a Sino-Japanese joint enterprise.

Group IV, consisting of one article, was designed to prevent China from ceding or leasing to any third power any harbor, bay, or island along the Chinese coast.

Group V, consisting of seven articles termed as "wishes," was drawn up to cover miscellaneous items: the Chinese Government's employment of Japanese political, financial, and military advisers, etc.

While the first four groups may be properly regarded as "demands" that the Government strongly desired to realize, Group V was regarded from the outset as being merely expressions of wishes or suggestions, which Japan hoped China would try to materialize. Should China have agreed to all of these demands, Japan was willing to negotiate for the return of German rights and privileges in Kiaochow Bay to China, on condition that the latter agree to the establishment of an exclusive settlement for Japanese residents.

In presenting her demands to China, Japan explained that "the object of the negotiations on questions between Japan and China is to ensure the maintenance of peace in the Far East, normalizing the unstable conditions arising from the Japanese-German War," and that "the Japanese Government would act resolutely to achieve its objectives by every possible means."

In the negotiations which followed between Chinese Foreign Minister Lou Cheng-ching and Minister Hioki, China adopted her usual intransigent policy, suggesting an article-by-article discussion, while Japan persisted on immediate action and on comprehensive discussion. The most difficult subject for negotiations involved the vital question of strengthening Japan's position in South Manchuria and Eastern Inner Mongolia, contained in Group II. Group V was also regarded as an important, though difficult, topic for discussion, but the Japanese Government never regarded Group V as demands to be enforced at all costs but merely miscellaneous wishes or suggestions which, if accepted, would strengthen Japanese interests. Japan had no intention of enforcing these wishes, regarding them in the light of "if China refuses, they can not by their very nature be pressed for acceptance."

In spite of the fact that Japan had been maintaining her special interests in South Manchuria and Eastern Inner Mongolia, approved by successive Russo-Japanese Secret Conventions and tacitly acknowledged by Great Britain and the United States, China from the very start of the negotiations vehemently opposed Japan's demands on land ownership, right of residence, mining rights, railway interests, and advisory rights.

Moreover, by maintaining that Manchuria and Mongolia were two entirely separate regions, China insisted that Japan had no right of claim on Eastern Inner Mongolia. Thus, the heated discussion between Japan and China remained deadlocked for more than two months.

In view of China's virtual rejection of Japan's demands concerning Eastern Inner Mongolia, Minister Hioki cabled Foreign Minister Kato, suggesting the use of an ultimatum as the only effective weapon. While the negotiations seesawed back and forth, China presented her last counterproposals to Japan's revised demands, in which:

1. China generally agreed to the whole of Japan's demands regarding Shantung Province, but requested the unconditional return of the leased territory of Kiaochow Bay.

2. China refused to recognize land ownership and per-

petual lease in Manchuria and demanded that Japanese residents abide by court orders under Chinese laws pertaining
to police, taxation, and land affairs.

3. China rejected Japan's principal demands concerning
Eastern Inner Mongolia, the core of which was the Sino-
Japanese joint enterprise in agriculture and mining rights.

4. China rejected the whole of Japan's demands contained
in Group V.

Foreign Minister Kato initially believed that even without
contravening treaty obligations, it would be sufficient for
Japan to employ certain coercive measures against China,
specifically either expediting or postponing the date of actual
rotation of Japanese troops in Manchuria and Tsingtao. Kato
did not feel it urgent to act upon Hioki's request for an ultimatum.

However, in face of the strong attitude adopted by a group
of *genro,* favoring an ultimatum as a simple and decisive
method of diplomacy, and President Yuan's suggestion that
an ultimatum be issued to save his face, further progress in
the negotiations appeared hopeless.

Having concluded that China's final counterproposal of
May 1 precluded any successful diplomatic maneuvers, the
top Kasumigaseki policy makers unanimously voted the following day, May 2, 1915, in favor of an ultimatum. After
receiving the Imperial sanction, Japan delivered the ultimatum to China on May 7.

That memorable document gave China twenty-seven hours
to accept Japan's revised demands, or "the Imperial Government will take such independent action as they deem necessary to meet the situation." China accepted the demands
early on May 9 and the treaties and notes were duly signed
and exchanged by Minister Hioki for Japan and Foreign
Minister Lou Cheng-ching for China on May 25, 128 days
after the presentation of the original demands on January
18, 1915.

The negotiations in 1915 resulted in the signing of two treaties and the exchange of thirteen notes. In these treaties and notes, the Chinese Government agreed (1) to recognize the extension of the leases of Port Arthur and Dairen and of the South Manchuria Railway lines to ninety-nine years (the exchanged notes fixed the dates of the Port Arthur-Dairen lease as 1997 and the lease of the Antung-Mukden branch line as 2007); (2) to grant to Japan the right to construct the railways and to work certain coal mines and iron mines in Manchuria; (3) to permit Japanese subjects to lease land for commercial, industrial, or agricultural purposes in Manchuria; (4) to approve any future agreement between Japanese capitalists and the Han-Yeh-Ping Company. In this connection, there was to be no confiscation or nationalization without the consent of the former, and the latter was to restrict its foreign loans to Japanese sources only.

It should be added here that all items in Group V, regarded as "wishes" and not essential demands, were withdrawn from the ultimatum. While Premier Okuma was of the opinion at the Cabinet meeting that Group V should be included in the ultimatum if Japan were to rely solely upon the method of duress, Foreign Minister Kato insisted that the demands, if accompanied by an ultimatum, should be reasonable and acceptable to the world powers. Since the requirement of armed force should be confined to irrevocable demands, he strongly favored elimination of Group V from an ultimatum.

Japan's possible motives in the Sino-Japanese negotiations naturally came under the close scrutiny of the world powers. Cognizant of this fact, the Japanese Government, soon after opening talks with China, not only notified Great Britain on the outline of the respective items contained in Groups I to IV, but also later transmitted this information to the United States, France, and Russia. However, since the points contained in Group V were from the very outset regarded as "wishes" and not essential demands, they were not only omitted from Japan's notifications to the British and other

Governments, but no reference was made to their existence.

The Chinese Government, however, in January, 1915, unofficially communicated to the Western powers the so-called "secret demands" in Group V, the contents of which were sensationally divulged by the American and Chinese press.

Although severely rebuking China for using subtleties, Japan, at the same time, rejected charges that the items contained in Group V—the entire contents of which were subsequently transmitted to Great Britain, the United States, France, and Russia—were exorbitant demands.

The Anglo-American attitude concerning the Sino-Japanese negotiations of 1915 on Japan's "Twenty-One Demands" to China is of special importance. The British Government, on receiving Japan's notification, expressed its desire to be consulted in case Tokyo intended to present demands which might affect the acquired rights of British subjects in China, and hoped that Japan would desist from presenting China with any demand that might infringe upon the latter's independence and territorial integrity.

On March 3, Foreign Minister Grey intimated that, while Great Britain was only directly concerned with her railway interests in South China within the context of Japan's demands to China, that issue was actually of minor importance. Of greater concern was the possible political complication which might arise from the negotiations. Great Britain, however, was prepared to sympathetically consider Japan's activities to expand her influence in China, especially in Manchuria.

Then on April 26, Lord Grey, on receiving Japan's final draft amendment, expressed the hope that Japan would avoid any rupture of diplomatic relations with China, but that should the items contained in Group V lead to a severance, public opinion in Great Britain would regard the act as being contrary to the spirit of the Anglo-Japanese Alliance.

Shortly thereafter, on May 6, Great Britain restated her desire that Japan would not take any coercive measures towards China without prior consultation with Britain. As a party to the Anglo-Japanese Alliance, Britain's concern was regarded as friendly. In fact, Lord Grey, in a statement to Parliament, expressed satisfaction at the reported conclusion of the Sino-Japanese negotiations which had nearly jeopardized the spirit of the Anglo-Japanese Alliance.

The attitude of the United States, in sharp contrast, was distinctly hostile. On March 19, 1915, Secretary Bryan sent a lengthy protest in reply to Japan's notification of the demands made to China, stating "while the activities of the United States and her subjects in China were not solely political, they have been establishing their footholds in missionary work, education, and commerce for more than several decades. In addition, the United States, on account of the fact that she is maintaining her broader treaty rights in China, could not help entertaining a grave concern over certain items in Japan's demands toward China."

In a protest in behalf of his country, Bryan raised no objection to Japan's demands either on the question of Shantung contained in Group I or on the question of Manchuria and Mongolia contained in Group II. With regard to the question of the Han-Yeh-Ping Company in Group III and the questions of school hospitals and railways as well as the right of missionary work in Group V, Bryan admitted that they were not specially related to the present interests of the United States and her subjects in China.

However, the question of arms and the question of Fukien Province, he felt, were contradictory to the principle of Open Door for commerce and industry. Furthermore, the questions of police presented in the form of "wishes" in Group V would only complicate the situation.

In short, the United States Government informed the Japanese Government that it had no objection to sixteen items, including the questions of Shantung, South Manchuria, and Eastern Inner Mongolia. It lightly protested against two items of the remaining five demands as incompatible with the

Open Door principle, and against three other items as being detrimental to the political independence and administrative entity of China.

In this connection, an exchange of views on the question of Fukien Province did take place between Japan and the United States, relating to the latter's alleged desire to improve a harbor in Fukien for a naval coaling station. It was reported at the time that an American firm was actually negotiating a contract with China for the improvement of the harbor in question. Although Japan was willing to consider the latter's wishes, she requested, in return, a United States promise not to allow its citizens to construct directly or indirectly any installation in the said region. Bryan disclaimed any such purpose or desire on the part of the United States.

The Japanese Government, not fully satisfied with the American attitude, asserted that it could not agree to any project to construct naval installations or railways and mines which would invite the influence of the Western powers into this region. Secretary Bryan replied that, in view of the national character of the United States, it would be hardly possible to make a promise to this extent.

Under these circumstances, Secretary Bryan on May 6 dispatched telegrams to both the Japanese and Chinese Governments, recommending that they make some concessions. But on the following day Japan presented her ultimatum to China in a final bid to check China's delaying and evasive tactics.

Writing on May 13, after the Chinese Government had accepted Japan's demands, Bryan sent a note to Japan affirming that the United States "cannot recognize any agreement or understanding which has been entered into or which may be entered into between the Governments of Japan and China, impairing the treaty rights of the United States and its citizens in China, the political or territorial integrity of the Republic of China, or the international policy relative to China commonly known as the open door policy." This move was not based on any intention to raise a new question, but only as a "prior notification" and "for the record."

The articles contained in the Sino-Japanese Treaties and Notes of 1915, on closer examination, reveal no aggressive intent aimed at infringing the fundamental principles of equal opportunity and Open Door or monopolistic ambitions. Under most of the articles, the Western powers were to have an equal share in the benefits and welfare stemming from the treaty, and all such questions as the extension of leases and the noncession agreements were to be amicably settled in accordance with the needs of the Western powers.

Notwithstanding, the reason why the Sino-Japanese Treaties and Notes of 1915 became the target of world wide criticism as a typical and concrete expression of Japan's aggressive designs may be attributed more to Japan's unskillful diplomacy in achieving her objectives than to the actual contents of the Treaties.

Retrospectively speaking, it was a mistake to have kept the contents of Group V secret at the beginning from the Western powers, including Great Britain. Secondly, it was a faulty judgment on Japan's part to have made her demands directly to the President of the Republic of China instead of transmitting them through China's legitimate diplomatic channels (far from preserving the secrecy of the contents, this step facilitated the disclosure of Group V to outside sources). Thirdly, Japanese insistence on immediate action in concluding the negotiations was also among the factors which incurred universal denunciation that "the methods resorted to by Japan were contrary to her traditional virtues."

The most serious diplomatic blunder was undoubtedly Japan's presentation of an ultimatum, despite the fact that the Western powers were disposed to accept, with a few exceptions, the items contained in Group V, and there was every possibility that China would eventually have reached a settlement satisfactory to Japan. If the ultimatum were sent merely to satisfy the request of the Chinese Government, to save its face, further comments would become superfluous.

It is undeniable, too, that the Japanese politicians were ignorant of, if not indifferent to, the future consequences of pressuring China with an ultimatum.

CHAPTER 25

World War I and the Versailles Peace Conference 1914-1919

WITH the outbreak of World War I, the French and Russian Governments proposed the conclusion of an alliance between Japan, on the one hand, and France and Russia, on the other, as well as a quadruple alliance of Japan, Great Britain, France, and Russia. Japanese Foreign Minister Kato, after conferring with British Foreign Minister Grey, declined to entertain the said proposals, preferring to defer the question until after the war.

Meanwhile, Japan received a formal invitation from the British Government in 1915 to adhere to the London Declaration, an agreement among Great Britain, Russia, and France of September, 1914, holding the participating powers to a promise not to enter into a separate peace and to consult each other upon peace plans before the discussion of peace terms for the purpose of allaying Russian anxieties. Japan, after due deliberation, informed the Governments concerned of her adherence to the Declaration on October 19, 1915.

After joining the Allied Powers as a belligerent, Italy also became a party to the London Declaration, thus making it a five-power war pact between Japan, Great Britain, France, Russia, and Italy. Although the Russian Revolution in 1917 eliminated Russia from the *entente,* her place was taken over by the United States. It was these powers which eventually constituted the Allied and Associated Powers, commonly called the "Big Five," at the Paris and Versailles Peace Conference.

At the time the Second Russo-Japanese Agreement was concluded, there were already a number of influential advocates of an alliance between Japan and Russia. In the winter of 1914, the four *genro* Inouye, Yamagata, Matsukata, and Oyama, having thoroughly deliberated on the question, forwarded a resolution to Prime Minister Okuma urging the conclusion of an alliance with Russia. Although Foreign Minister Kato appeared reluctant to accept the proposition of the *genro,* his successor, Viscount Ishii, former Ambassador to France, did not hesitate to give effect to his cherished opinion. The Fourth Russo-Japanese Agreement and the Secret Convention were thus concluded on July 3, 1916.

Heading a special Japanese war mission to America in September, 1917, Viscount Kikujiro Ishii initiated negotiations with Secretary of State Robert Lansing on the question of China. After successfully overcoming the objections to the wording of Japan's interests in China, the two countries affixed their signatures to a joint declaration, the so-called Lansing-Ishii Agreement, approving Japan's special interests in China, the official notes of which were exchanged between Secretary Lansing and Viscount Ishii at the State Department on November 2, 1917.

By this diplomatic move, Japan was able to complete a system of alliances and agreements for the attainment of her continental development. It became increasingly clear that Great Britain, the United States, France, and Russia were compelled to recognize Japan's special interests in China through general treaties or the exchange of official notes.

Simultaneously, Japan separately concluded special secret conventions with Great Britain, France, and Russia, respectively, in return for her assistance during the war, holding them to their promise to support Japan's demands at the Versailles Peace Conference for the transfer of German interests in Shangtung as well as the German islands in the South Pacific north of the Equator.

In other words, by these general treaties and special war-time secret conventions, Japan was in a position to success-fully press her claims at the Peace Conference at any time. It may safely be said that Japan's success at Paris and Versailles owes a great deal to these secret conventions.

During World War I, Japan pursued her China policy with unusual vigor. Soon after the conclusion of the Sino-Japanese Treaties and Notes of May 25, 1915, based on Japan's Twenty-One Demands towards China, Yuan Shih-kai, the first President of the Republic of China, acceded to the throne under a resolution of the National Assembly which had been moved by the House of Councillors. The Japanese Government, with the support of her allies, Great Britain, France, Russia, and Italy, suggested a postponement of Yuan Shih-kai's accession to the throne, but the latter showed no inclination to comply. This Japanese attitude provoked the opposition of the Kuomintang leaders and other elements and soon led to the outbreak of the third revolution. In these circumstances, Yuan was forced to cancel his enthronement in March, 1916.

The Terauchi Cabinet, in the days that followed, lent its support to Tuan Chi-jui. For almost two years from 1917 to 1918, Japan granted a tremendous number of credits to China, for instance, the Yokohama Specie Bank's successive reform loan, the Ssupingkai-Chengchiatun Railway loan, the Kirin-Changchun Railway loan, the Transport Bank loan, the Wire Telegraph loan, the Kirin-Heilungchang Provinces Gold Mine and Forestry loan, the Kirin-Hoeryong Railway loan, the Four Manchurian and Mongolian Railways loan, the Two Shantung Railways loan, the Peking-Tientsin District Flood Damage loan, the Kiaochow-Tsinan Railway loan, the Shantung Province Public Property and Salt Industry Compensation loan, the Nanking-Kiukiang Railway loan, the Peking-Suiyuan Railway loan, the so-called Nishihara loans, and the War Participation loan.

The total value of these loans came to ¥180,000,000, of

which ¥129,660,000 were in the form of Central Government loans, ¥16,250,000 were district loans, and ¥34,141,500 comprised company and private loans. In view of the fact that for the previous several decades Japan had advanced loans to China amounting to only ¥120,000,000, the size of the latest series of loans is absolutely astonishing.

Then in May, 1919, shortly after the signing of the Brest-Litovsk Treaty following the outbreak of the Russian Revolution, Japan and China entered into the Sino-Japanese Military Agreement in order to determine the scope of cooperation of their armies and navies against the common enemy. It was widely rumored that on the strength of this agreement, Japan was to be vested with the right of constructing fortresses, railways, dockyards, and arms factories in China, even with the power to control the Chinese Treasury.

While the Japanese Government positively denied the rumor, the lack of any foundation for such a report became obvious when the text of the Agreement was later published.

To dispel public censure that the aforementioned loans as well as the Sino-Japanese Military Agreement were intended as a lever against the Kuomintang by the Tuan Chi-jui Cabinet, the succeeding Hara Cabinet was forced to proclaim a nonintervention policy towards China. In any event, it is undeniable that Japan did follow a positive policy towards China during the Great War, marked by unusual activity.

Unfortunately, this policy was not rationally or methodically executed, and invited unnecessary suspicion of Japan among the Chinese people. Besides inviting the antipathy and distrust of the various powers, Japan's attitude also left a number of thorny diplomatic questions for future settlement.

The signing of the Armistice on November 11, 1918 signified the end of World War I and the defeat of Germany. The formal Peace Conference of Versailles began on May 7 and the Treaty of Peace was signed on June 28, 1919. At the Peace Conference, China demanded that the Sino-Japanese Treaties and Notes of 1915, resulting from Japan's Twenty-One Demands, should be placed on the agenda of the Conference as the signing of these Treaties and Notes originated during the World War.

However, the Chinese proposal concerning the question of Manchuria in the said Treaties and Notes was rejected as of minor importance, but the question of Shantung, centering around Tsingtao, was treated as an important item of the agenda. The Chinese Government insisted that it was justified in demanding the direct return of Shantung from Germany since the Shantung Treaty of 1915 was signed under coercion. Moreover, all treaties between Germany and China had already been renounced at the time of China's participation in the Great War.

Such Chinese assertions, however, yielded no results. Article 156 of the Versailles Treaty stipulated, in compliance with Japan's demand, that Germany should abandon all rights and privileges concerning Shantung to Japan. Opposing this stipulation, China attempted to insert a reservation into the signing of the Peace Treaty, but failed to receive approval.

Under such circumstances, China was not among the signatory powers of the Treaty of Peace on June 18. At the same time, the cautious stand of the United States Government against a number of understandings relating to the disposition of the question of Shantung of 1915 and 1920, moved Japan to declare in the additional agreement that her policy was aimed at the eventual return of Shantung Peninsula, reserving only the right of establishing the settlement at Tsingtao with respect to German economic interests and general conditions. Be that as it may, Japan's diplomacy at the Versailles Peace Conference appeared to be mainly a continuation of her World War diplomatic policy and was successful at least in preserving her interests in China.

CHAPTER **26**

The Washington Conference and its Aftermath 1919 - 1931

WHILE Japan's conduct at Versailles may be properly described as "successful," at the Washington Conference, held from November, 1922, to February, 1923, she was unable to maintain her new position gained during the war in China. An indication of subsequent developments was clearly revealed, prior to the Washington Conference, during the negotiations on a new international banking consortium in China, signed on October 15, 1921. The said negotiations made Japan realize that her chances of preserving South Manchuria and Eastern Inner Mongolia as her spheres of influence and maintaining their special status were becoming increasingly slim.

In 1919, the United States put forward a plan for the formation of a new international banking consortium to undertake loans to China. This plan having been accepted by the State Department, identical notes on the proposal for a new consortium for China, to include American, Japanese, British, and French financial groups, were communicated *mutatis mutandis* to the Japanese, British, and French Ambassadors in Washington on October 8, 1919. Japan reacted by proposing a certain reservation as contained in the Odagiri-Lamont communications. Manosuke Odagiri, the Japanese financial representative, proposed that "all the rights and options held by Japan in the regions of Manchuria and Mongolia, where

Japan has special interests, should be excluded from the arrangements for pooling provided for in the proposed agreement." He explained that this claim was based upon "the very special relations which Japan enjoys, geographically and historically, with the regions referred to, and which have been recognized by Great Britain, France and Russia on many occasions."

The Japanese proposal, being regarded as an important political question, immediately became the subject of negotiations between the Governments concerned. Joining the United States in strongly opposing Japan's overture, Great Britain adopted an even more positive attitude than the United States despite the existence of the Anglo-Japanese Alliance.

Taking a step further, the British Government on August, 11, 1920, published a memorandum stating that one fundamental object of the American proposition, already approved by the British, Japanese, and French Governments, was to exclude any special demand in any special sphere of influence, and to open up the whole of China to the joint activities of the international banking consortium. The memorandum went on to say that this object could not be attained by the powers concerned without their sacrificing economic priority in their respective spheres of influence.

Japan then had to explain her reasons for excluding South Manchuria and Eastern Inner Mongolia as follows: (1) Japan not only had close relations with South Manchuria and Eastern Inner Mongolia politically and economically, but the enterprises established in the said regions affected the vital question of Japan's national defense; (2) since any infiltration of Russian influence detrimental to Japan would be by way of Manchuria and Mongolia, the latter's interests in the said regions were a matter of life or death; (3) consequently, Japan's vital interests in South Manchuria and Eastern Inner Mongolia were of an entirely different nature from those of other powers.

Both Great Britain and the United States, however, expressed their disapproval of Japan's "formula" concerning the reservation of Manchuria and Mongolia, claiming that Japan's intention was designed to acquire economic monopoly at the expense of the interests of other powers, or was an attempt to establish a territorial division as a sphere of influence based on political exclusivism. After patient point-by-point negotiations, an understanding was finally reached with regard to the following points: (1) the South Manchuria Railway and its existing branches, together with their subsidiary mines, did not come within the scope of the Consortium; (2) the projected Taonan-Jehol Railway and the projected railway connecting a point on the Taonan-Jehol Railway with a seaport were to be included within the terms of the Consortium Agreement; (3) the Kirin-Hoeryong, the Chengchiatun-Taonan, the Changchun-Taonan, the Kaiyuan-Kirin (via Hailung), the Kirin-Changchun, the Shinminfu-Mukden and the Ssupignkai-Chengchiatun Railways were outside the scope of the joint activities of the Consortium.

Thus, while unsuccessful in inserting in the final Consortium Agreement a specific clause that would reserve her special interests in South Manchuria and Eastern Inner Mongolia, Japan did receive vague assurances from the United States, Great Britain, and France that they would not countenance operations inimical to Japanese interests in Manchuria and Mongolia. These general understandings finally cleared the way for the formal signing of the Consortium Agreement, which took place in Paris on October 15, 1920.

If the aforementioned proposition for the formation of a new international banking consortium was designed to check Japan's financial and economic advances in the Far East, it can similarly be assumed that the idea for the Washington Conference was aimed at preventing Japan's political and military expansion in the said area. Although a more detailed reference to the Washington Conference is beyond the purpose of this book, the Conference itself marked the first step in the reorientation of Japan's foreign policy in the Pacific area, especially in the Far East. In this connection, from the standpoint of Japan's continental policy, the Washington Conference achieved such significant results as the conclusion of the Nine-Power Treaty, the solution of the question of restoring Shantung, the question of the Twenty-One Demands, and the question of China's full tariff autonomy.

The question of Shantung was settled by direct Sino-Japanese "conversations," but the negotiation itself was carried out through the good offices and under the intent observation of Charles Hughes of the United States and Arthur J. Balfour of Britain. Under the Shantung Treaty, signed after strenuous talks between the Japanese and Chinese representatives, Japan relinquished her right to establish an exclusive settlement which China had earlier approved in the exchange of Notes in May, 1915, and the priority rights to supply capital goods and materials and foreign assistance that Germany once possessed.

Japan also agreed to restore to China the former German leased territory of Kiaochow within six months after the Treaty came into force, and pledged to withdraw the Japanese guards at Tsingtao within thirty days and the Japanese troops along the Kiaochow-Tsinan Railway within six months.

China, on the other hand, took active steps to nullify the so-called Twenty-One Demands, including the restoration of Port Arthur, Dairen, and the South Manchuria Railway in 1923, the year of the termination of the lease by the earlier stipulations of the Treaties of 1915. Ku Wei-chin, the Chinese representative, went further to insist on the invalidity of foreign settlements and their retrocessions before the time limit, while Dr. C. T. Wang, singling out the Sino-Japanese Treaties and Notes of 1915, urged that the said Treaties and Notes be reconsidered and nullified.

In reply, the Japanese delegate, Masanao Hanihara, clearly informed the Chinese delegation that Japan had no intention whatever of abandoning "the important rights which Japan acquired and maintained legally, justifiably and at tremendously heavy sacrifices." Nevertheless, recognizing the necessity of compromising to some extent, the Japanese Government delegate Kijuro Shidehara on February 2, 1922, the day following the publication of the Shantung Treaty, declared that Japan would voluntarily renounce the following interests stipulated in the Sino-Japanese Treaties and Notes of 1915:

1. The loan for railway construction in South Manchuria and Eastern Inner Mongolia, as well as the right of priority for loan guaranteed by various taxes as security.

2. Priority rights for employment of advisors and instructors in South Manchuria.

3. The reservation made for future negotiations on the draft of Group V.

The Japanese Government took another step on February 6, 1922, by participating in the signing of the Nine-Power Customs Convention, supporting China's desire for restoration of the tariff autonomy. Among other concessions made at the Washington Conference by the powers, including Japan, were the adoption of the so-called Fourth Resolution relating to the abolition of the practice of consular jurisdiction and the withdrawal of foreign postal agencies from China.

Furthermore, Japan pledged to reduce her troops, except the military forces, for the maintenance of transportation in Manchuria and the Peking-Tientsin area. Thus, as far as Japan was concerned she not only lost her foothold and various interests acquired during or even before the World War, but even took steps on her own volition to relinquish her gains. The Washington Conference can thus be described as a first step in Japan's reorientation of her continental foreign policy.

After the Washington Conference, the main plank of Japan's continental policy towards China was the execution of the letter and spirit of the Conference agreements and resolutions. Popularly known as the "Shidehara Policy," the four principles as enunciated in the Diet on January 18, 1927, by Foreign Minister Baron Kijuro Shidehara may be summarized as follows:

1. To respect the sovereignty and territorial integrity of China, and to scrupulously avoid all interference in her domestic conflicts.

2. To promote the solidarity and economic rapprochement between the two nations.

3. To show sympathy and benevolence for the just efforts made to realize the declared aspirations.

4. To maintain an attitude of patience and tolerance toward China's present situation and, at the same time, to protect Japan's legitimate and essential rights and interests by all reasonable means at the disposal of the Government.

It is undeniable that tensions between China and Japan eased as a result of Shidehara's declaration, and the feelings of distrust and suspicion of the Western powers towards Japan's foreign policy also began to subside. On the other hand, China's attempts to take advantage of Japan's soft and cooperative policy resulted in frequent and unjust trampling of Japanese interests. This increasingly aggressive attitude of China towards Japan naturally fostered the growth of much discontent in Japan.

Meanwhile, Baron Tanaka, who took over the reins of the Ministry of Foreign Affairs in April, 1927, was urged to adopt a positive policy towards China. Negotiations were started between Japan and China in order to make Manchuria and Mongolia a region where both the indigenous and foreign peoples could live in peace. In these negotiations, China pursued her usual policy of evasion and delay and prevented any progress.

When the Hamaguchi Cabinet came into power, Baron Shidehara, who again assumed the position of Foreign Minister, attempted to continue his peaceful and cooperative policy towards China. However, his tenure was interrupted by the outbreak of the Manchurian Incident on September 18, 1931, said to have been caused by the blasting of the

South Manchuria Railway at Liu Tiao Kou by the Chinese troops.

Whereas the apparent cause of the Manchurian Incident was China's flouting of Japan's honor and interests, imposing upon Japan's tolerance and relying on Anglo-American support, the root cause is traceable to the Washington Conference. The agreements and resolutions stipulated at the Conference encouraged China to adopt a hostile policy towards Japan and misled her to believe that her provocative conduct would not invite retaliation.

It is perhaps no exaggeration to say that the powers which participated in the Washington Conference unconsciously planted the seeds of upheaval in the Far East for several decades to come, by providing China with the minimum of restraints in order that they could establish an order that would serve their own interests.

Subsequent events which are now a part of the tragic history of the Far East have vividly demonstrated the farsighted judgment of United States Secretary of State Cordell Hull who once poignantly warned that the revision of the Washington Treaties by orderly processes is a matter of acute urgency for stabilizing the Far Eastern situation.

Appendix
Chronological Treaty Highlights

1895 Treaty of Shimonoseki (Sino-Japanese Peace Treaty)
1902 First Anglo-Japanese Alliance
1905 Taft-Katsura Agreement (Japanese-American)
1905 Portsmouth Treaty (Russo-Japanese Peace Treaty)
1905 Second Anglo-Japanese Alliance *offensive and defensive; recognizes Japan's paramount interests in Korea*
1905 Treaty of Peking (Japan-China) *China transfers Russian holdings to Japan*
1907 Franco-Japanese Agreement
1907 First Motono-Iswalsky Agreement (Russo-Japanese) *divides Manchuria into spheres of influence*
1908 Root-Takahira Agreement (Japanese-American) *reaffirms Open Door principles*
1910 Second Motono-Iswalsky Agreement (Russo-Japanese) *mutual assistance pact*
1911 Third Anglo-Japanese Alliance *third-party arbitration clause*
1912 Third Russo-Japanese Agreement *divides Inner Mongolia into spheres of influence*
1914 London Declaration
1915 Twenty-One Demands (Sino-Japanese Treaties and Notes)
1916 Fourth Russo-Japanese Agreement
1917 Lansing-Ishii Agreement (Japanese-American) *approves Japan's special interests in China*
1919 Versailles Peace Treaty
1921 Four-Power Treaty (Japan, U.S., Great Britain, France)

1922 Nine-Power Treaty (Japan, U.S., Great Britain, France, China, Italy, Belgium, Netherlands, Portugal)
1925 Soviet-Japanese Treaty

Index

Abaza, Admiral, 57, 133, 137
Afghanistan, 40, 43, 151, 154, 224
Aigun, 348; *see also* Chinchow-
 Aigun line
Alexander III, Tsar, 47, 49, 51, 56
Alexieff, General, 133, 134, 142
Alexieff, Russian financial adviser,
 54
Amau statement, 273
Amur Railway, 357
Amur River, 53, 88
Amur Steamship Company, 48
Anglo-American arbitration treaty,
 205–206, 207–208, 209, 212, 362–
 363
Anglo-Chinese alliance, 40–41, 42,
 43
Anglo-Chinese Corporation, 353
Anglo-French Entente Cordiale,
 153–154
Anglo-French-Russian-Japanese al-
 liance, proposed, 226–227
Anglo-French-Russian Secret Trea-
 ty of 1915, 230, 232
Anglo-German Agreement, 91–92,
 103, 182, 321; interpretation, 93–
 99; Japanese reaction, 92; negoti-
 ations, 86–90
Anglo-German alliance, proposed,
 81–82

Anglo-Japanese Alliance, First, 40,
 41, 47, 65, 148, 150, 153, 317;
 concluded, 123, 323; international reactions, 125–127, 130;
 negotiations, 72–76, 110–124; official document, 124–125; text,
 127–129
Anglo-Japanese Alliance, Second,
 167, 330–331, 339; international
 reactions, 169–170; negotiations,
 155–168
Anglo-Japanese Alliance, Third,
 202, 208, 227–228, 363, 374;
 Chinese Revolution, 365; international reactions, 212; League
 of Nations, relationship to, 260;
 negotiations, 205–208; revision
 question, 259, 265–266; terminated, 272; text, 209–211
Anglo-Japanese Declaration to the
 League of Nations: First, 260;
 Second, 261
Anglo-Russian Agreement of 1899,
 85, 321, 349, 353
anti-Japanese immigration law,
 183, 300
Antonoff, Russian correspondent,
 296
Antung-Mukden Railway, 357–
 359, 369, 373

393